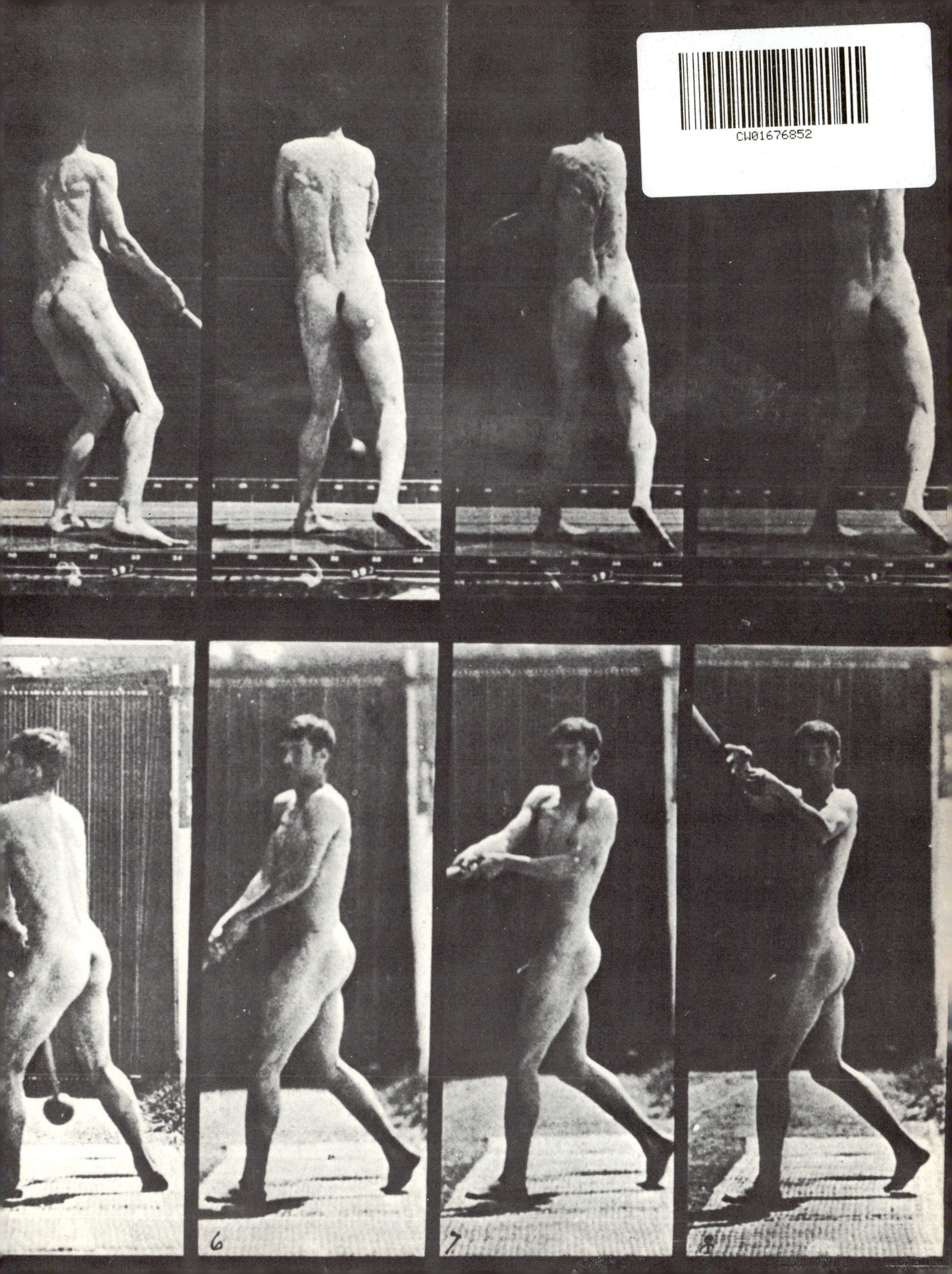
6
7
8

Head and Figure Modelling

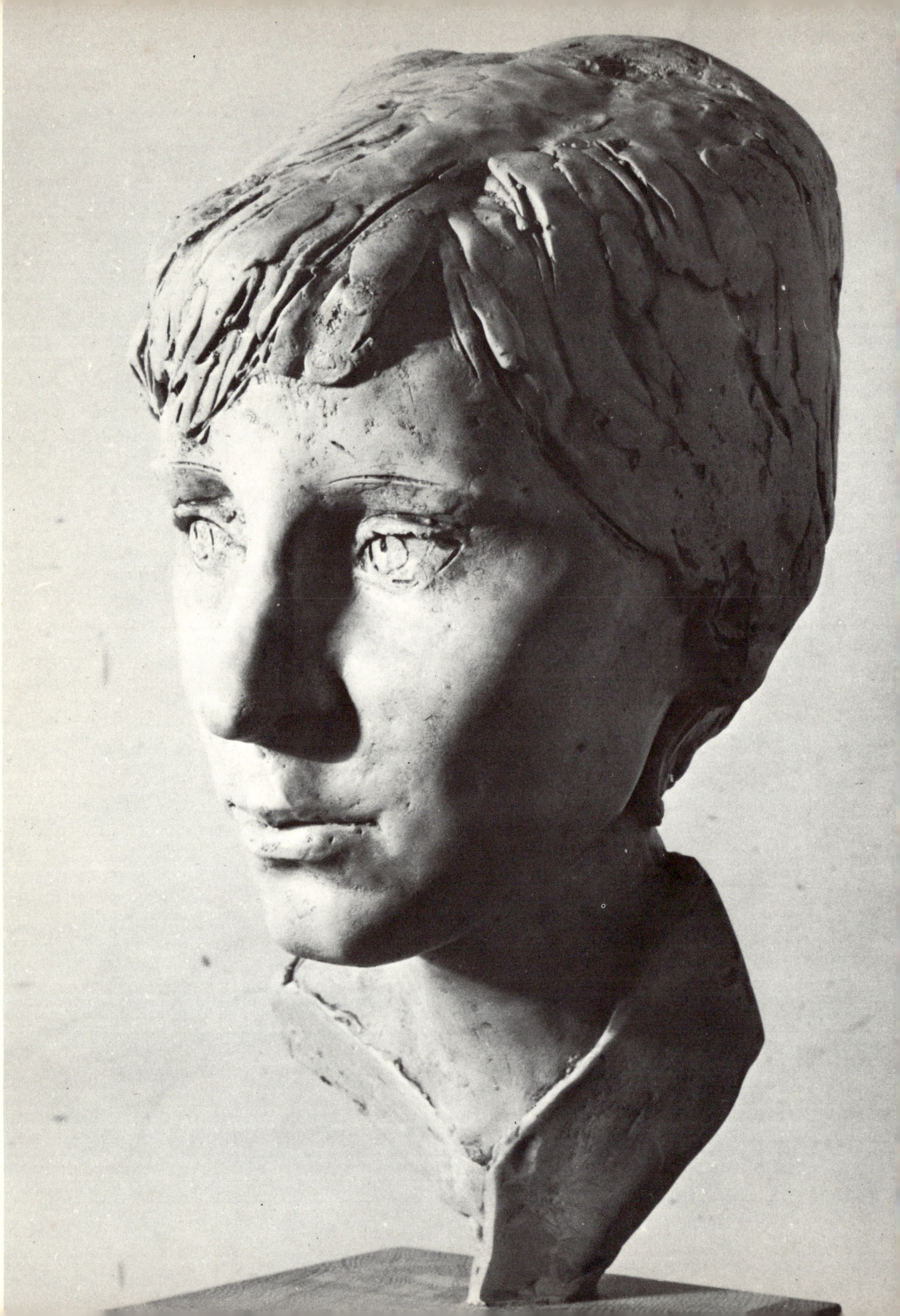

Head and Figure Modelling

John W Mills

B T BATSFORD LTD LONDON

Frontispiece
Portrait of Anna GRP
John W Mills
Collection D Turner
photograph B Pletts

Endpapers
Man swinging bat, plate 55 from
The Human Figure in Motion by
Eadweard Muybridge
Dover Publications Inc, New York

First published 1977
ISBN 0 7134 32586
Filmset in 12 on 13 point 'Monophoto' Spectrum by
Keyspools Limited, Golborne, Lancs
Printed in Great Britain by
The Anchor Press Ltd Tiptree, Essex
for the publishers B T Batsford Ltd.
4 Fitzhardinge Street, London W1H 0AH

Contents

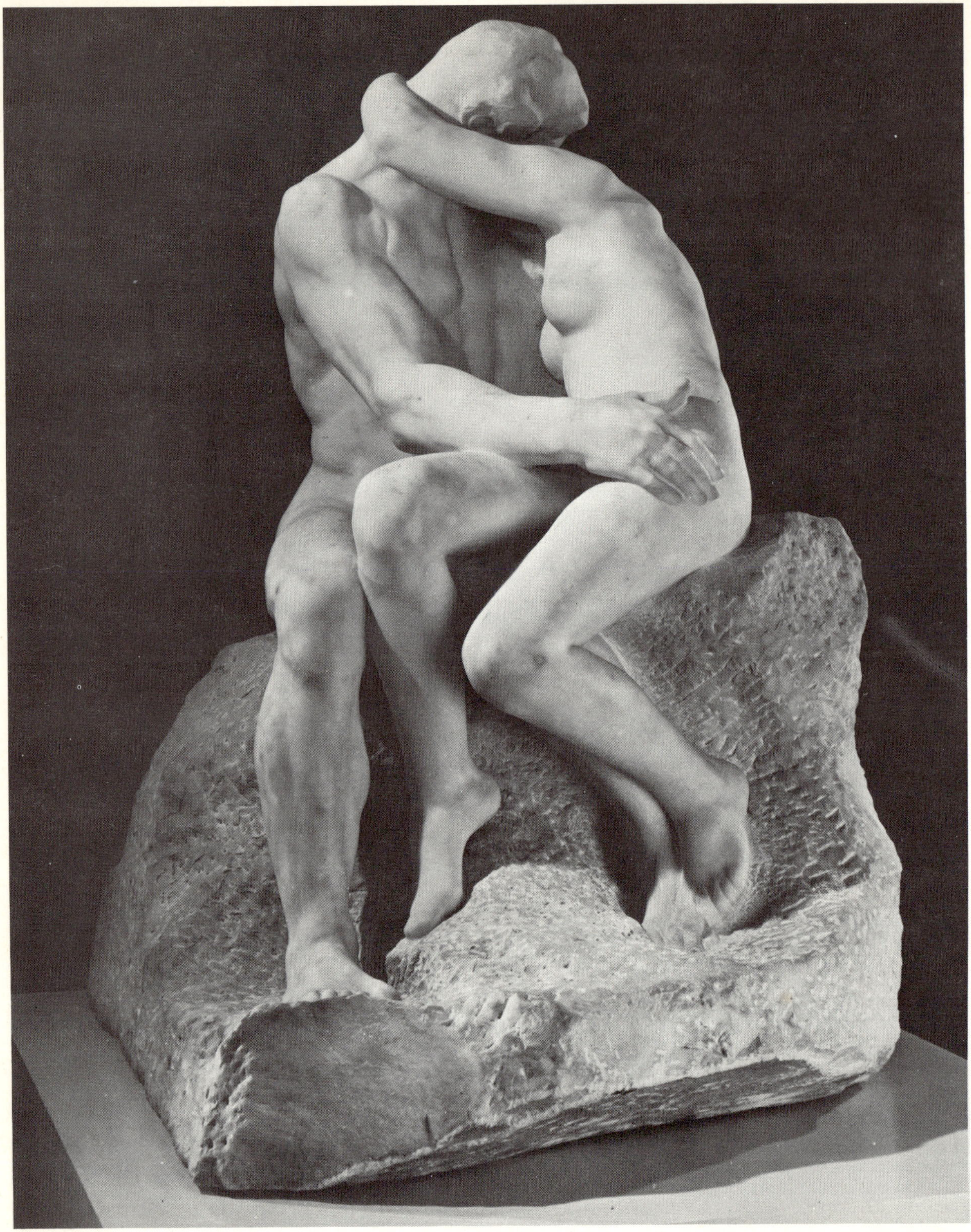

Preface

Writing this book is of great importance to me, because it has given me the opportunity to put into words my feelings and observations regarding figurative sculpture. Figuration is my chosen field of activity in sculpture, and the making of specific, identifiable images is my preoccupation. I have for long felt the need to communicate my feelings in a tangible and, I hope, helpful form, as an aid to furthering the cause of figurative sculpture. Teaching, at all levels and for too long, has been based on the premise that 'what I am about to tell you, you do not know and do need to know'. This premise relates to all skills, academic and practical, and although useful and successful as a one-off ideal, has become a poor pedagogical device, because of its dependence on persuasion. Persuasive lecturers and dogmatic demonstrators have done untold harm in art schools all over the world, using this technique. Check the idiom in which you find yourself working, and determine the influences; if there is only one, think again! I have seen, too often, students grouped around a model, thoughtlessly copying the subject as though to prove their implied ignorance. The same students however do not easily mistake one person for another, they do not neglect visual impact and tactile stimulus when selecting a partner of the opposite sex. They recognise their own image in the mirror each day and can easily recognise an abnormal figure on sight; so what do they really not know?

The academic norm that has grown up in art schools is based on classical precepts, which are in themselves questionable in that they are based on later analyses of Ancient Greek forms and images. These analyses produced academic formulae such as those on proportion referred to in chapter 5. They produced also standard poses for models based on Ancient Greek sculptures, poses that used to feature in Life Modelling examinations. Formulae for heads were worked out too, similarly based on Classical Greek examples, a school of sculpture not remarkable for its portrait sculpture, being more concerned with general ideals. A

The Kiss Marble
Auguste Rodin
The Tate Gallery, London

general formulae can only be useful as a guide; a study of tribal images will convince you of a wider world of imagery. The art school life class that attracts so many people with little imagination, was a compulsory study for me and my contemporaries, and for some became a crutch with which to prop up a flagging confidence and sterile powers of invention. This potentially useful feature of art school activity I would like to see used sensibly as an aid and not as a means of escape.

The life model should be used for reference only; posed after careful selection to enable an image, already decided upon, to be more finely drawn. Such images should be born in the mind of the sculptor, ideas growing out of experience and observation, found and practised in every day life by every one. The sculptor is different to other people only in that he expresses himself best by making three dimensional equivalents to his ideas. His everyday life includes eating, sleeping, loving, arguing, communicating with or ignoring his fellows, in the same way as any other person. His source material is this same everyday world we all live in, with all its advantages and disadvantages. Ideas and images must grow out of this common experience.

I have included in chapter 1 a brief appraisal of some figurative sculptures, not by any means a survey and very partial, reflecting my own taste. I make no excuses for doing this because I am able to express only a personal point of view. I have also included photographs of my own sculpture, rather in the manner of presenting credentials. I hope these examples encourage confidence in my ability to make a sculptured image, and back up my text on the techniques of study and modelling the head and figure. Taste and approval are so personal, reflecting background, exposure to images of all kinds, and to other people's ideas, that to mention them at all can lead to endless and fruitless debate—far safer between the covers of a book. I am conscious of this fact, and so have restricted my selection of examples to those that have or seem to have a general appeal, and have used them to illustrate my points as well as to embellish these pages.

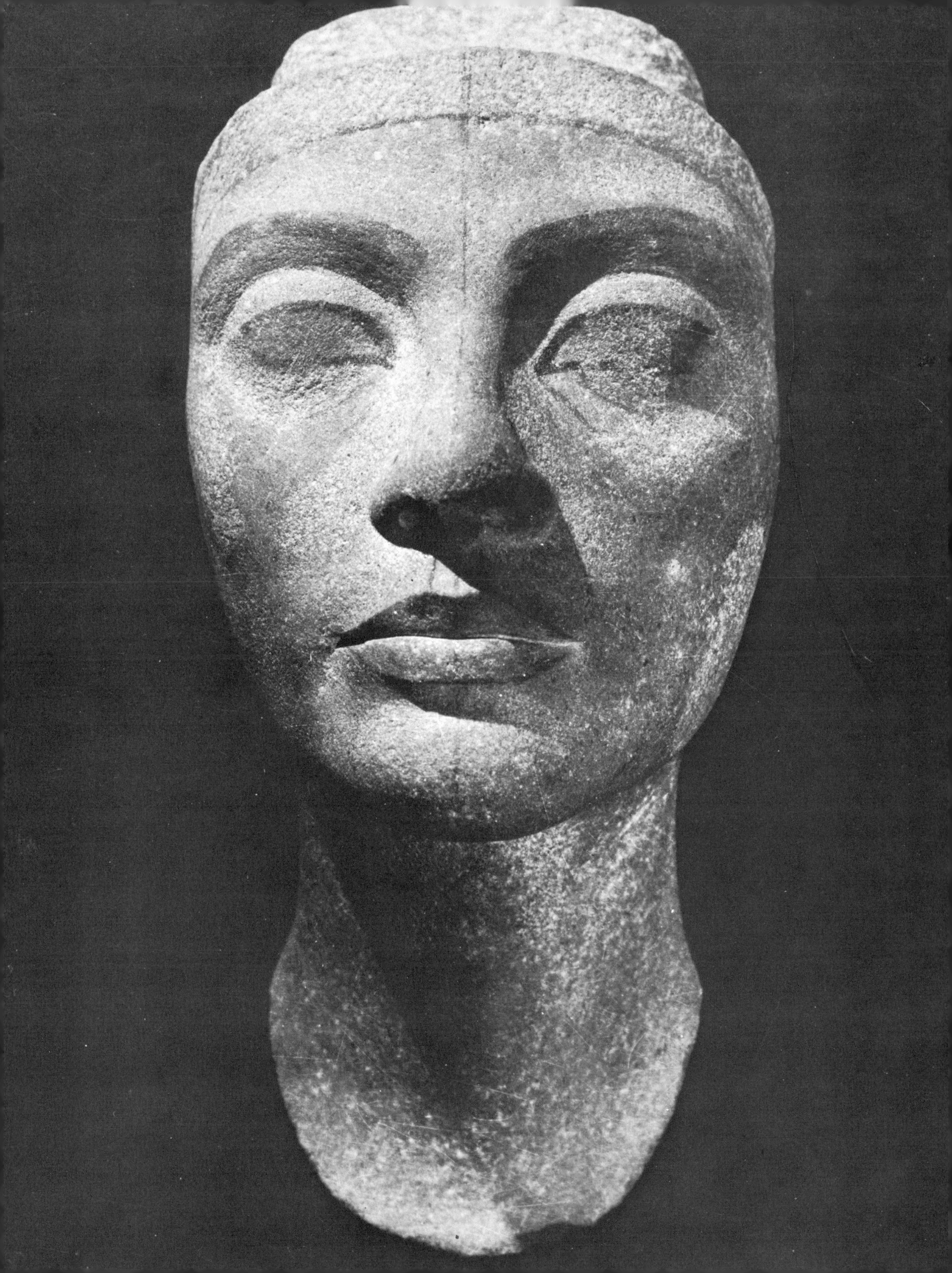

1 The head and figure in sculpture

The character and shape of man has preoccupied artists since prehistory. Students of the fine arts cannot avoid the study of figurative painting and sculpture, no matter how concerned they may be with means of expression that are apparently abstract, having no obvious reference to the human form. Contemporary idiom often reflects fashion and not an individual need to express an image sincerely felt, stimulated by observation, committed to memory and made manifest in whatever materials best suit it. The filter, that is the artist, embodies sufficient potential to make that image unique in as much as the artist is unique.

Of course there have been, and will continue to be, fashions in figurative sculpture. Some people naturally are innovators, others are consolidators, and others merely copyists. My object is to encourage confidence, by confiding technical facts, so that the student might seek to achieve images that truly reflect his own personality and not that of others.

To be influenced is not a bad thing. But to be influenced by one example only, can be detrimental to personal statements. Accumulative knowledge is not the sole province of science, and to investigate as wide a range of examples in figurative sculpture as possible, can lead to a proper use of influence. Such study from the subject will demand of the artist personal decisions which, coupled with technical accomplishment, will result in a personal statement.

This to my mind is a sensible goal, and as an aid to this kind of study I will discuss some modelled sculptures that successfully illustrate the marriage between image and technique, intention and statement. I will not do this in historical chronology, because this would falsely imply influences between sculptors that cannot be substantiated. Museums house fine examples of modelled figurative sculpture, and so as one uses a museum to wander through, to be attracted by specific items that in turn demand greater study, so these examples are chosen. Auguste Rodin is probably the most accomplished expressive modeller in the

Queen Nefertiti
Cairo Museum
See page 28

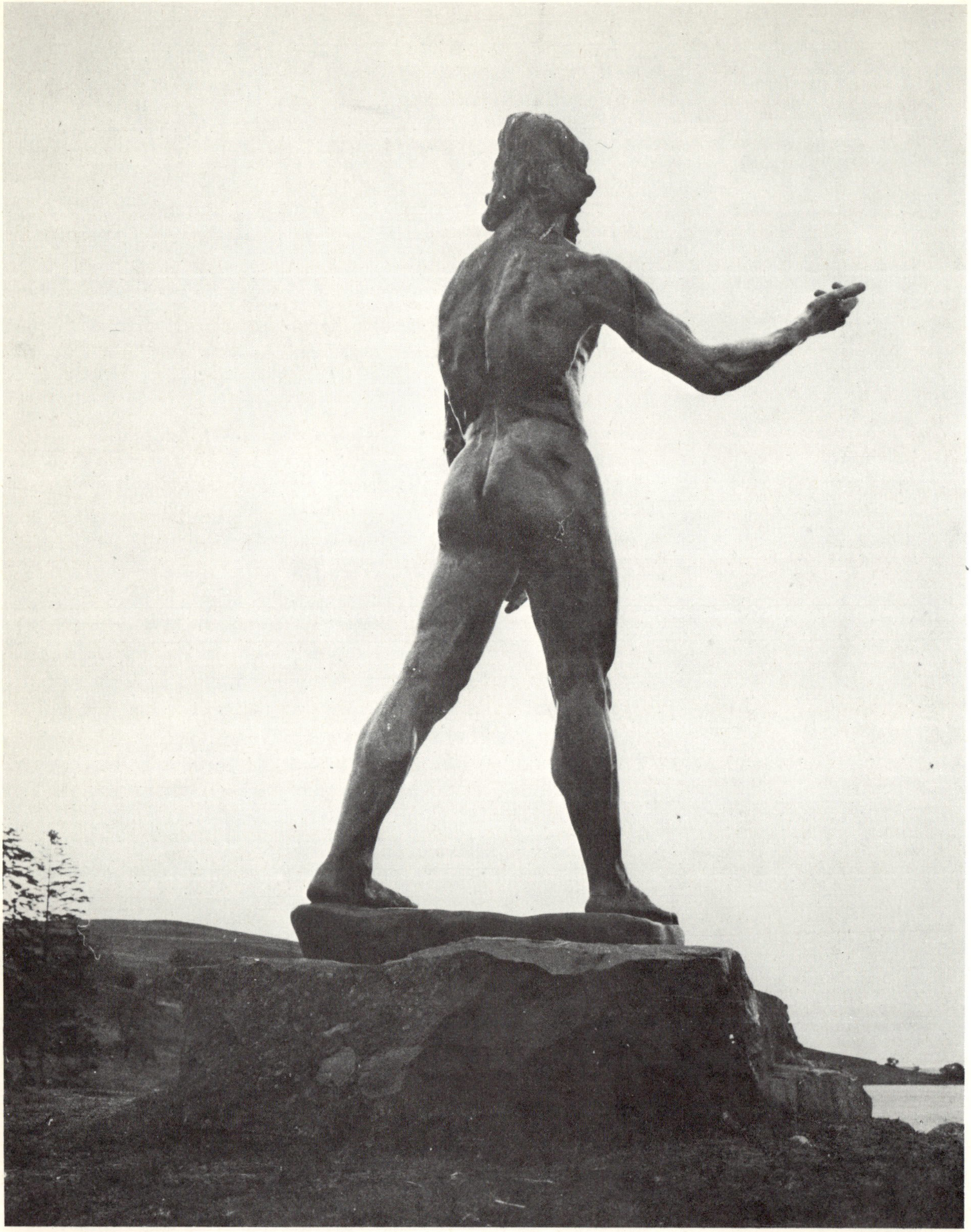

history of western european sculpture. He was to clay, wax and bronze, what Michelangelo was to marble. They both demonstrated technical freedom of the highest order, and both used their facility to the best possible effect. Rodin's sculpture *John the Baptist,* is an interesting example both of figurative sculpture and the use of the model. Accused of casting from life his *Age of Bronze,* Rodin decided to make a figure that was larger than life size, to prove his expertise as a modeller and refute the accusation of fraud. *John the Baptist* was the result and, together with his sculpture *L'homme qui marche,* became a key monument in the history of figurative sculpture.

Page 12
Page 14
Page 14

In making these sculptures Rodin used the model for reference, rather than as a phenomenon to be copied. The *Age of Bronze* is more a copy, but the later sculptures are a result of using the model as reference material only. Research and study, produced sculpture that embodies features derived from life, but organised in such a way as to evoke a sense of reality in a static form. Clay is manipulated, squeezed, kneaded, pushed, smoothed and burnished until it looks and feels like a real arm or torso, head, leg or foot. The image becomes an equivalent to not a duplicate of reality.

Page 15

The clay study *River God* by Michelangelo evokes a similar feeling. It feels real although features are exaggerated. On the other hand, the small wax anatomical studies attributed to Michelangelo, are of a different order, and represent three-dimensional research into physiological fact, needed to gain the confidence so necessary to achieve a sense of reality without copying.

Donatello is another sculptor of superb technical accomplishment who made images of power and moment, equal to the people about him, who were his reference library. This naturalism based on experience was to become a rare thing in painting and sculpture. To some extent the work of Donatello and friends became the basis for academic disciplines, that were eventually brought to the point of sterility, to be usurped 400 years later by the impressionist and later movements in the fine arts.

Page 20
Page 22

The Donatello *David* is an elegant and refined image, and is so convincing an evocation of a youth as to cause modern speculation on the artist's sexual preoccupations. This sculpture reminds one of the figure modelled years later by Degas known as *The Little Dancer Aged Fourteen.* This too is a lucid equivalent to real experience, modelled smaller than life size. In chapter 3 I have written of exercises aimed to train the visual memory, a practice used by Degas. He made three-dimensional aids to assist his painting, and his work as a whole correlates memory and obser-

St John the Baptist Bronze
Auguste Rodin
photograph John W Mills

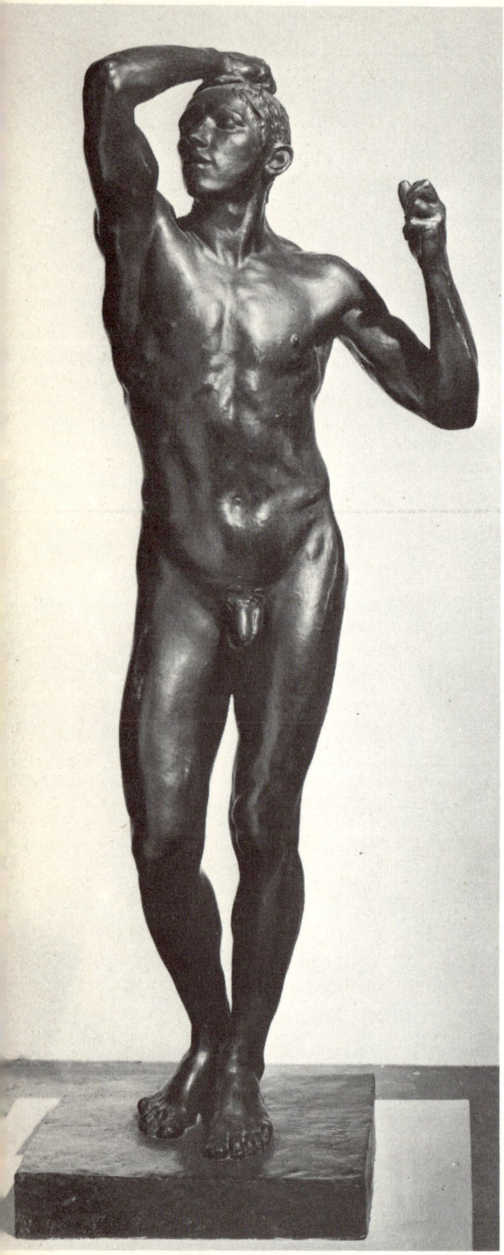

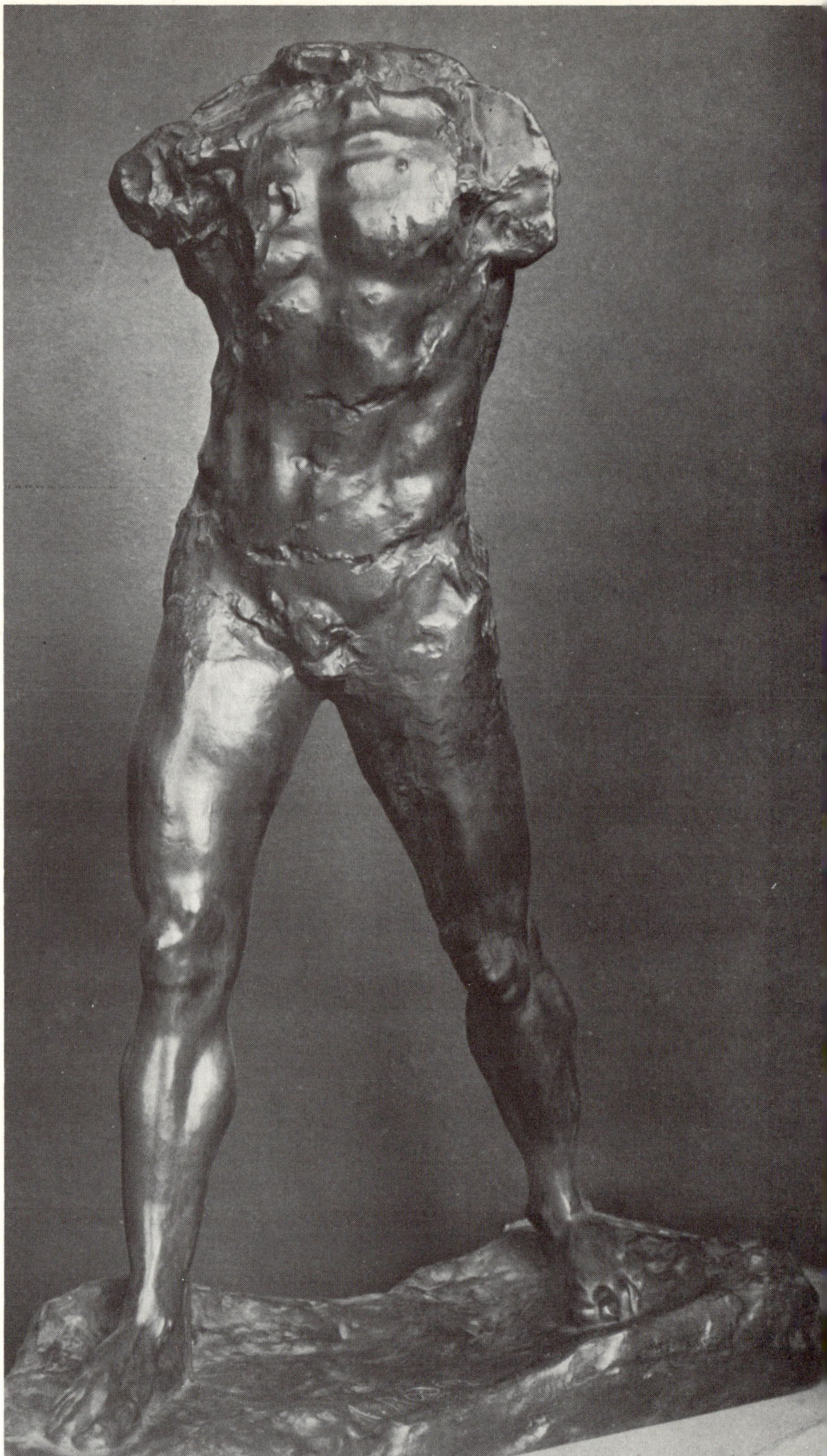

The Age of Bronze   Bronze
Auguste Rodin
The Tate Gallery, London

L'homme qui marche   Bronze
Auguste Rodin
Museé Rodin, Paris

Page 22

vation to an intense degree. *The Little Dancer Aged Fourteen* is his largest and most complete sculpture, but alas its weaknesses lie in the fact that Degas was singularly inept at three-dimensional construction and made the wax in opposition to the poor armature that was supposed to support it. So we have a sculpture that offers two lessons, one of positive observation, the other of poor attention to technical skill that almost destroyed the work, saved only by friendly sculptors coming to his aid.

Pages 24, 26, 27

Marino Marini can be seen as perhaps following Donatello in the Italian Renaissance traditions. But he managed to break the thread of slavish influence and academic rigidity to make such personal sculptures as *Juggler, Pomona* and *Judith.* To a large degree Marini in the 1950's prompted a sensuous attitude to figurative sculpture, both in Europe and the USA, that had been stifled by academic discipline. His contemporaries Giacomo Manzu and Emilio Greco continue this love, but with a difference. Marini feeds from sculptural influences recognising the power of a subject in relation to well-tried sculptural language; Manzu on the other hand is more concerned with responses to his immediate companions. Greco achieves a tactile quality in his sculpture, that compliments their whimsy. This quality is arrived at by smoothing and refining the surfaces and forms to cor-

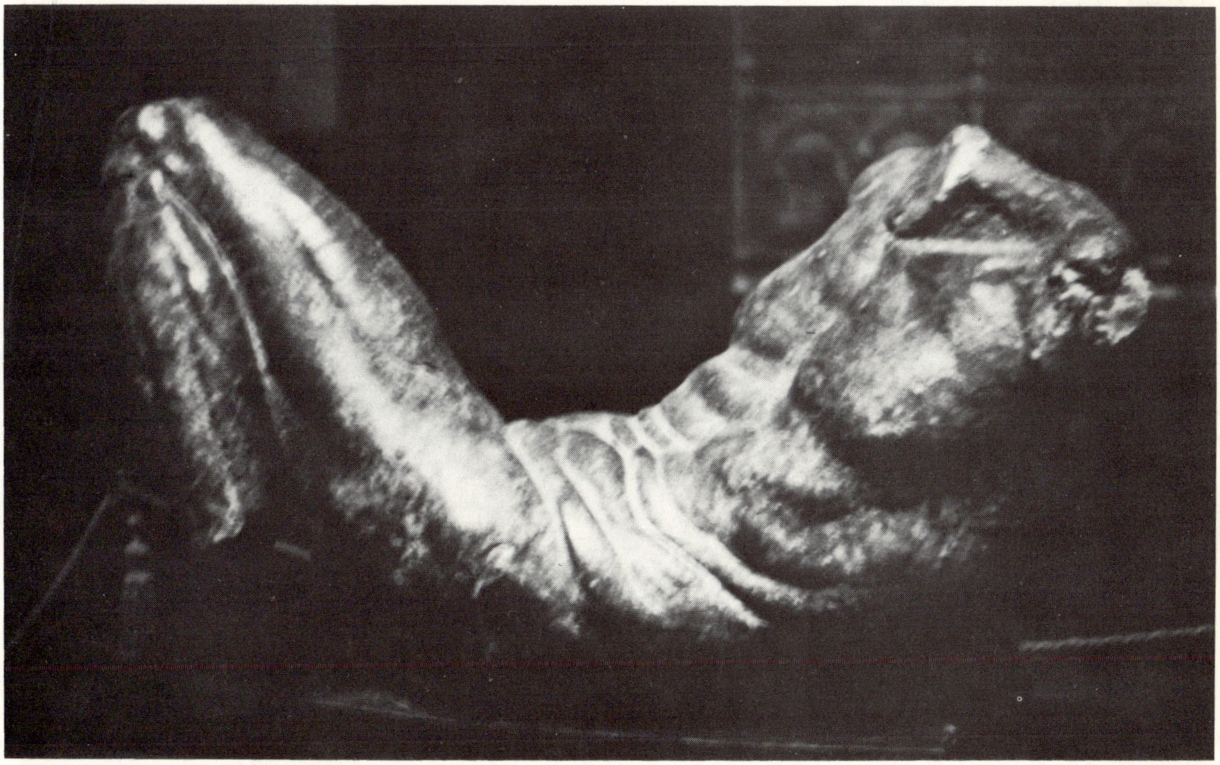

River God
Michelangelo
Academia Florence
photograph John W Mills

respond to sensual dreamlike memories. Marini makes figures of strong formal qualities that dominate the observed phenomena, to achieve images with powerful impact. Manzu seems to coerce the clay and wax into three-dimensional evocations of the people he loves and the friends he has about him. Even his large commissioned works have this intimate quality.

Page 29

Medardo Rosso, another Italian sculptor, although working predominantly in Paris, contemporary with Rodin, used figures almost incidentally. They are used to engender the atmosphere of a particular place and at a particular time. The quality of his observation and modelling facility is apparently removed from academic tradition, but as a good ballet dancer requires skill and discipline to dance freely, so Rosso's images are freely expressed, because of his training.

Pages 32, 33

Life modelling and the traditions associated with the Life Studio are described in chapter 5, but its influence cannot be too strongly stated. It is a fact that anatomical study and study from the nude became, and still remains to some extent, the academic norm by which artistic prowess was judged. Landscape painting perhaps being the only exception. No art school was complete without such a studio, and no training complete without due time being given to drawing and modelling from the life model. I illustrate from my own experience at the Royal College of Art in 1958. It was the practice up till then to devote a great percentage of art school time to study in front of the life model, and my first year post-graduate study at the RCA was at least ninety per cent study from the naked human figure – Life Study. The shortcoming of such training is the narrowness of the study. The model is live, and sometimes very beautiful. The studio was more fully attended on the occasion of a beautiful model, but the study was not really life. Learning to work from a still model only, and then only able to work if the model is present, is indeed narrow-sighted. No matter how accurately this skill is achieved the result will be academic and not easily spiced up.

Study from the cadaver as an aid to a better understanding of anatomy, can lead only to an ability to draw cadavers. The examples offered by such great men as Da Vinci, Michelangelo and George Stubbs, are useful only if taken at more than face value. Dissection can only be useful if at first the figure is understood, so that it can be used to further clarify a statement and strengthen the impact. To test this, examine the work of these artists before their episodes of anatomical dissection and after. The visual impact does not change, articulated parts may be stated more clearly but little else changes.

Wax Study for a Slave
Michelangelo
Crown Copyright
Victoria and Albert Museum

The lesson to be drawn from both these academic disciplines is

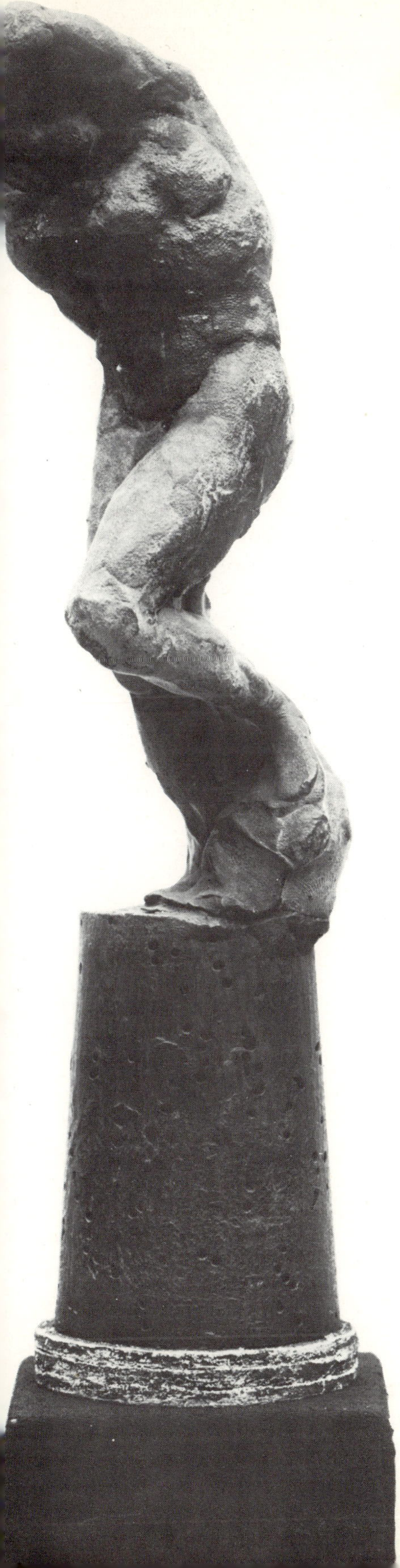

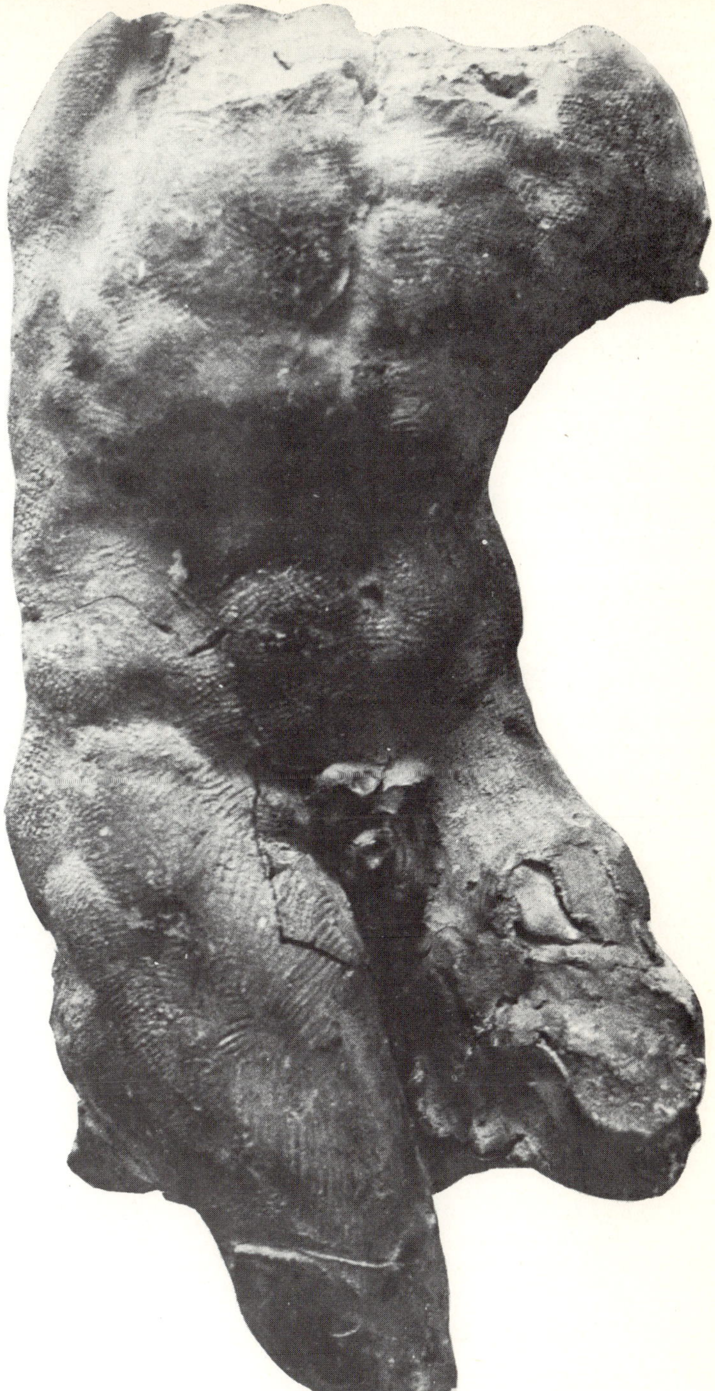

Fragment of maquette for the
Bearded Boboli Slave
Michelangelo
British Museum
photograph John W Mills

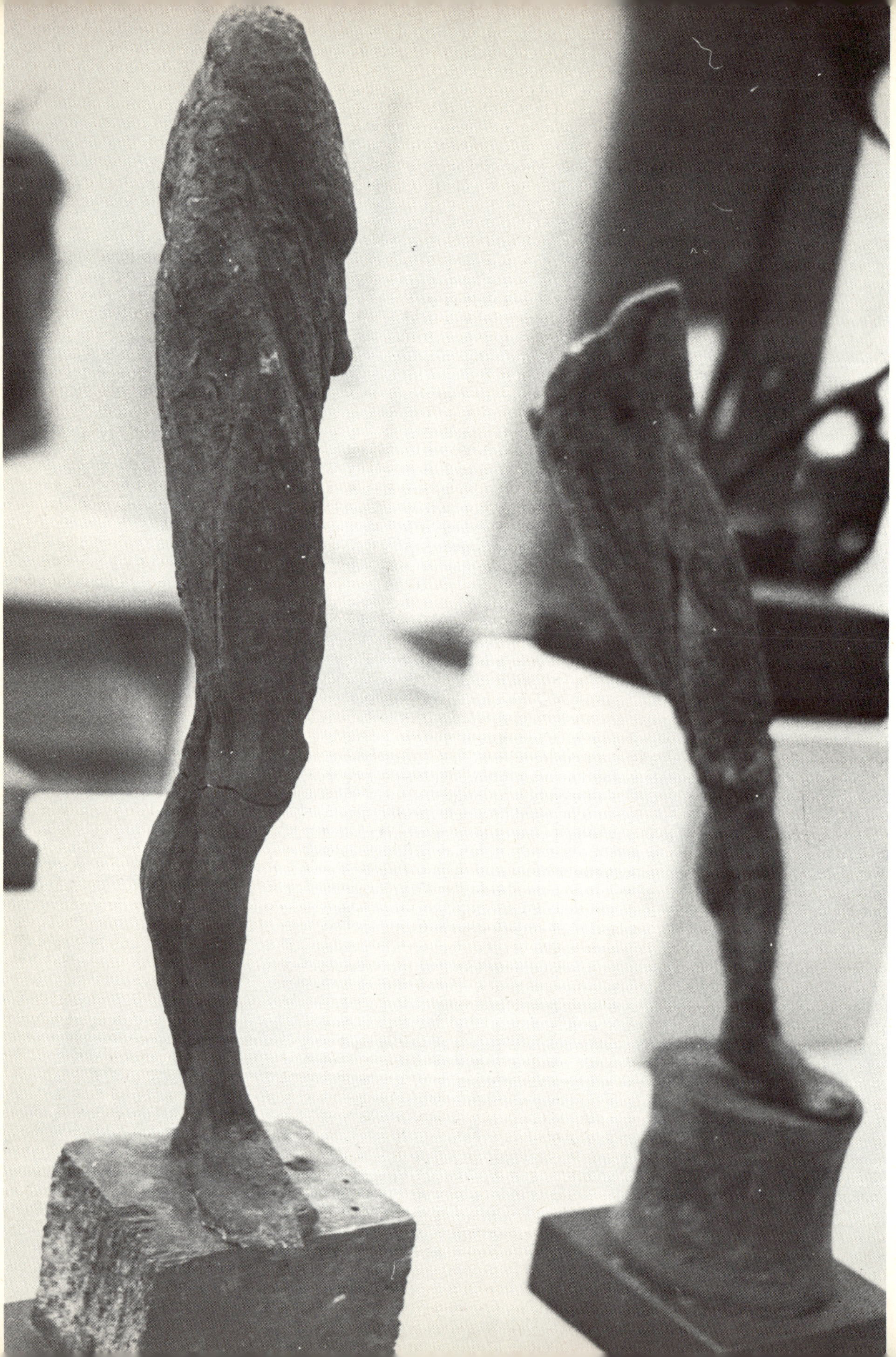

Left and right leg Ecarthe
sixteenth century,
Florentine Red Wax
Formerly ascribed to Michelangelo
Victoria and Albert Museum, London
photograph John W Mills

Left and right arm Ecarthe
sixteenth century,
Florentine Red Wax
Formerly ascribed to Michelangelo
Victoria and Albert Museum, London
photograph John W Mills

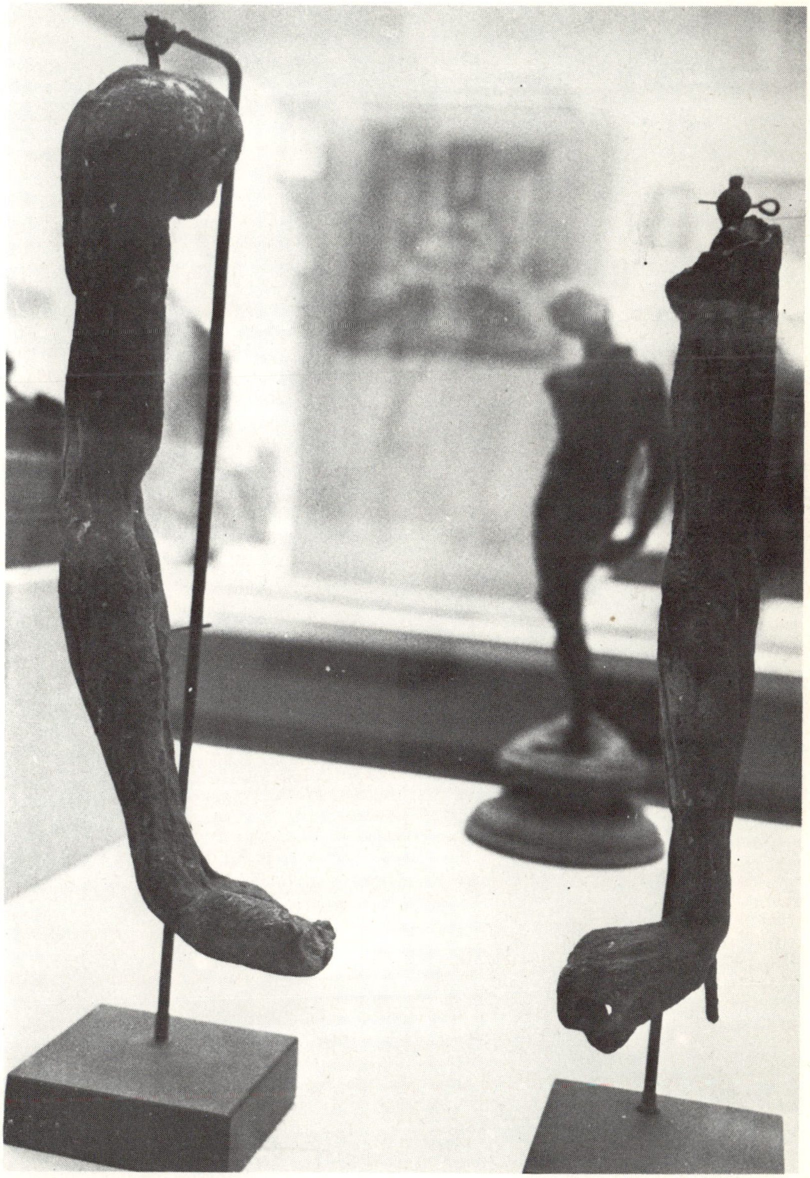

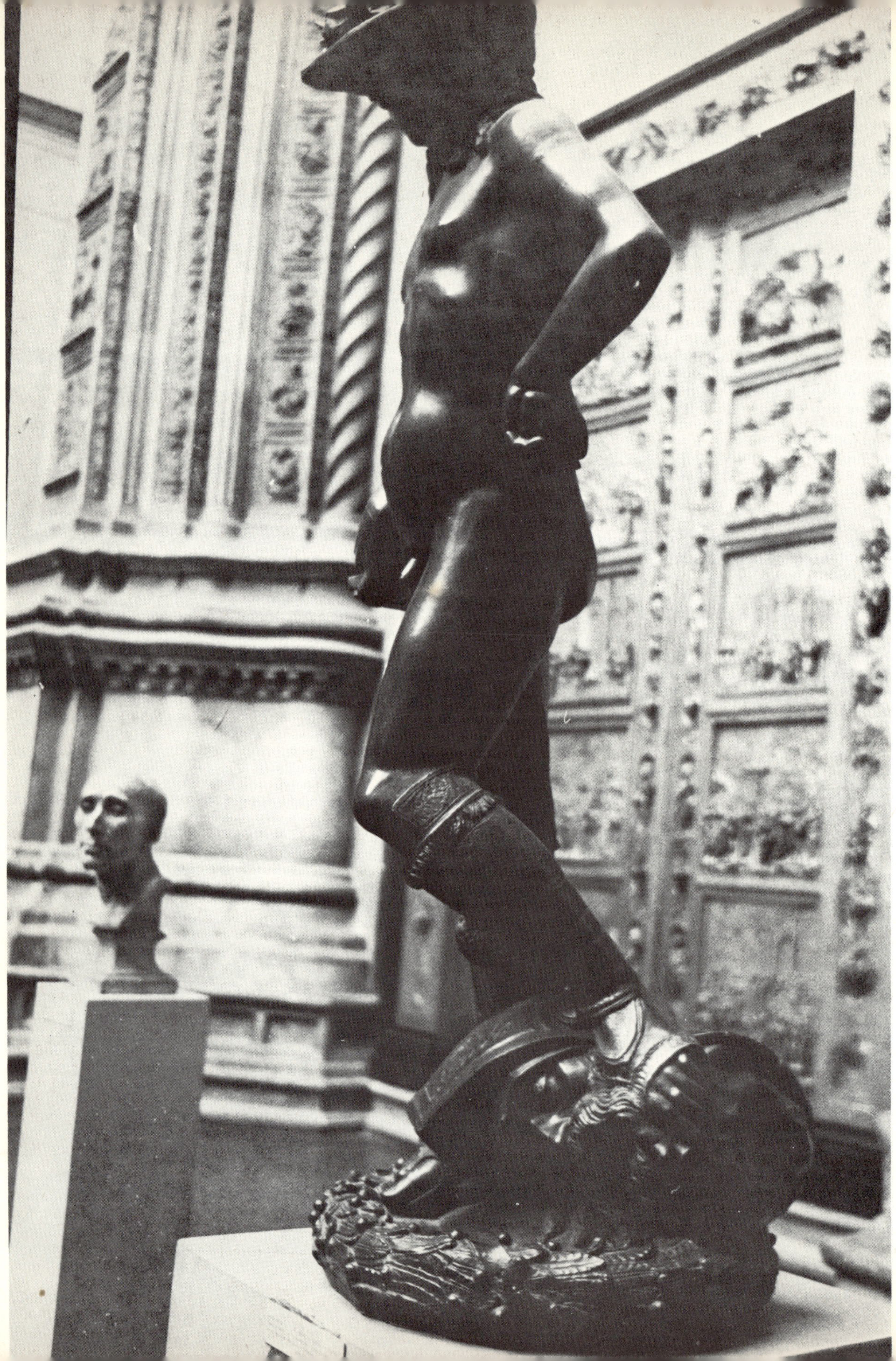

Left and right leg Ecarthe
sixteenth century,
Florentine Red Wax
Formerly ascribed to Michelangelo
Victoria and Albert Museum, London
photograph John W Mills

Left and right arm Ecarthe
sixteenth century,
Florentine Red Wax
Formerly ascribed to Michelangelo
Victoria and Albert Museum, London
photograph John W Mills

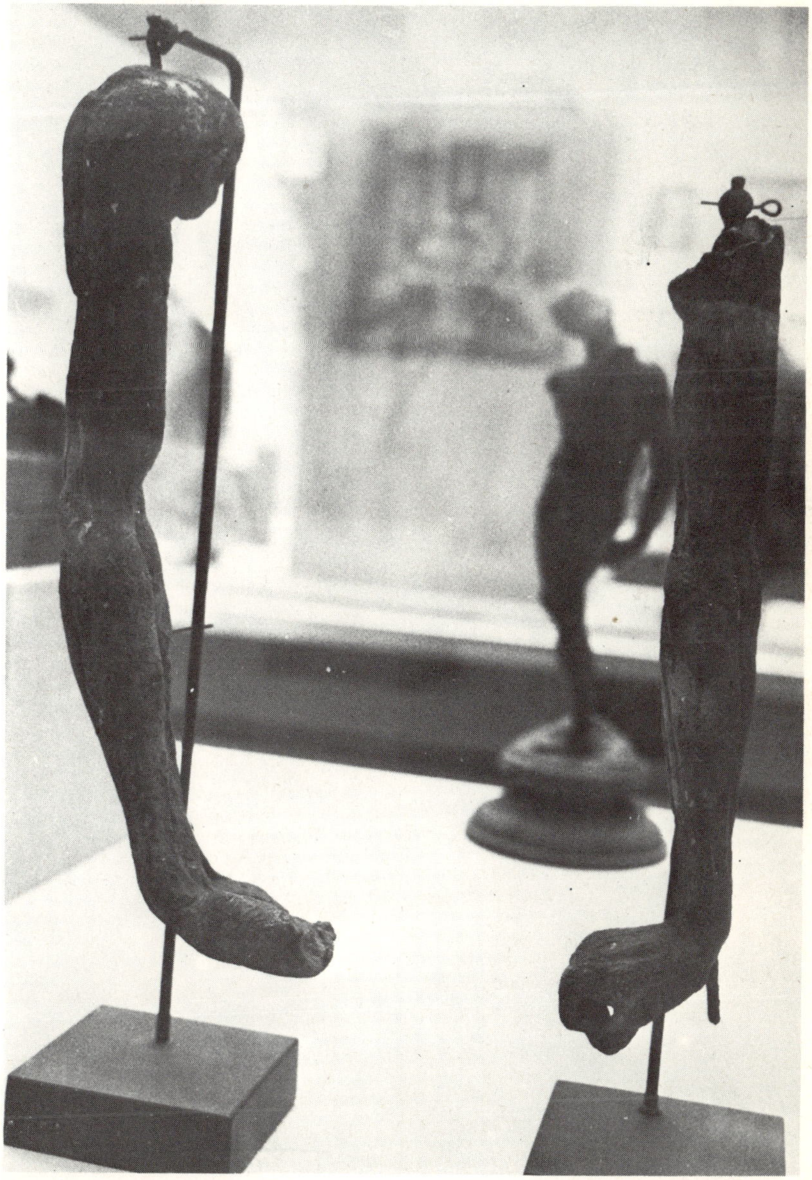

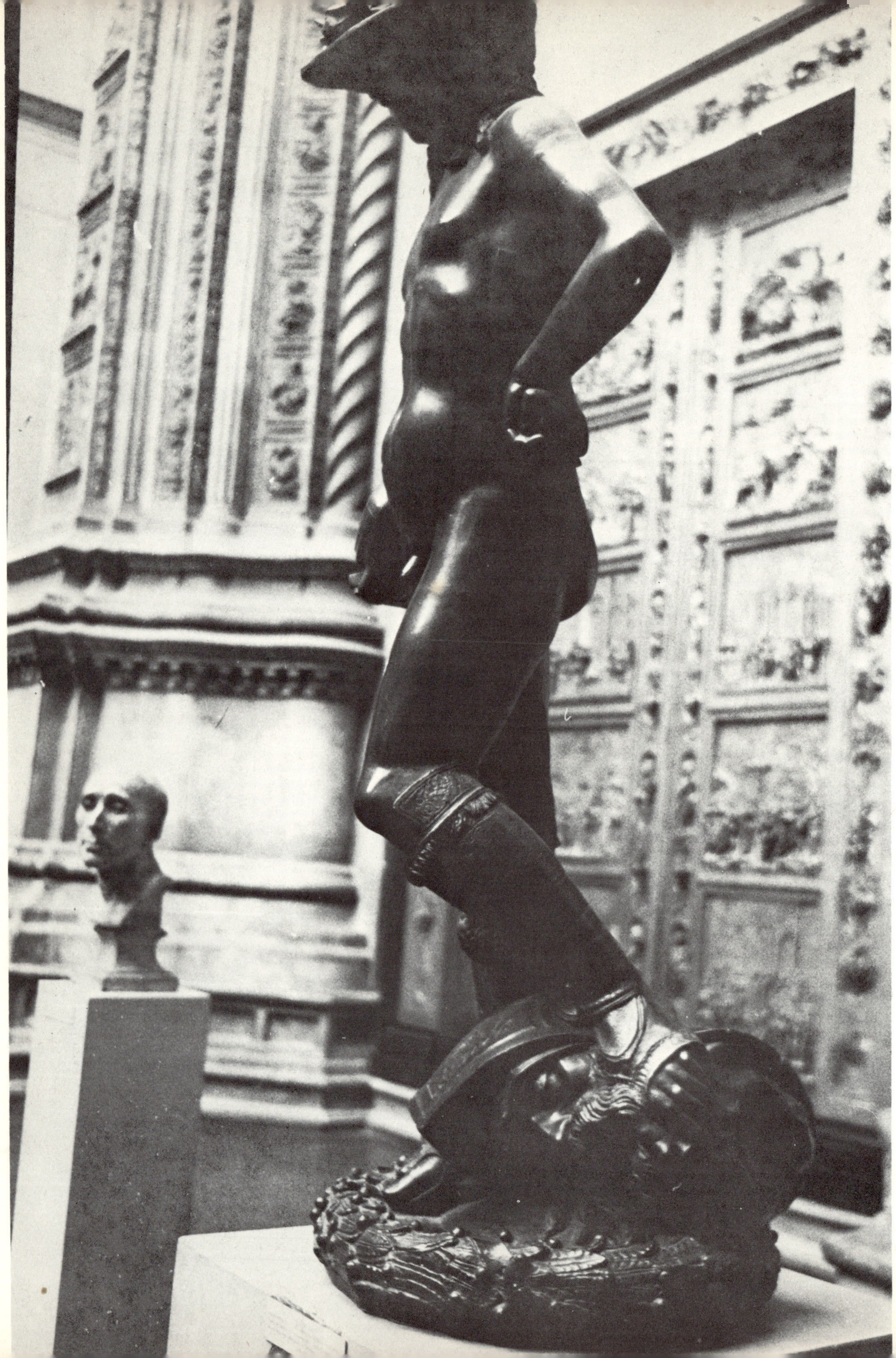

that neither is life in the useful sense to the visual artist, in his attempts to give form to an idea. Both disciplines may provide aids and useful reference but cannot be sufficient stimuli in themselves.

Jacob Epstein wandering around the sculpture studios at the Royal College of Art was heard to ask a student working on a life size figure 'are you working from a model?' and when answered 'no' he wandered away muttering 'I always work from a model'. Did he mean he couldn't work without a model in front of him at all times?

Page 30

The *Visitation* is a fine example of Epstein's work from the model, but the subject is forced to become an Epstein, helping to give form to his idea. The degree of objective study needed to make a portrait sculpture that is both accurate in recalling the visual physical character of the sitter, and is an interesting sculptural form, is a mysterious factor. Jacob Epstein possessed such skill, a marriage between facility, imagination and objective study that produced such heads as *Jacob, Kramer*. These portraits have impact of such power that they convince the onlooker of their reality. The image presented is true, an equivalent to reality, and in this respect is similar to Roman portraits. Sculptured Roman portraits such as those of the Emperors Hadrian and Claudius are

Page 30

Pages 34, 35

David Bronze
Donatello
Plaster cast in the Victoria and Albert Museum, London
photograph John W Mills
See page 13

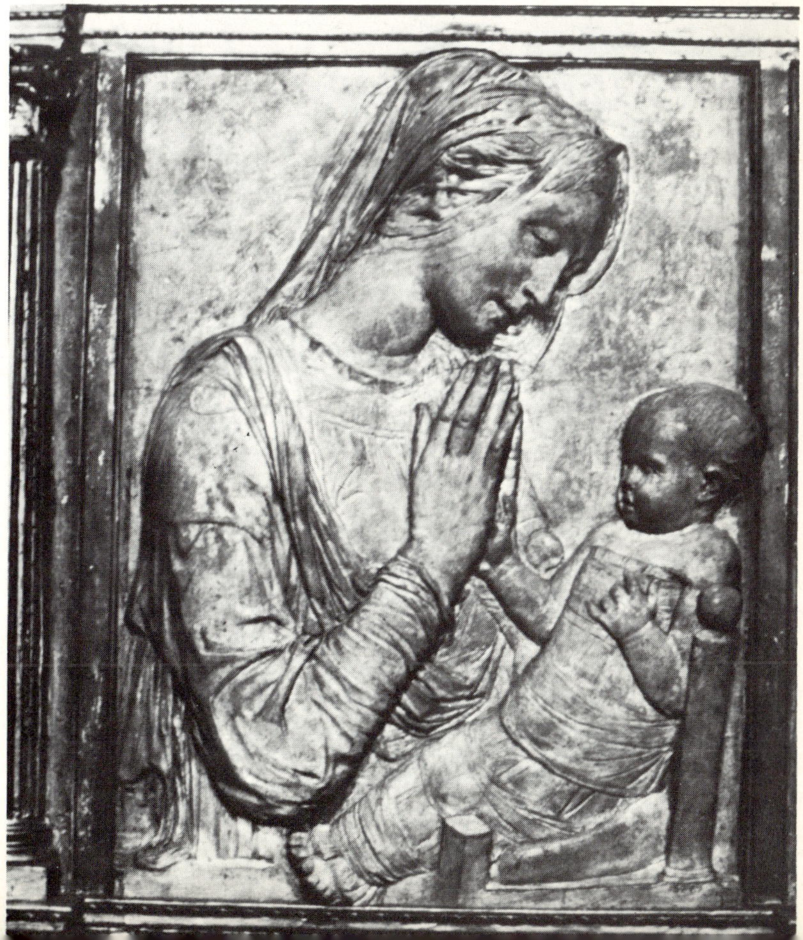

Virgin and Child
Donatello
Victoria and Albert Museum, London
photograph John W Mills

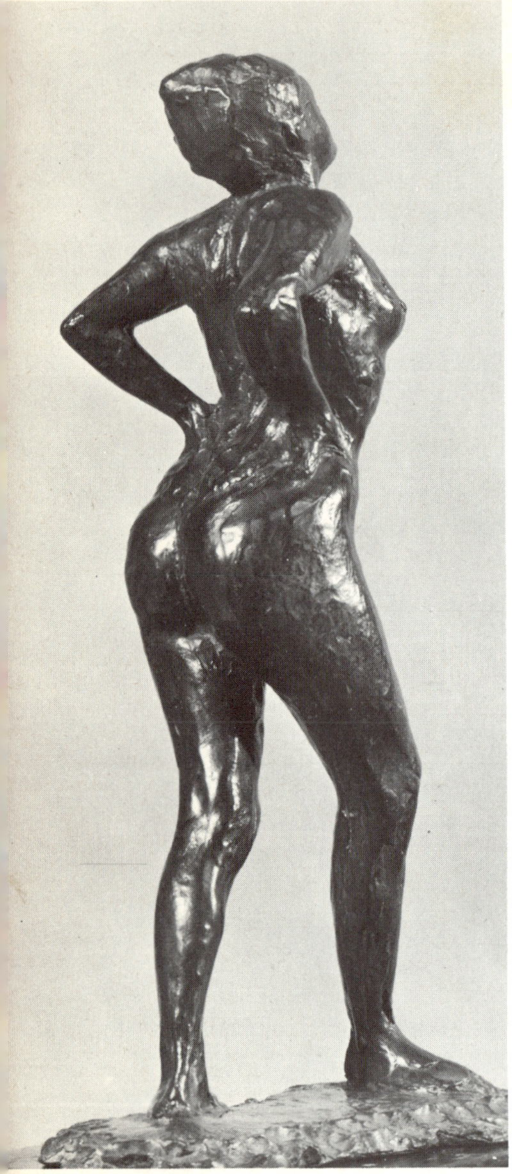

Nude with hands on
hips Bronze
Degas
The Tate Gallery, London

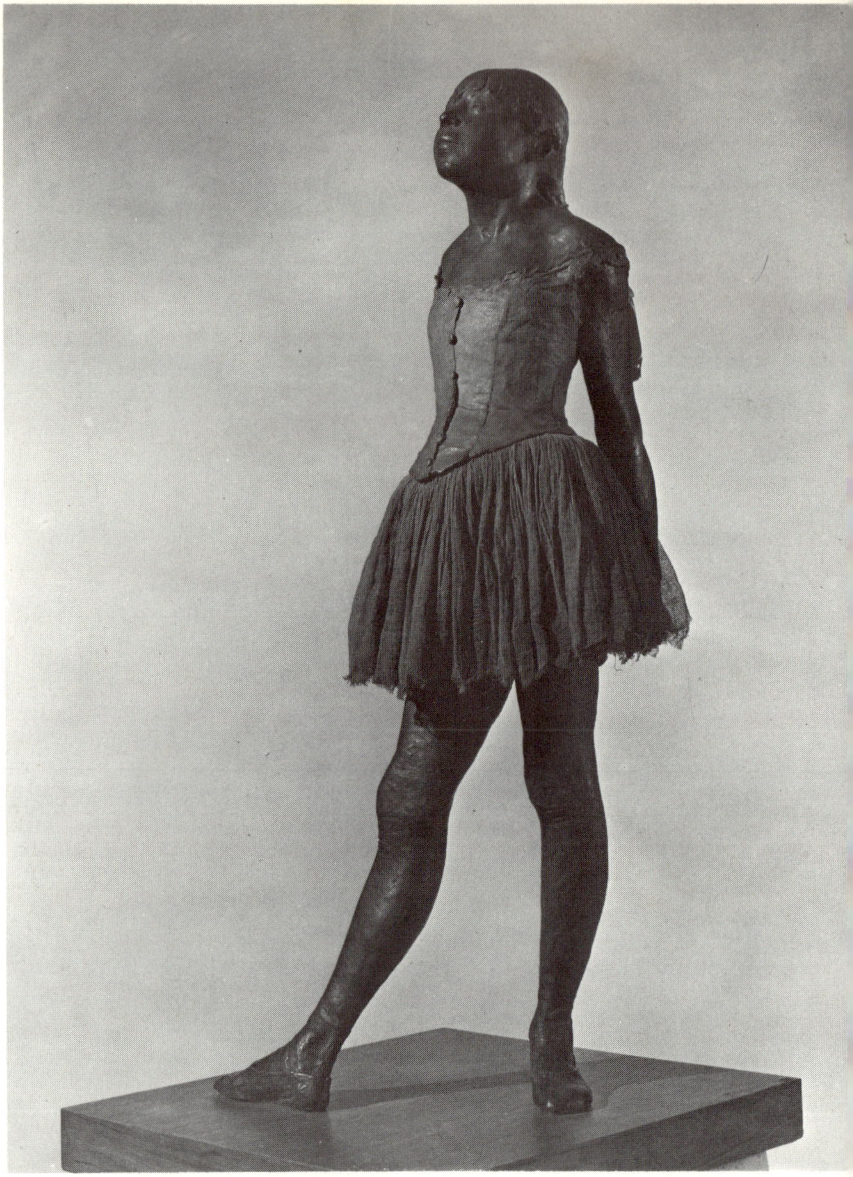

The Little Dancer Aged
Fourteen Bronze
Degas
The Tate Gallery, London *See page 15*

among the finest achievements in that art in european history. When examined in detail we find features are formalised, enlarged or altered in some degree or other, but the handling of the material to evoke a particular character is masterful always. Such a yardstick was used thereafter by Donatello, Rodin, Marini, Richier.

So called expressionism produces sculpture of a different ilk, using a degree of accidental form, to balance observation with an exciting extrovert handling of material. The excitement generated by this expressive attack on the media becomes, in some cases, more important than the image. Germaine Richier in her bronze *Page 36* *'L'Orage'* presents us with a mature control of this idiom. One wonders if it might not have been a gesture of despair against academic life classes. Elizabeth Frink makes sculpture which in many respects evokes a similar feeling, and her figure of the *Fallen* *Page 37* *King* demonstrates a marriage of idea, idiom and technique to make an astute reference to life. Giacommetti on the other hand makes equivalents to people who chance into his studio net, more out of indecision and hyper-sensitivity than by recalling moments *Pages 38, 39* of memory. In one respect Giacommetti presents a cast iron case against preoccupation with the model, demonstrating the fact that a statement made when confronted by and compared with the living model is always wrong. In the same way landscape is always better than a painted duplicate, simply because it is real, and reality in its infinite complexity is always better. The artist must filter what he needs to use at any one time. The same subject may preoccupy him for as long as he can gain useful information from it; this could be a life time. But once the stimulus is exhausted then he must move on to something new. He must explore acceptable alternative images to that of the original. When working on a particular subject an alternative treatment of surface, arrangement of forms, gesture or expression, will occur to the artist. These alternatives are evidence of the creative filter at work, so it is important to be aware of the alternatives in addition to the original conception. In this way it is possible to tap the source for as much stimulus and information as it is willing to reveal at any one time. Leaving the idea only when it no longer stimulates and provides alternative solutions. A study of art history impresses one with such lines of development detectable in the work of many great artists, such as Donatello, Michelangelo, Rodin and Henry Moore. Men obsessed it would seem with few subjects, but each exploited fully.

Academic norms are associated in a Western European background as much with ancient Greece as with the Renaissance. The classical proportion of figures from the Hellenistic Greek period

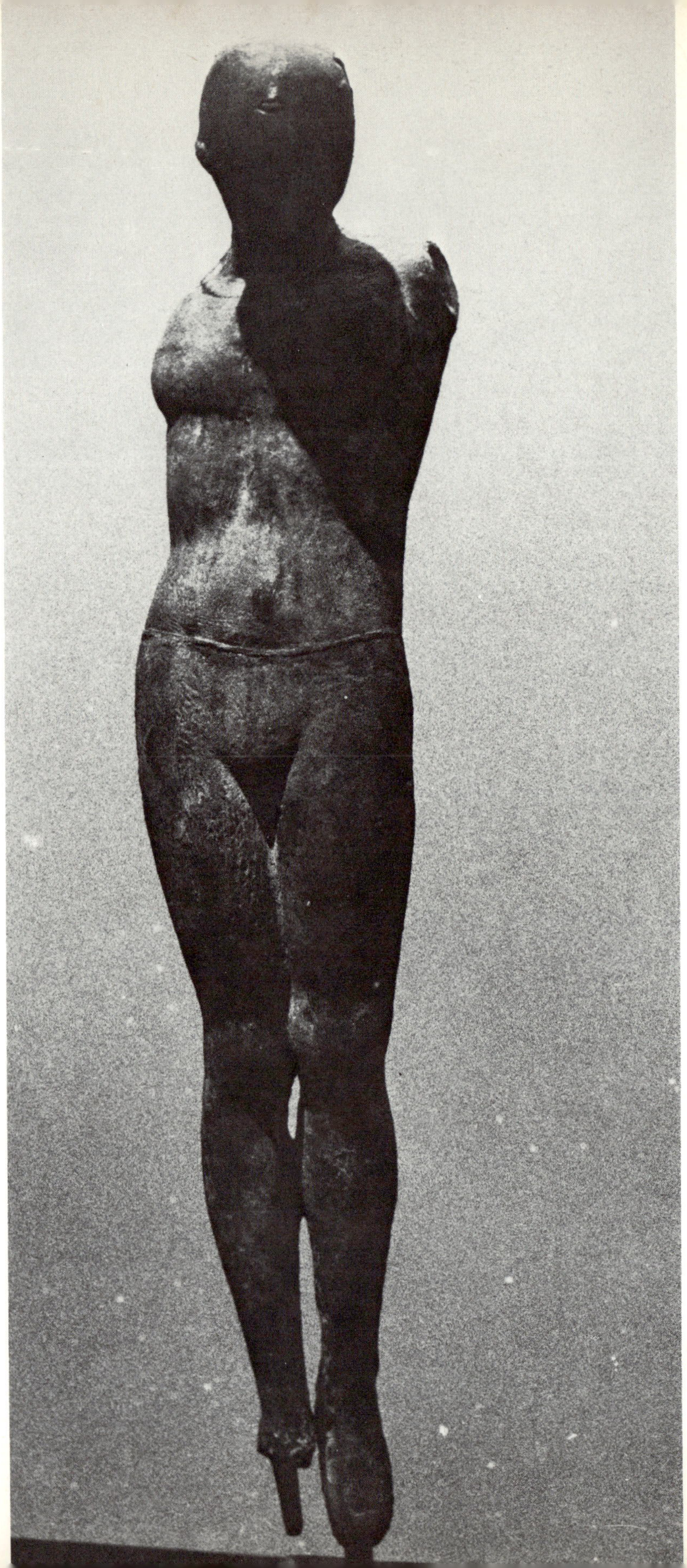

Juggler 1964 Bronze
Marino Marini
Chicago Institute of Fine Art
photograph John W Mills

became the guiding, if somewhat blinding, light to academicians, as bright as that of Michelangelo. No aspirant to fine figurative sculpture can avoid studying the Greeks, and in so doing learn many lessons. Hellenistic sculpture in particular seems to point towards, rather than mirror physical perfection of the human body. Such perfection was to become the goal for physical culturists, to build their bodies, using weight training, according to the pattern set by these sculptures. The scientist Sir Lawrence Bragg once stated that a possible explanation for these superb, nearly perfect, images was to do with reconciling advancing wisdom with physical decline; both occurring with age. If only we could enjoy both together, achieving thereby the ability to put into practice with a virile body, what we know to be right with mature thought. So, according to Bragg, Greek sculpture mirrors philosophy. Such sculptures are of course perfect examples of subjective objectivity. Objective study providing the information to be interpreted in favour of the subjective ideal. How did they manage it in such a particular manner? If likened to sculpture with a similar subjective drive, as witnessed in those from India, *Page 40* and in particular such female figures as *Parvati*, the achievements are equal but at the same time didactic. The Indian sculptures are sensuous and compelling, but formalised. Features mirror religious dogma, and possibly the predilictions of the sculptors, rather than physical reality. The assembling of parts is so masterful that convincing equivalents to reality are made, embodying all that flesh implies sexually, yet remaining remote.

The Italian Gothic sculptor Giovanni Pisano made sculptures of similar moment. In his case, too religious images are endowed *Page 41* with a sense of reality. See *Habbakuk*. His sculpture is so much a part of Tuscany and the Tuscan people, that the impact of his daily contact with his neighbours can be felt even today, his models seem still to be walking about the towns and villages.

The sculptured head is of a totally different order. Idealised heads are usually inferior products, surmounting grande figures, and designed to take a subordinate role. In Egyptian Colossi for instance, the head is formalised so that it is not the image maker, but simply a design element in the overall scheme. The head of *Page 34* Rodin's *Balzac* is the opposite, this feature is definately the focal *Page 45* point of the image. The head on Picasso's sculpture *Man With a Lamb* is of similar impact, and twentieth century figurative painting and sculpture owes much to the lessons given by Rodin and so well understood and passed on by Picasso. His unique contribution is in pointing out the lessons to be learned from history, and then by manipulating materials, inventing ways to assemble features, to be precisely evocative of the subject.

Judith, 1945 Bronze
Marino Marini
Kurtsthistrische Musea, Antwerp
See page 15

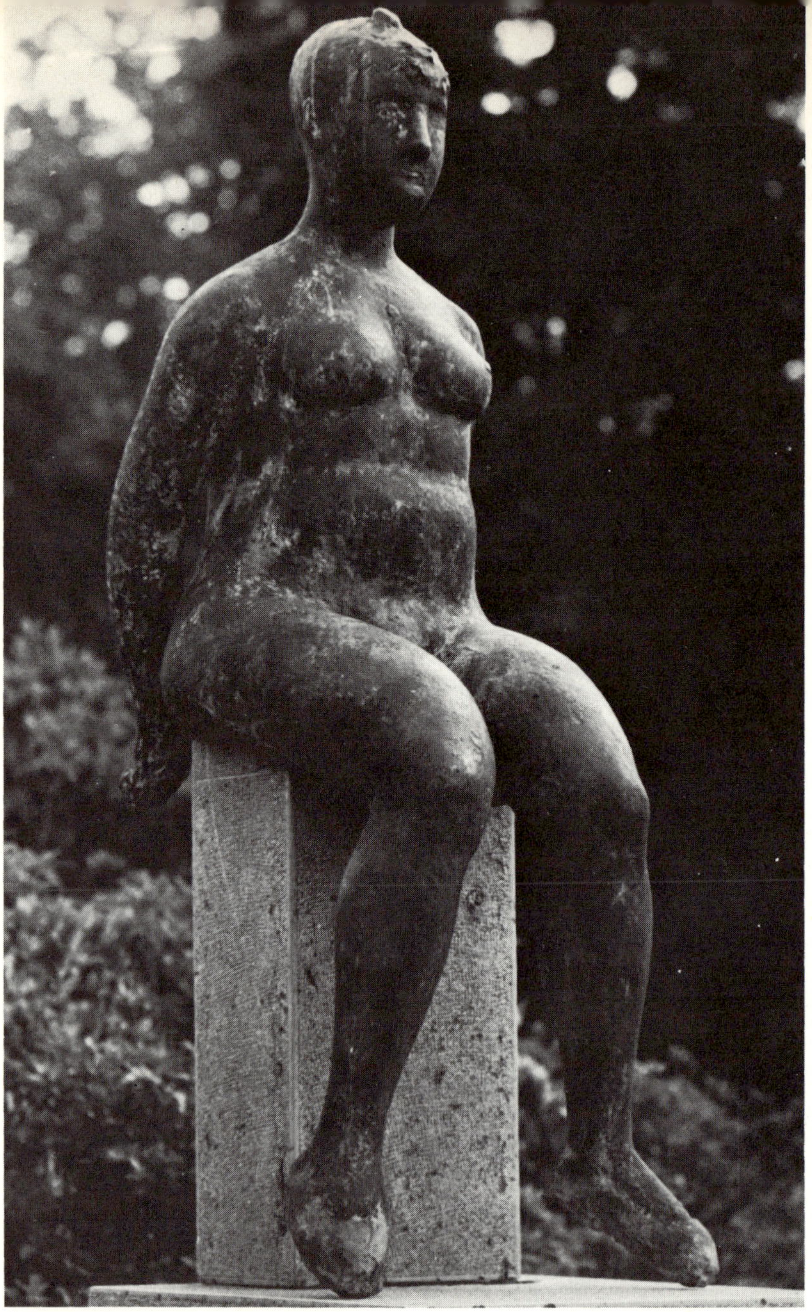

Pomona Bronze
Marino Marini
The Royal Museum of the Arts
J Rump Collection, Copenhagen
See page 15

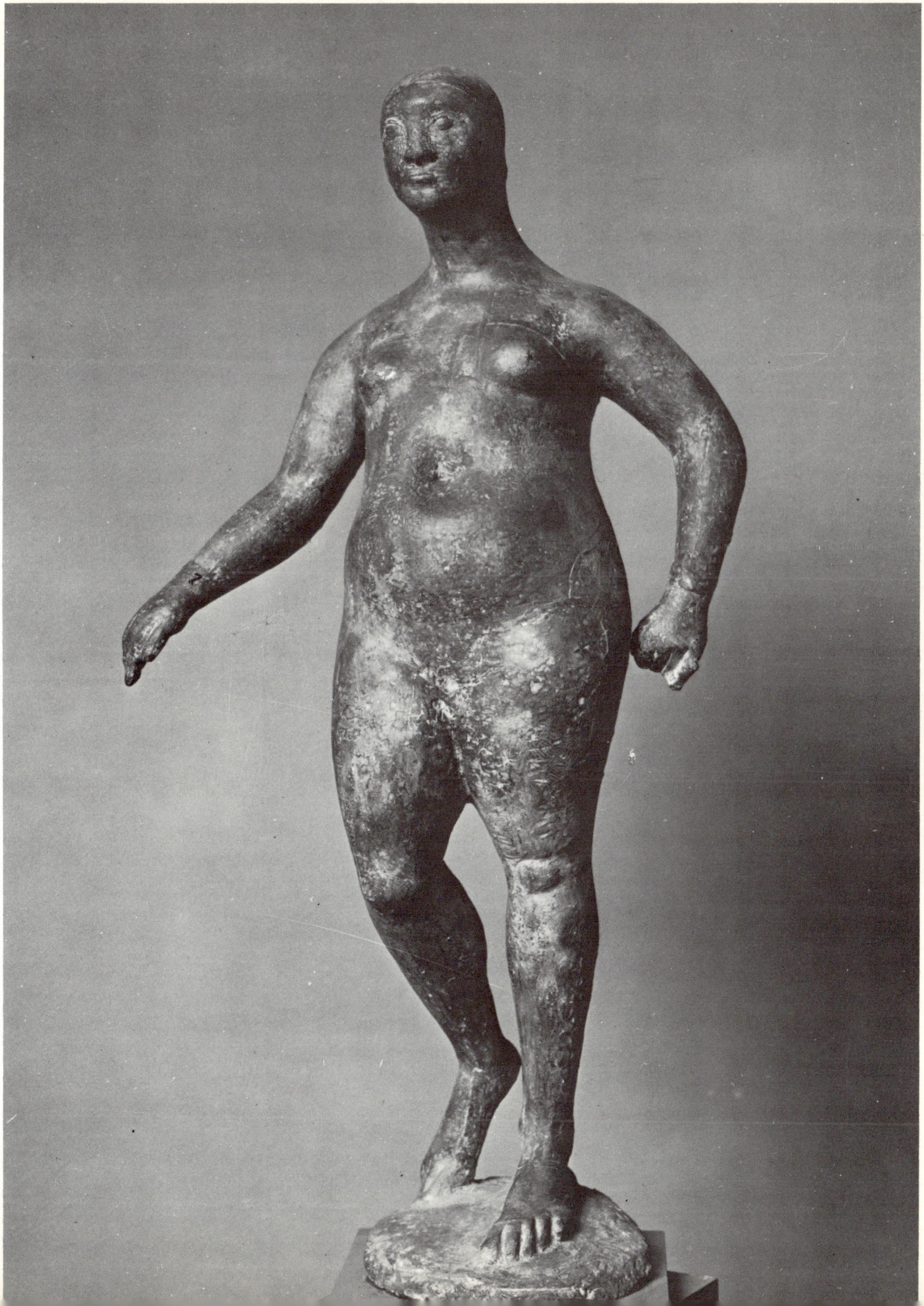

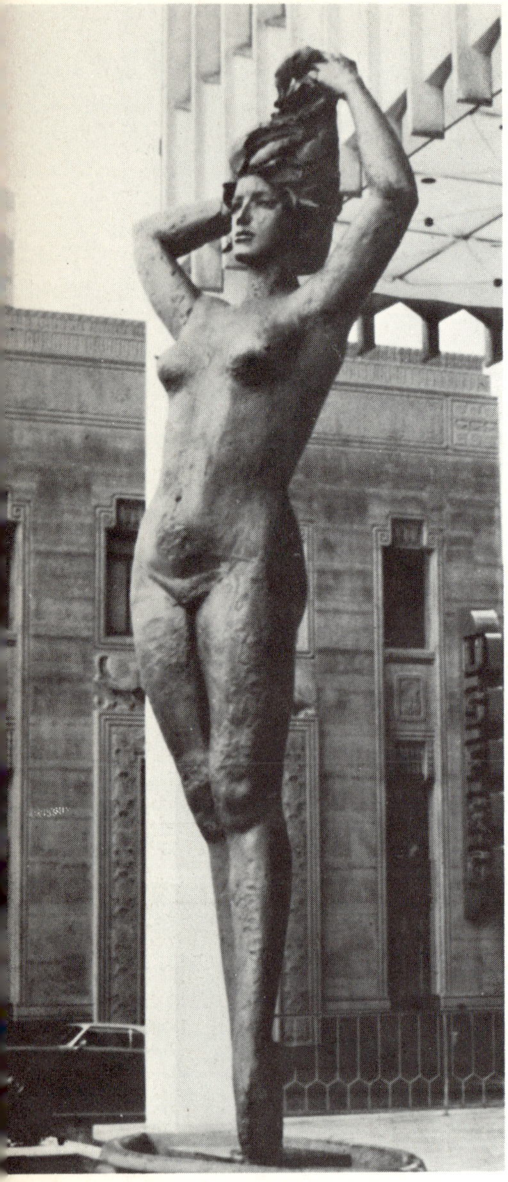

Dancer Bronze
Giacomo Manzu
Detroit
photograph John W Mills

Formalising facial features to make an integrated unit often leads to a formula which is evident in Greek, Indian and Egyptian sculpture in general, and can be appreciated more readily when an exception to the rule appears from one of the same cultures. Sculptures of the Pharaoh Akhnaton and his court present such exceptions. These images are powerful as sculpture and so accurate representations of the King and his court, that the modern medical diagnoses of their various illnesses have been possible. Their physical characteristics have been so well recorded, their oddities being used as stimuli.

Such physical oddity, enabling structure to be easily comprehended, is a prime factor in the choice of subject and sitter. Extreme examples of this are the numerous sculptures made of the starving and ill, the halt and the lame. Exaggerated anatomical features can be copied to produce superficially potent images. The selection of sitters for portrait in particular, and for life study in general, is often based on physical peculiarities and extremes. Features that give the artist a point of departure, a constant reference point, and thereby licence to exaggerate. It is difficult to make a sculptured image from a head that presents no outstanding feature. The difficulty Manzu apparently had making the portrait of Pope John was probably due in part to this, but the quality of the bronze figure gives an indication of how this deficiency can be overcome. The same sculptor modelling a subject of his own choice however produces a sculpture of a different quality.

The element of liking or disliking the sitter is a factor in commissioned portraiture that can present the sculptor with a problem. Portrait painters of the stature of Holbein, Goya, Velasquez or Rembrandt often dealt with this problem by studied use of sombre tones. Cleverly surrounding the sitter with painted quality effects that create a pictorial harmony, to distract from the sitter. The sculptor cannot do this. This constant problem is in part responsible for the perpetuation of academic norms. Canova, for instance, found it more profitable to produce portraits of Napoleon in the genre of ancient Greece, thus, unfortunately for us, avoided making a portrait of an odd little man. He avoided too the genre of Ancient Rome which would have demanded a greater adherence to the truth. The subject was therefore flattered. Flattering the sitter was, and still is, the most important factor in a poor portrait. When the sitter is confronted by a three-dimensional likeness of himself, it has a great impact, because it is not reversed as a reflection in a looking glass. It is another person yet also the same person, and this fact makes it hard to respond favourably at first. Winston Churchill's reaction to his portrait by

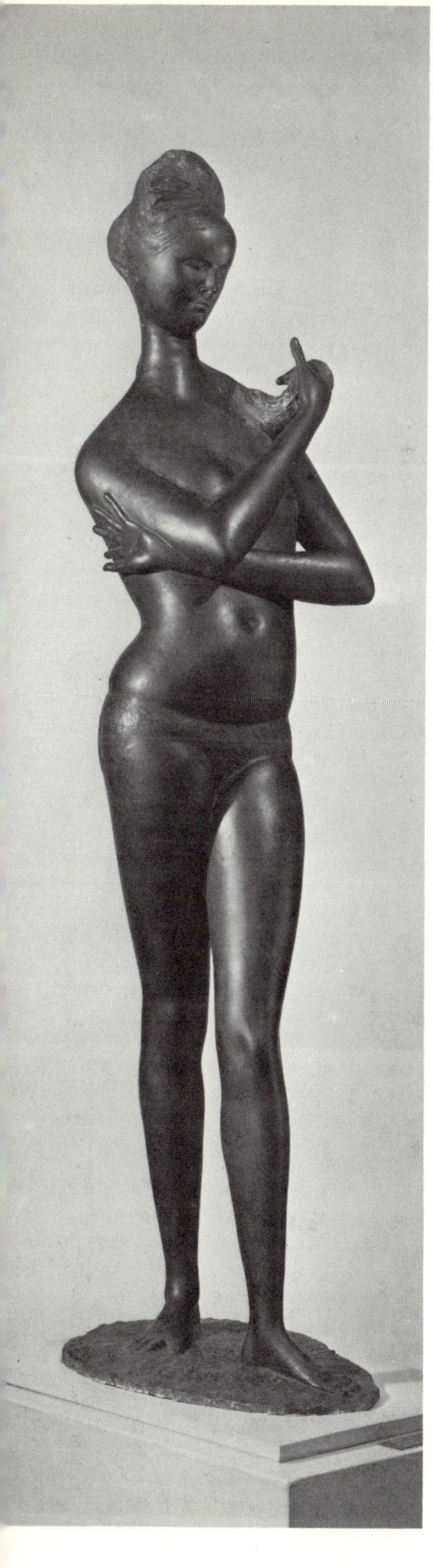

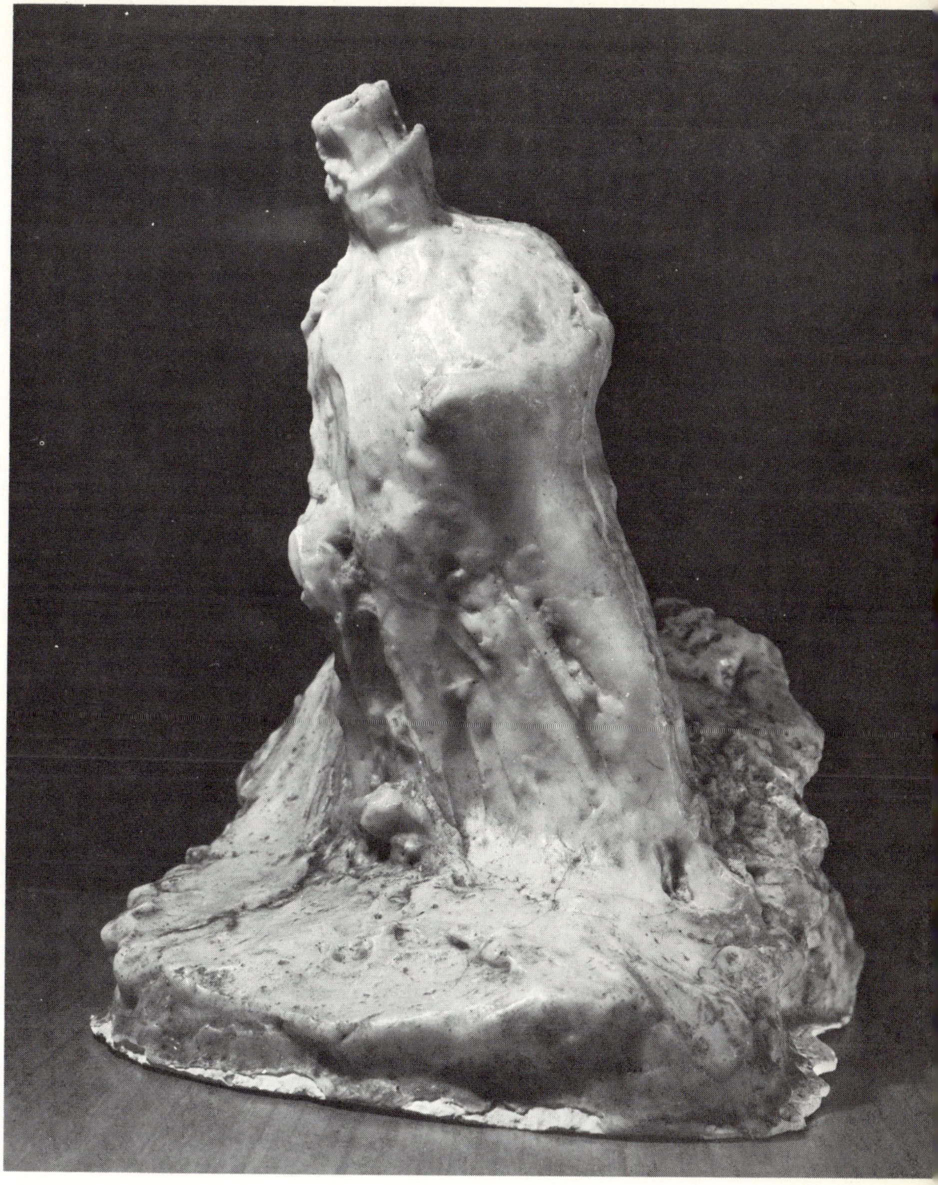

The Bookmaker 1894
Wax over plaster
Medardo Rosso
Collection, The Museum of Modern Art, New York. Acquired through the Lillie P Bliss Bequest
See page 16

Bather   Bronze
Emilio Greco
The Tate Gallery, London
See page 15

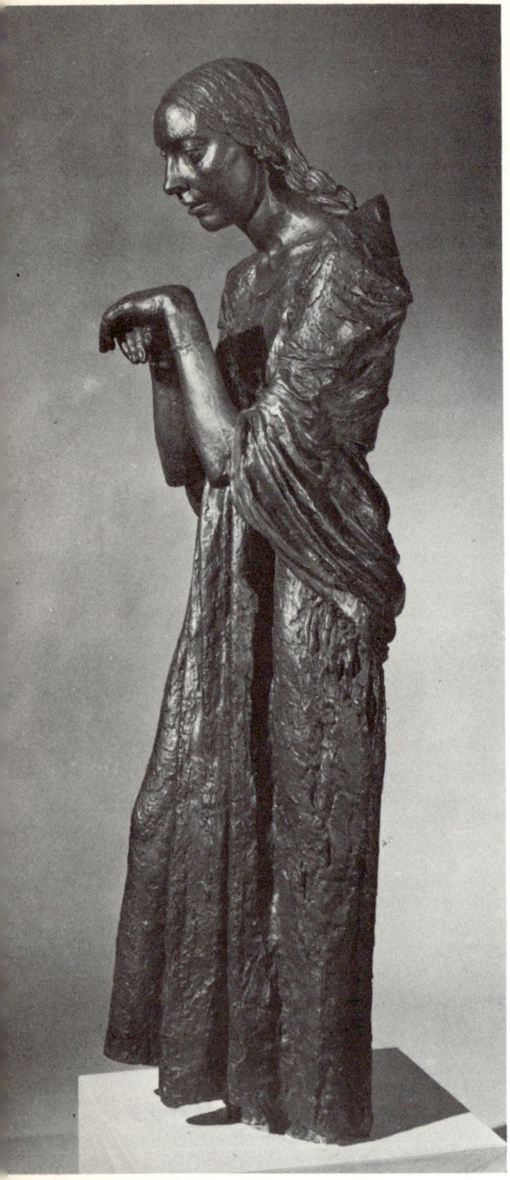

The Visitation
Jacob Epstein
The Tate Gallery, London
See page 21

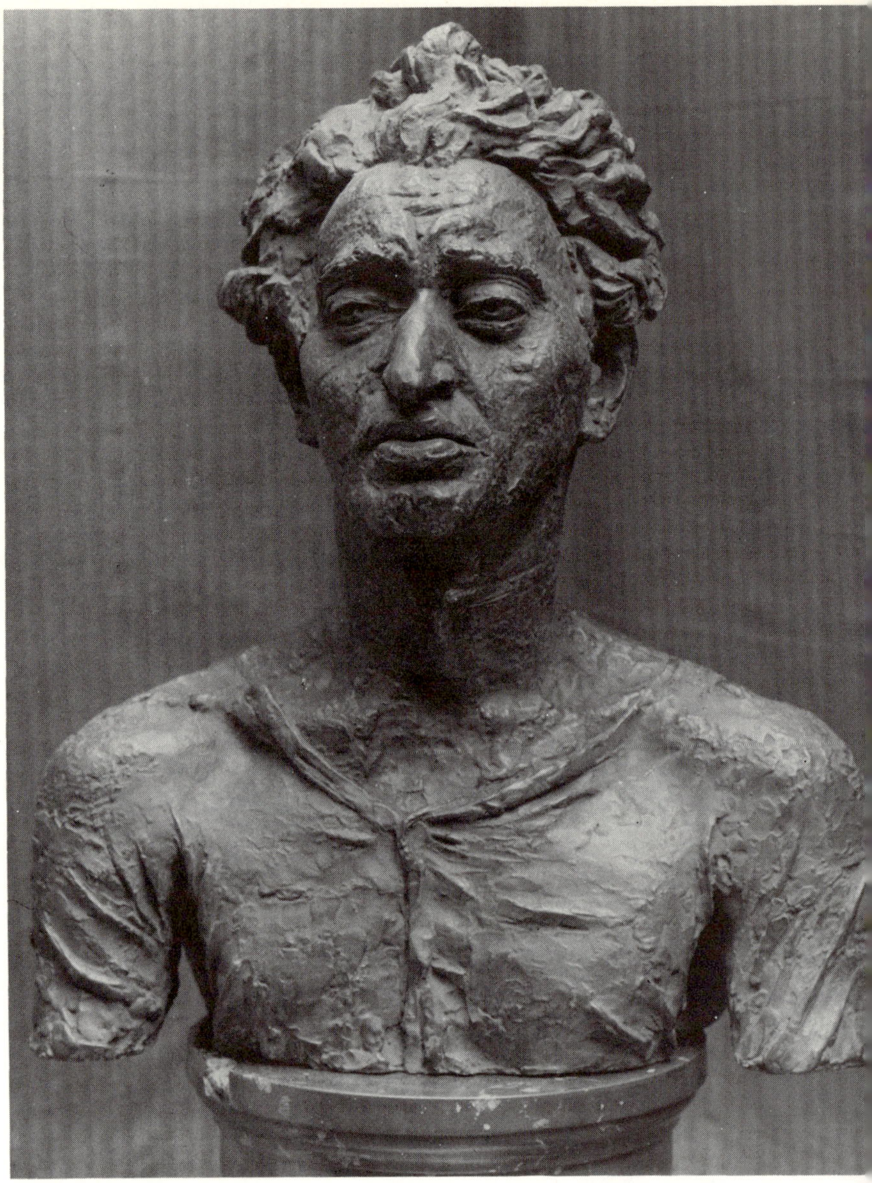

Jacob Kramer   Bronze
Jacob Epstein
The Tate Gallery, London
See page 21

Graham Sutherland and his clash with Jacob Epstein, offer counterparts to the Napoleon-Canova mutual admiration society. Both the Churchill likenesses were accurate and relentless, conflicting or coinciding with the sitter's opinion and image of himself. Both rejected by him.

Everyone has a memory of their reflected likeness, coupled to a concern, either a love or a hate, for a particular feature. This memory affects an appreciation of a portrait. The artist therefore has to be careful in his treatment of the sitter. Some sculptors avoid the issue altogether by modelling only chosen subjects, all of whom conform to a pattern. Others force the image of the sitter into a particular idiom to become only another one of a series. The honest thing to do, surely, is always to pay attention to the elements of choice, and select those features most typical of the sitter and balance their disposition and emphasis of detail according to the correct personal visual impact. This can only be the impression of that particular person upon the artist. An honest rendering will always be the best solution in the long run. If a client is offended by that, then perhaps he is no great loss, do not lose sleep over an inability to flatter a client. Most thoughtful clients will accept the portrait when wisely presented, and respond to a unique sculpture, even though it corresponds to their unique personality, and may at first seem unflattering.

Rodin in his old age said about portraiture that even with women the truth must be stated 'but not always all the truth'. The procedure in working from a head or figure he explained: 'on beginning their work they (the artists) should exaggerate characteristic features. The exaggerations are necessary to establish the structural expression. It is only by graduation of these more characteristic traits that the relative values of all the parts can be determined'.

The following chapters deal with the materials of modelling and their related skills, as well as with the esoteric skills of anatomy and observation both inside and out of the studio. In this respect it is not a conscious effort to force a student into a particular way of doing things, although I am very conscious of my personal bias. I feel that if an idiom can be detected too soon in a students work it may indicate a shortcoming in the nature of that student's study, and this should be as broad as possible for as long as possible. His tutor should assist him in this broad endeavour and not push him towards a mannered and narrow influence.

The British sculptor Eric Gill once said 'it is best to study from the naked model, it is better to do it later in life, when the experience of living has filled the mind'. The broader the study the greater the experience and the more likely is the mind to be filled with personal things.

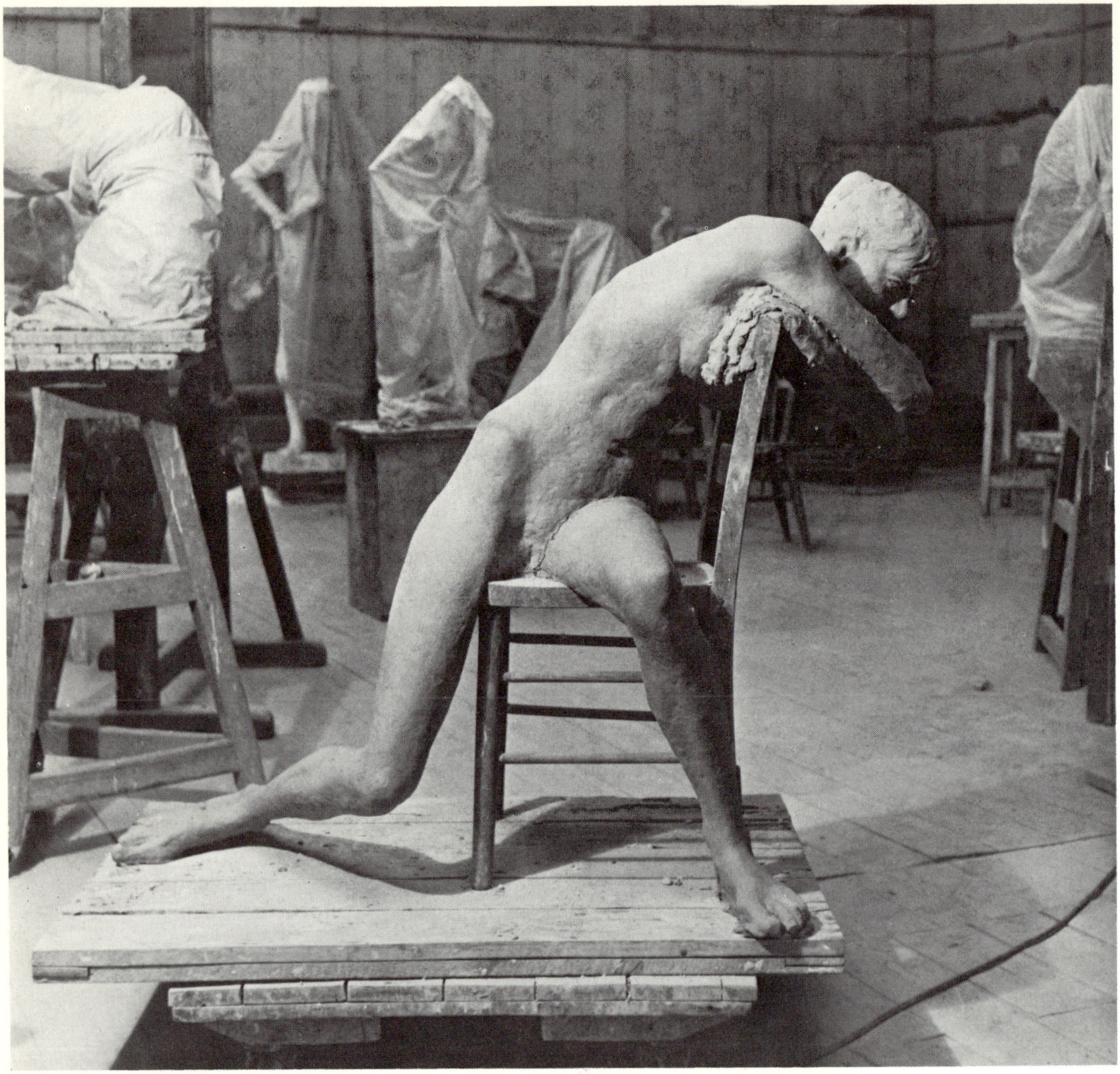

Life Study 1958 at the
Royal College of Art
Clay
John W Mills
photograph John W Mills
Front view
See page 16

Back view

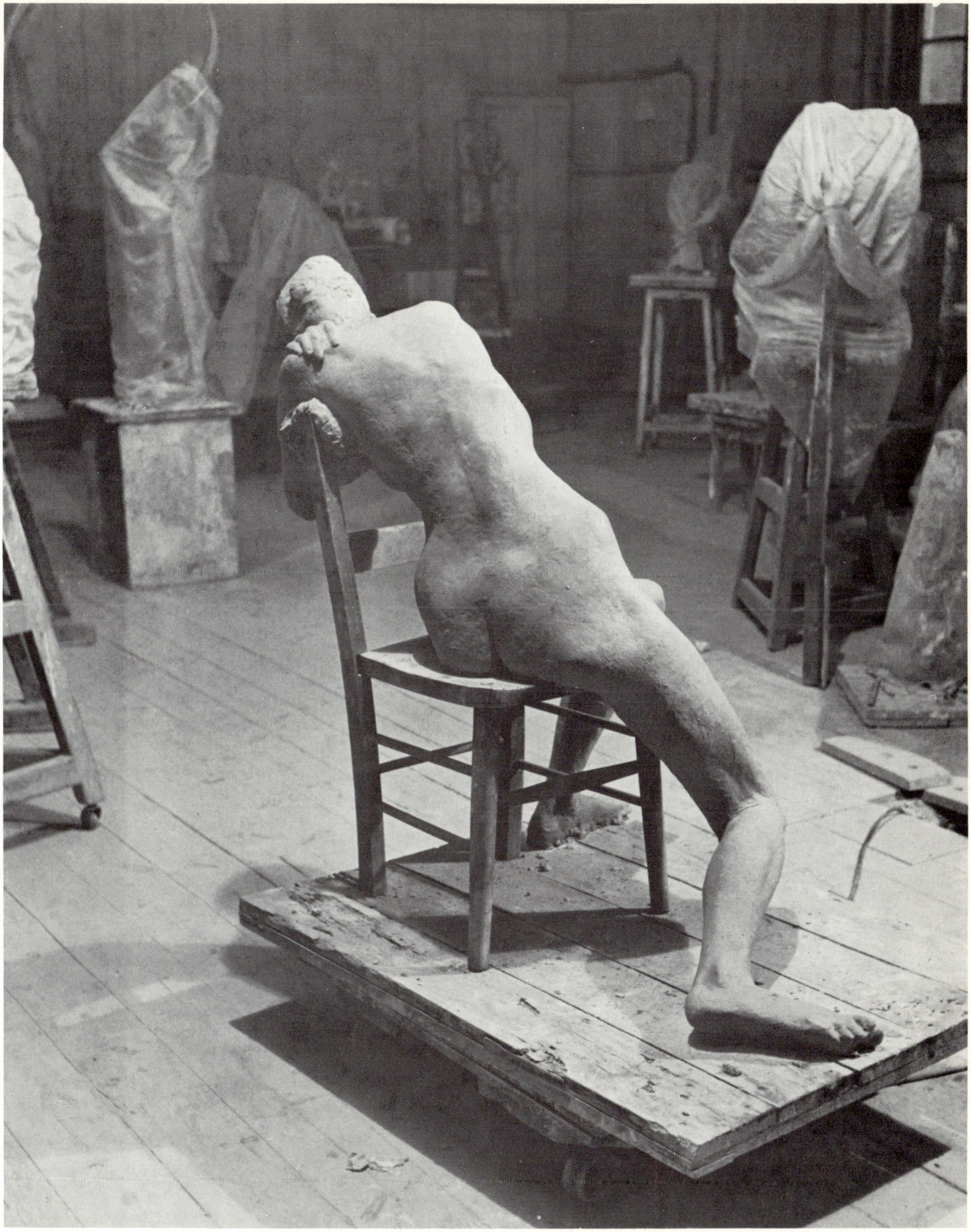

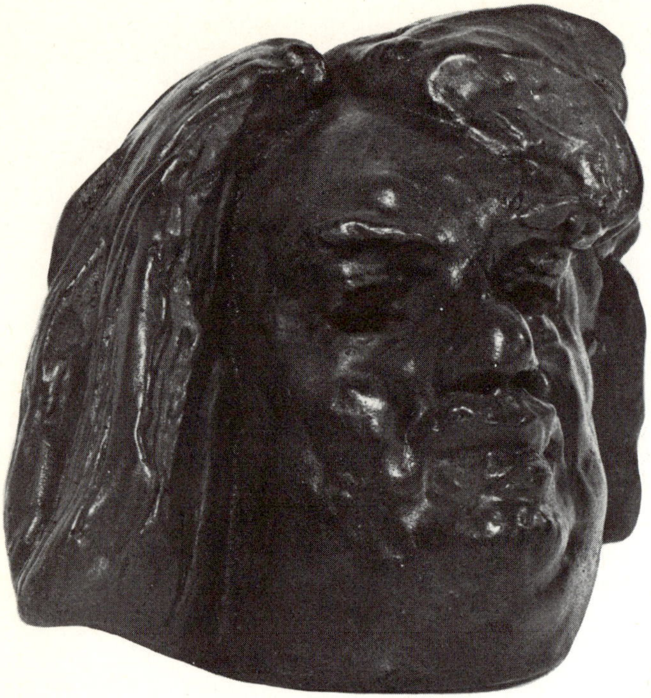

Study for Balzac Bronze
Auguste Rodin
photograph John W Mills
See page 25

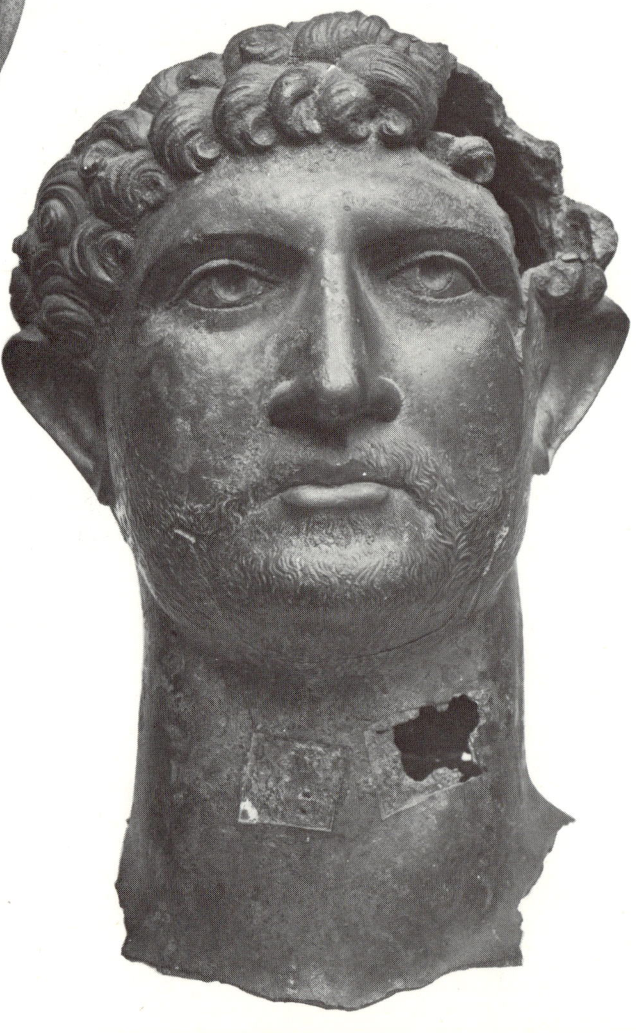

Head of the Emperor Hadrian
second century AD
British Museum, London
See page 21

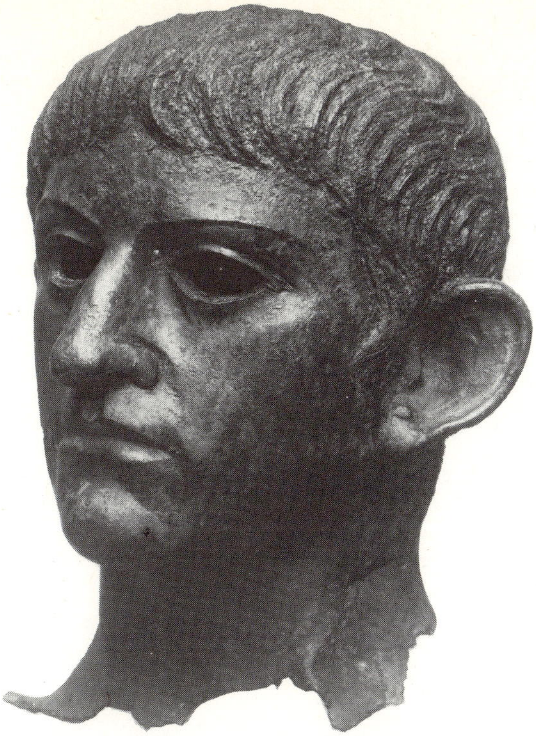

Head of Claudius, mid-first century AD
British Museum, London
See page 21

Dionysus Marble
From the Athenium Acropolis
British Museum, London
See page 25

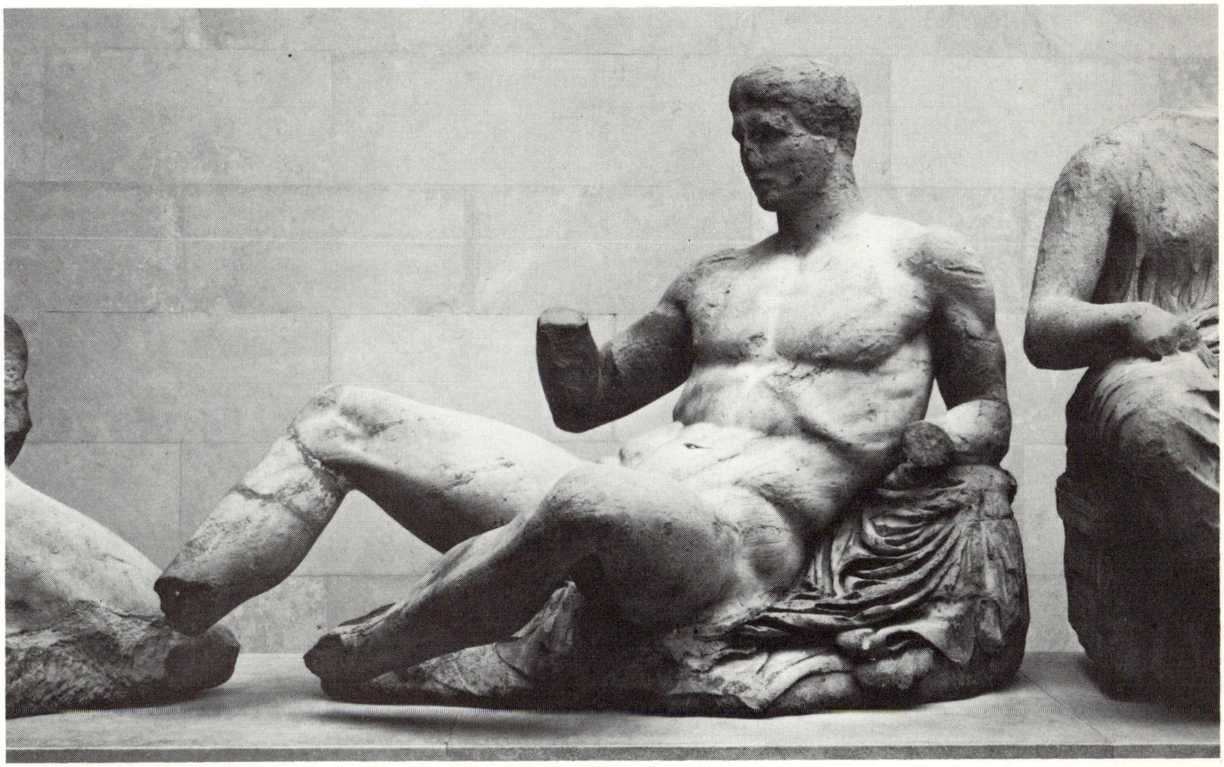

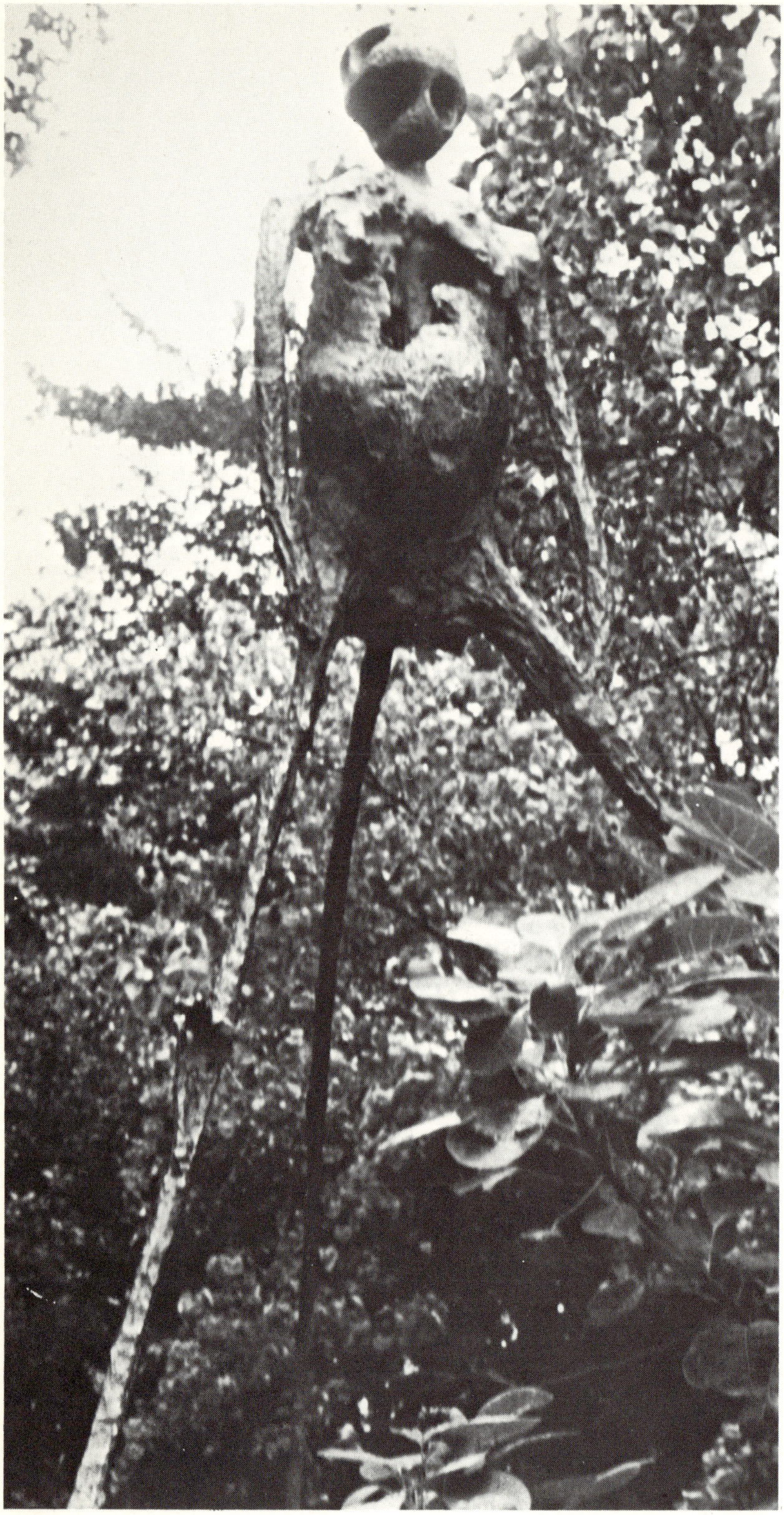

Shepherd of the Landes Bronze
Germaine Richier
photograph John W Mills

L'Orage Bronze
Germaine Richier
Musees Nationaux, Paris
See page 21

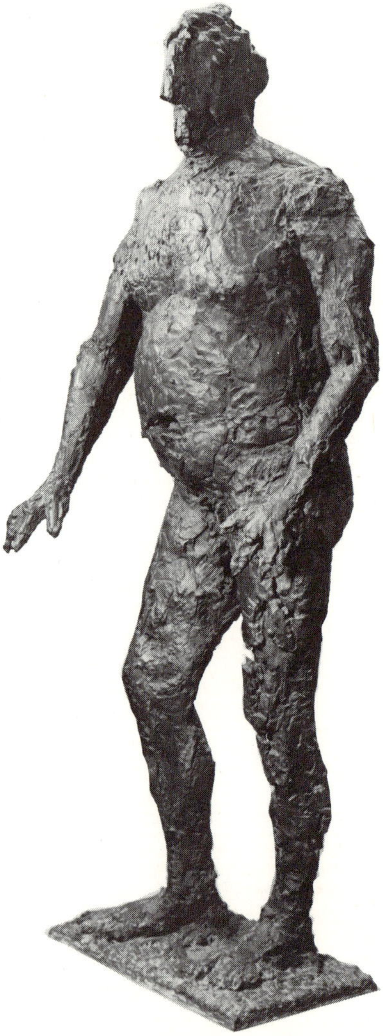

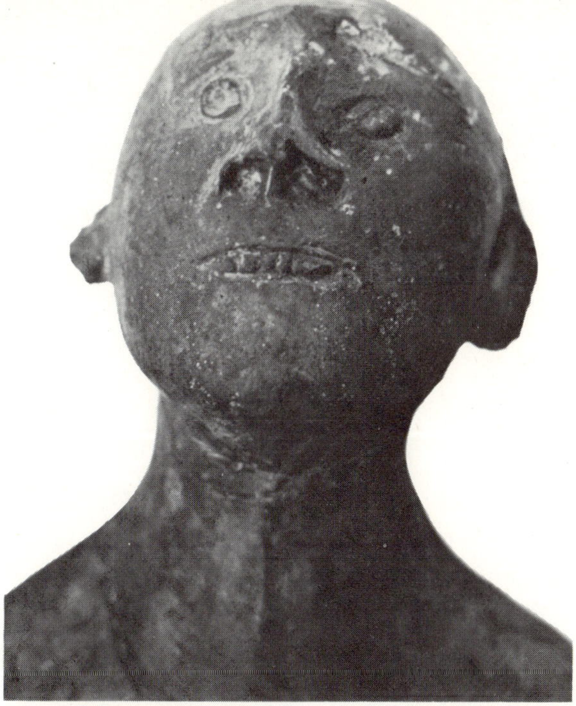

Dancer Bronze
Marino Marini
Albright-Knox Collection
photograph John W Mills

Fallen King Bronze
Elizabeth Frink
photograph John W Mills
See page 23

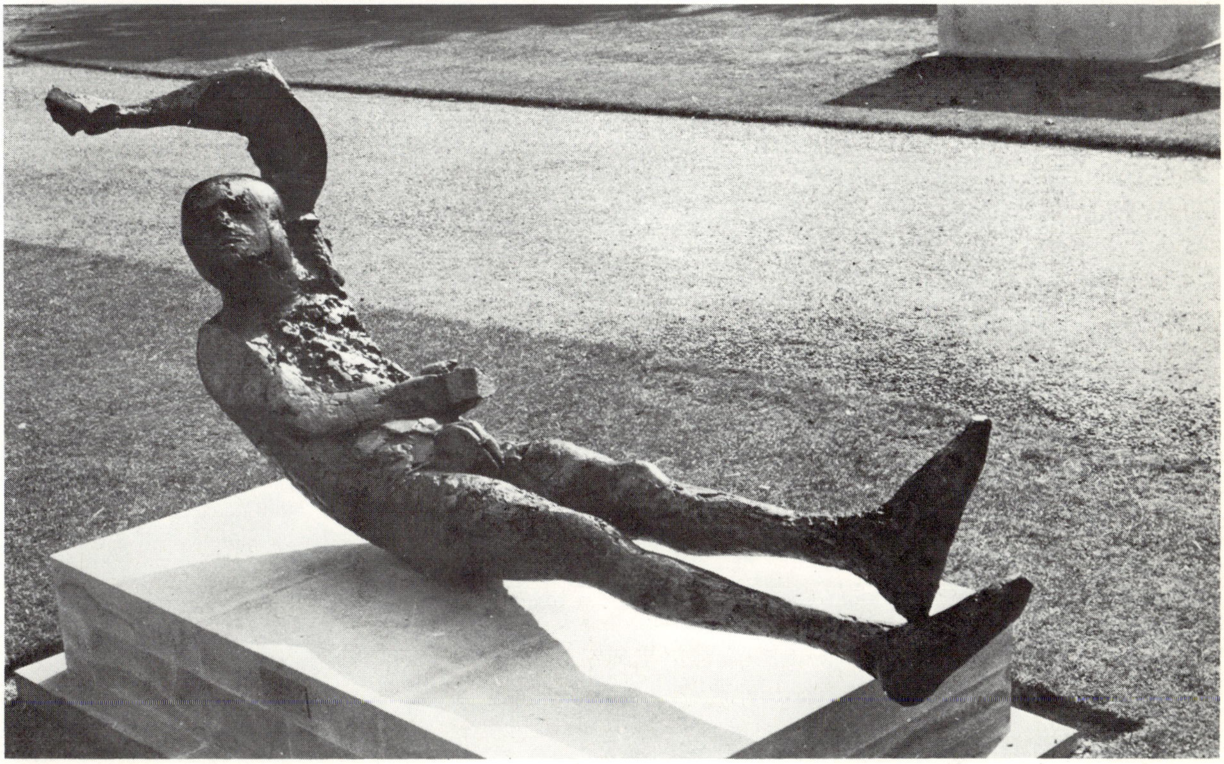

Head being modelled by Alberto Giacometti
photograph Franco Cianetti

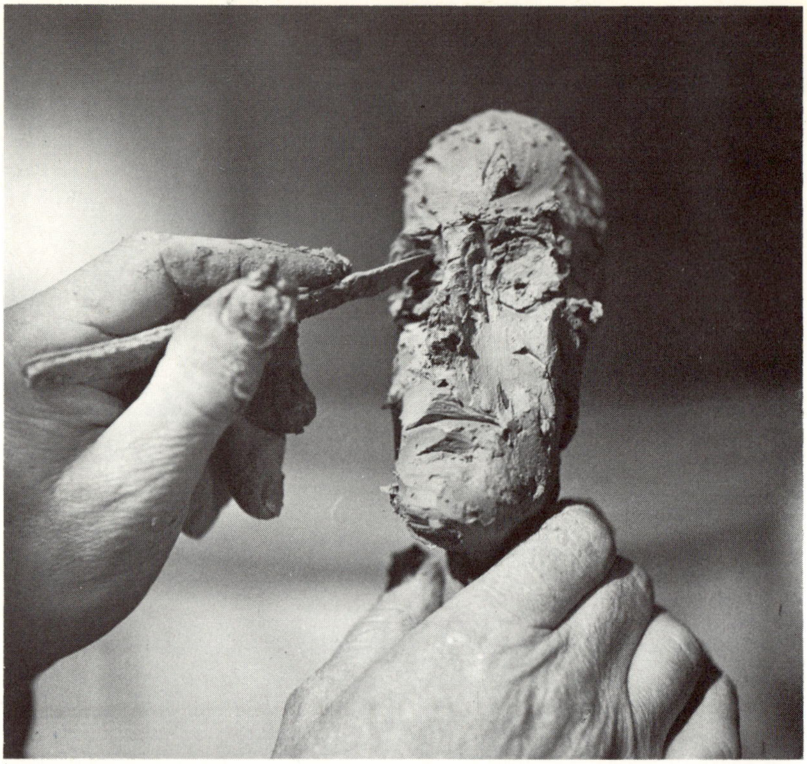

Sculpture with Sitter
Alberto Giacometti
photograph Franco Cianetti

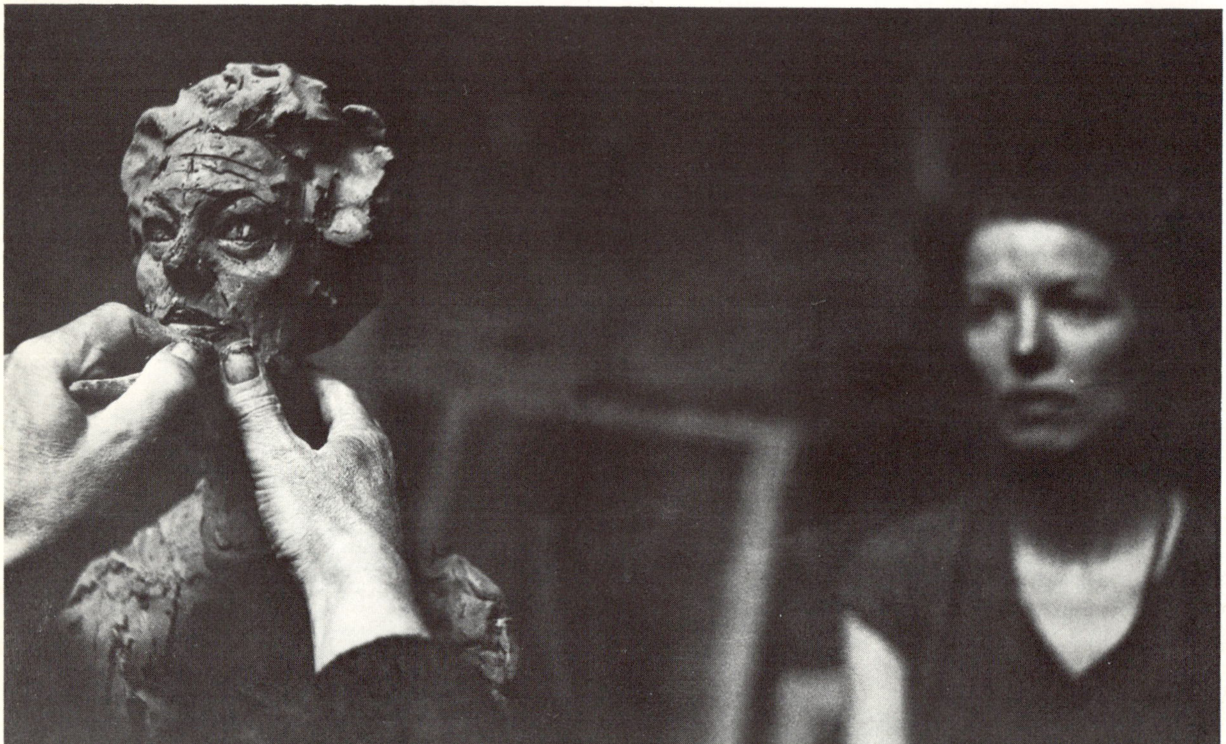

Chiavenna Head 1   Bronze
Alberto Giacometti
The Tate Gallery, London

Walking Man   Bronze
Alberto Giacommeti
Albright-Knox Collection
photograph John W Mills

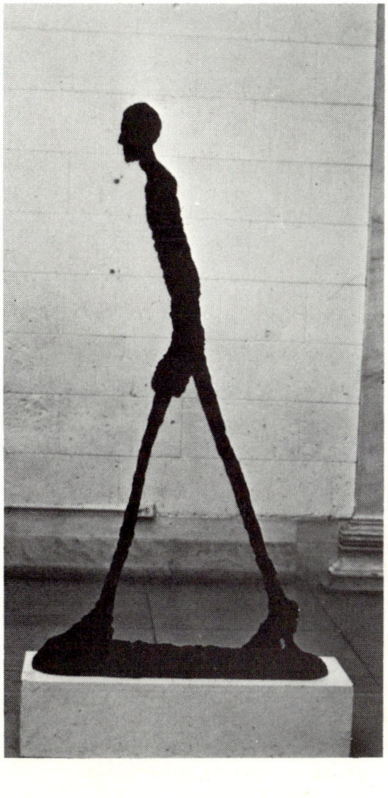

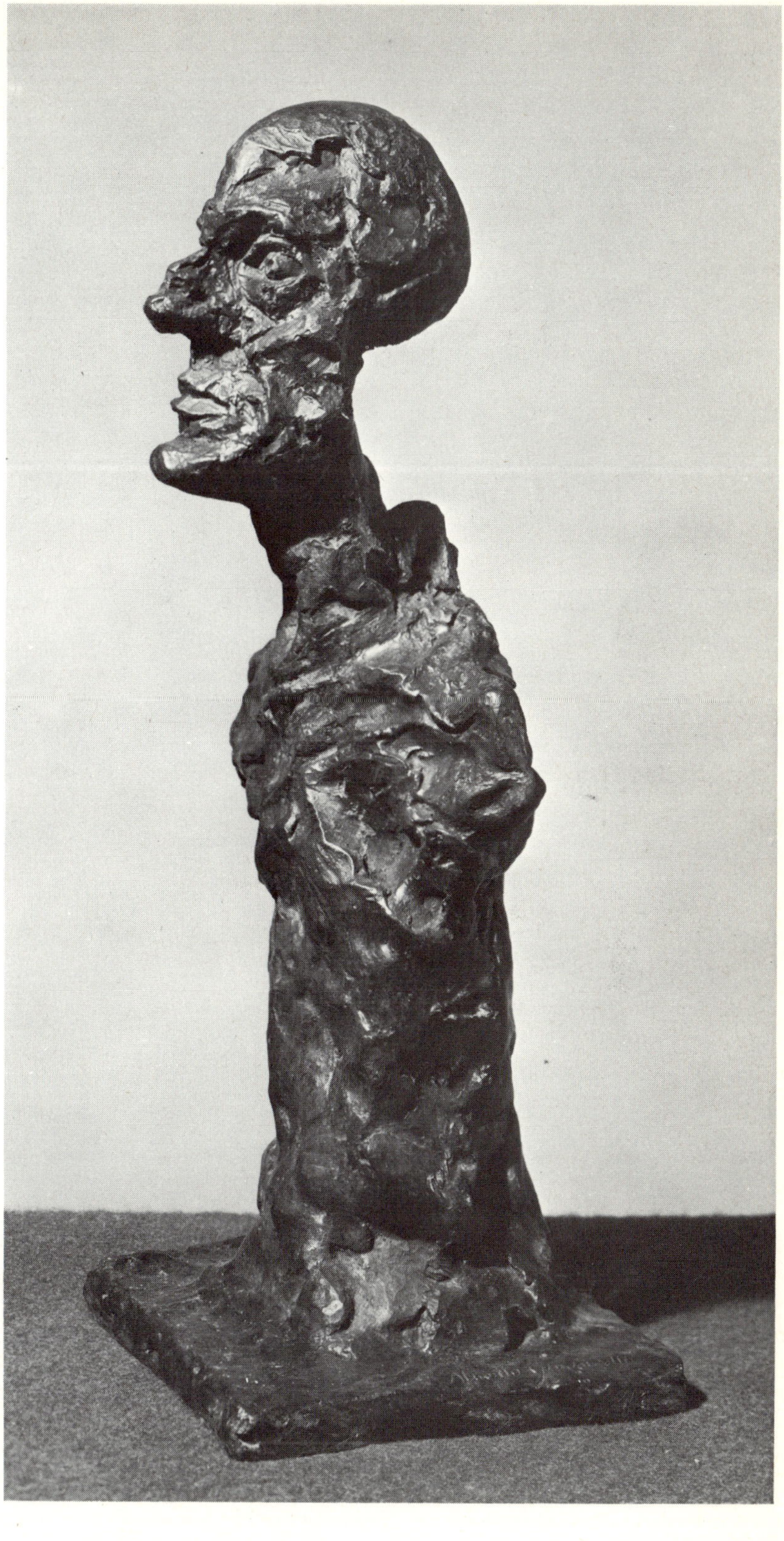

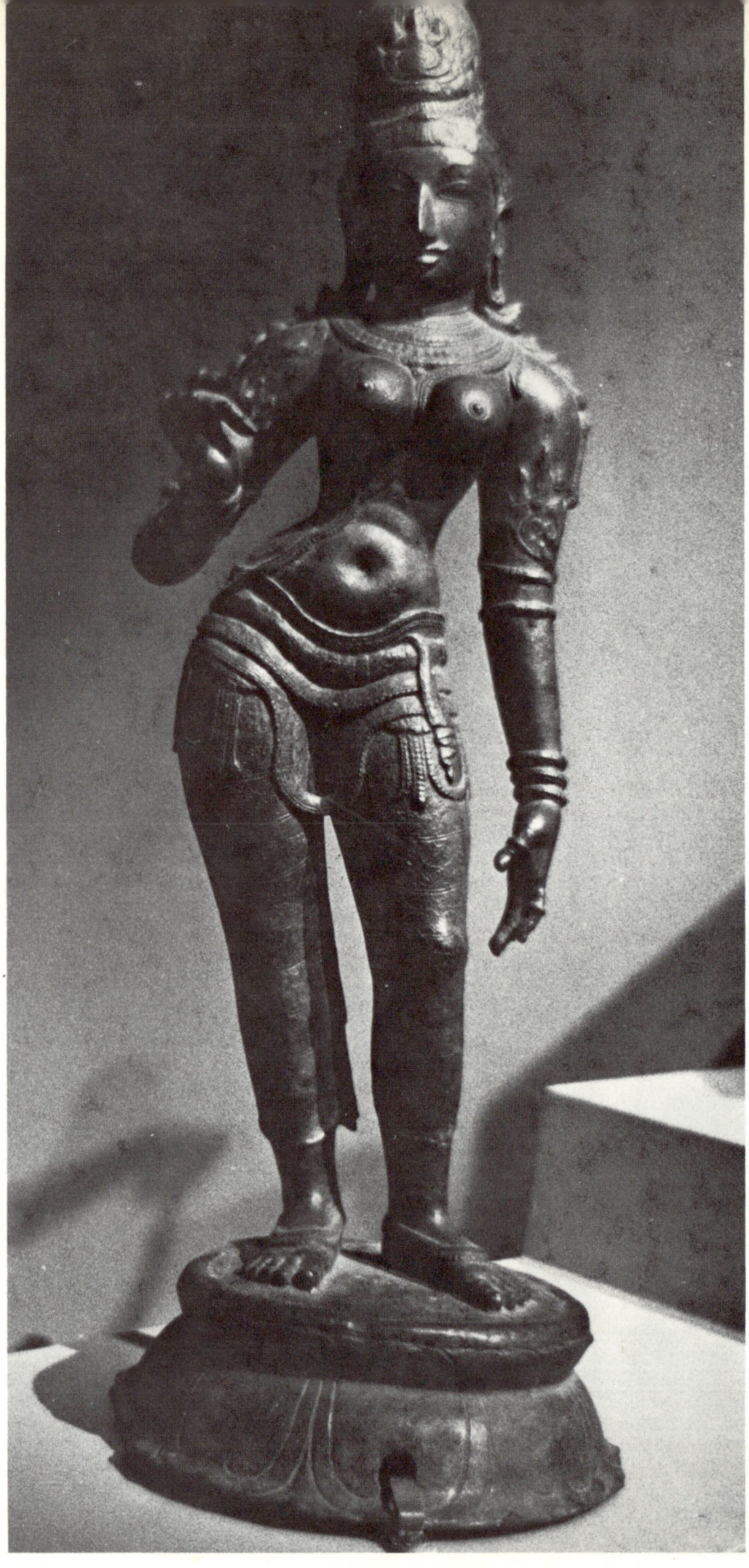

Parvati, consort to Siva Bronze
Madras State thirteenth-fourteenth century
Victoria and Albert Museum, London
photograph John W Mills
See page 25

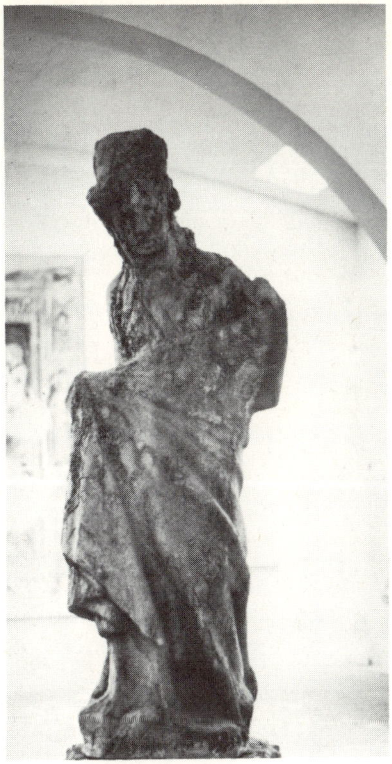

Figura di Santa   Marble
Giovanni Pisano
Museo Nationale, Pisa
photograph John W Mills

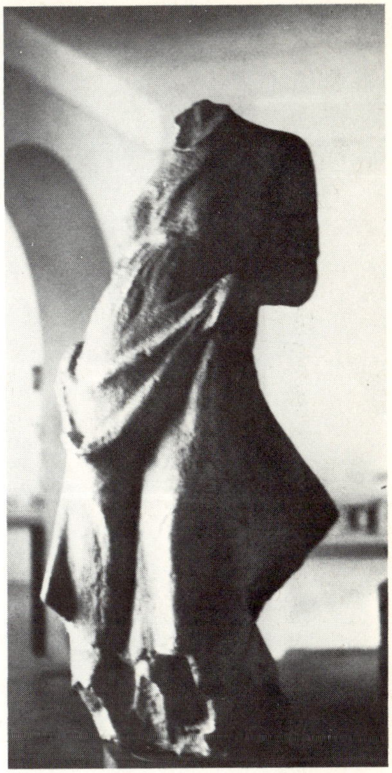

Figura Feminile Danzante
Giovanni Pisano
Museo Nationale, Pisa
photograph John W Mills

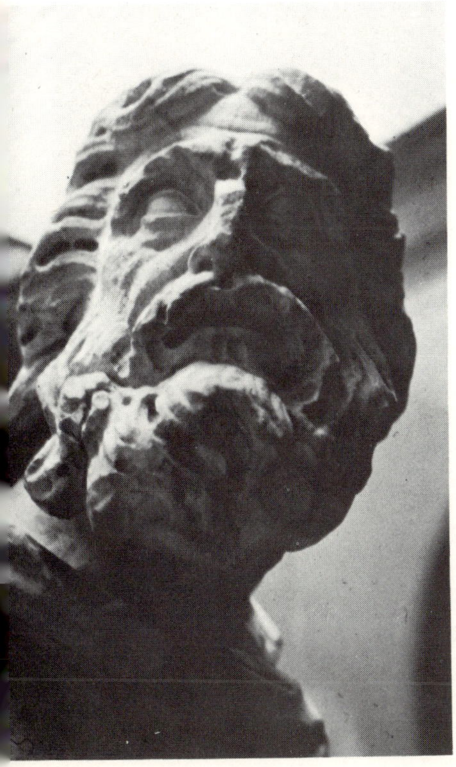

Habbakuk
Giovanni Pisano
Victoria and Albert Museum, London
photograph John W Mills
See page 25

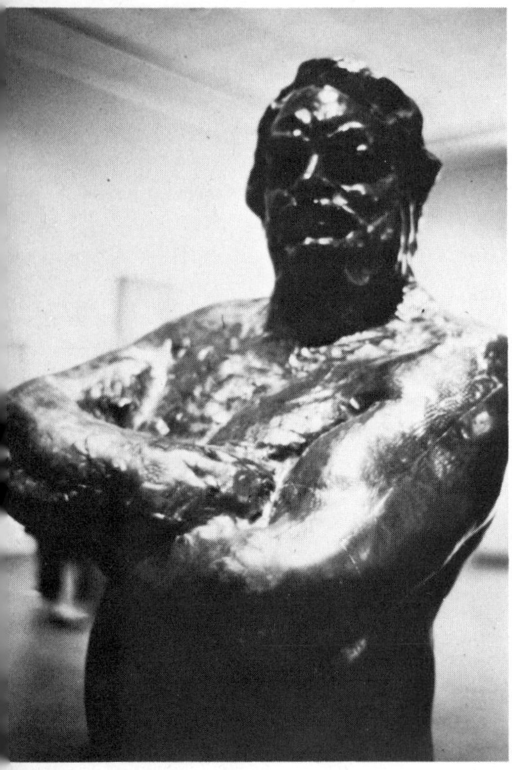

Study for Balzac Bronze
Auguste Rodin
Chicago Institute of Fine Art
photograph John W Mills

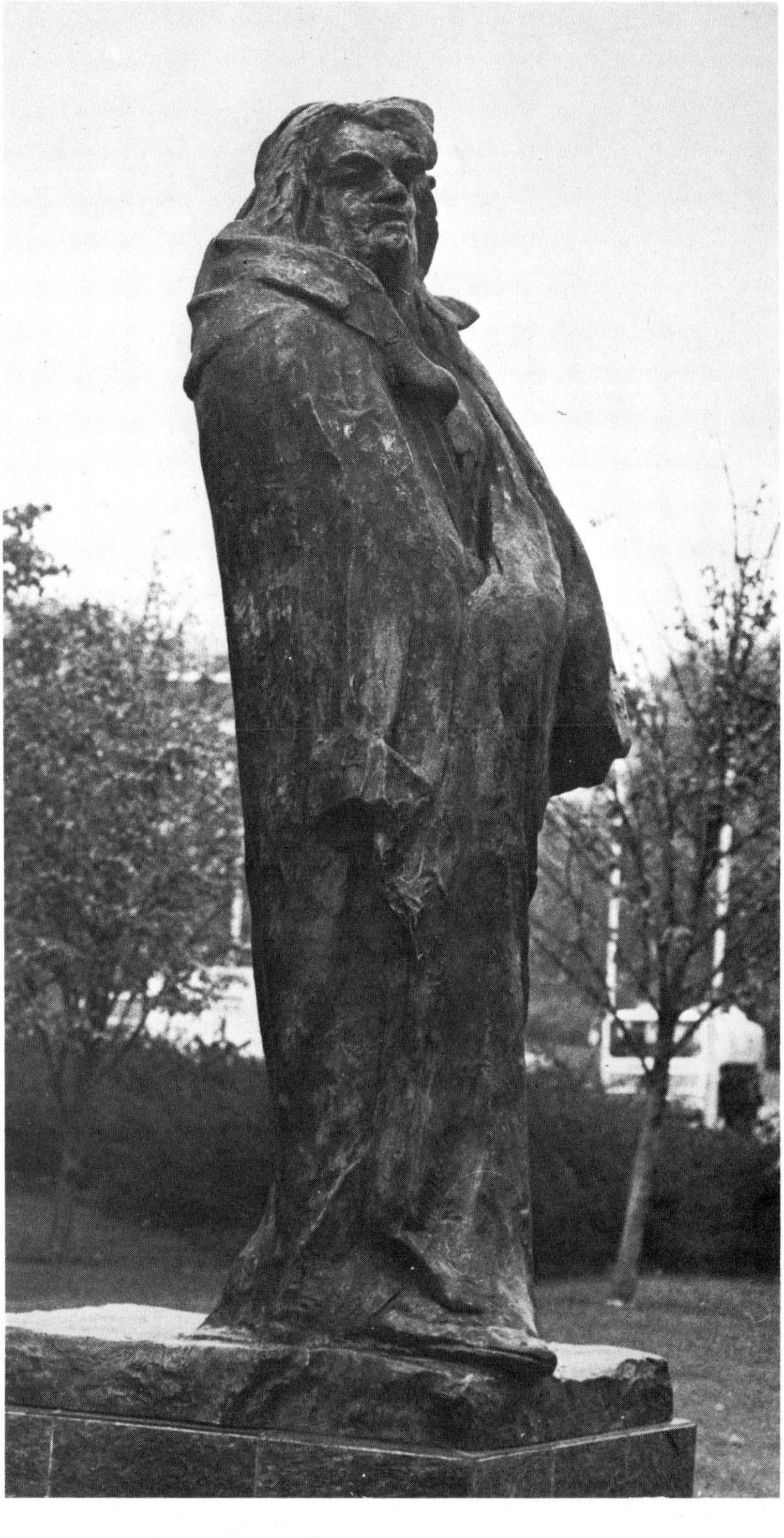

Balzac Bronze
Auguste Rodin
Kodak House, Hemel Hempstead
See page 25
photograph John W Mills

Detail opposite

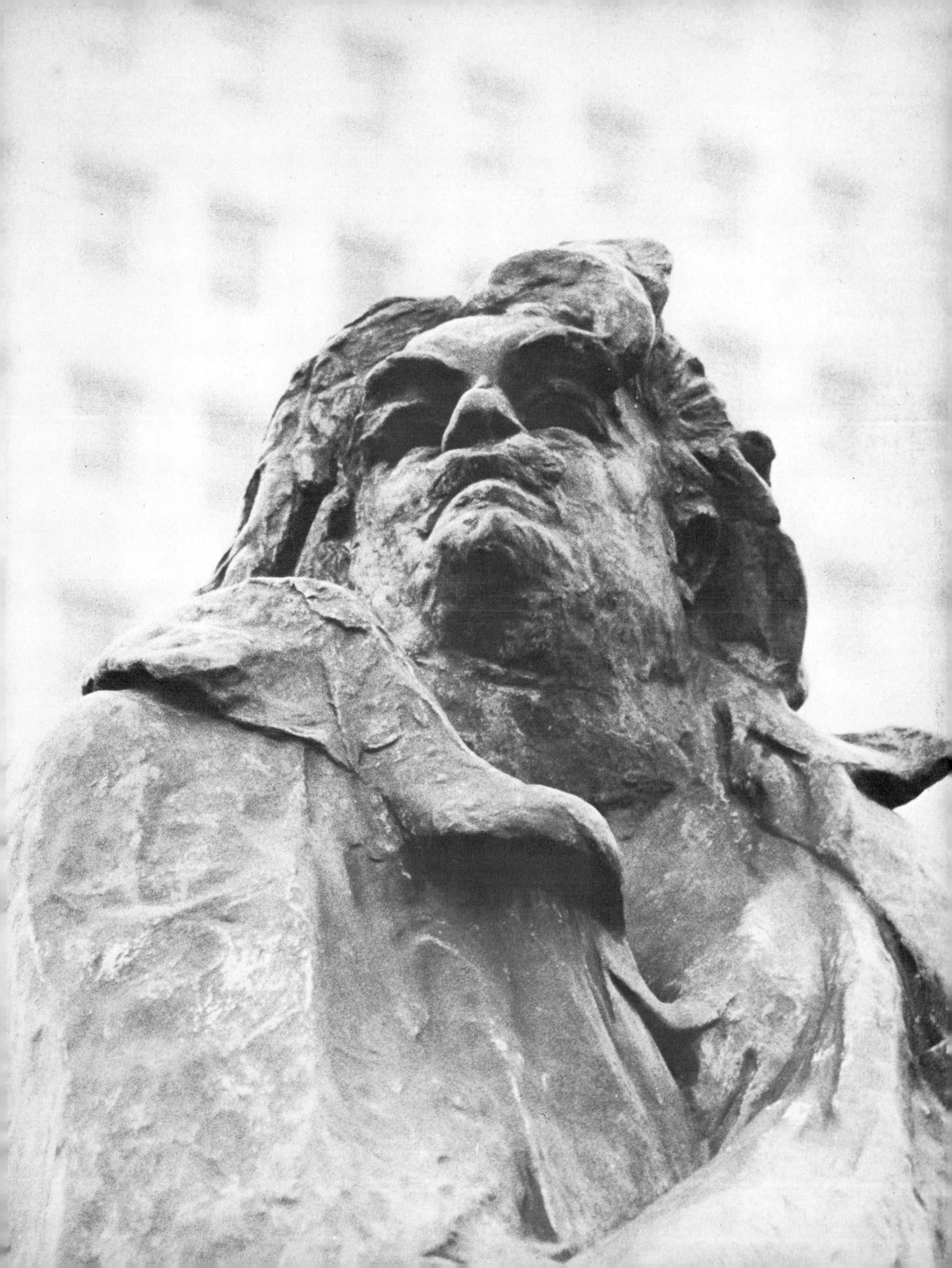

King Amenophis IV
later Akhnaton
Cairo Museum
See page 28

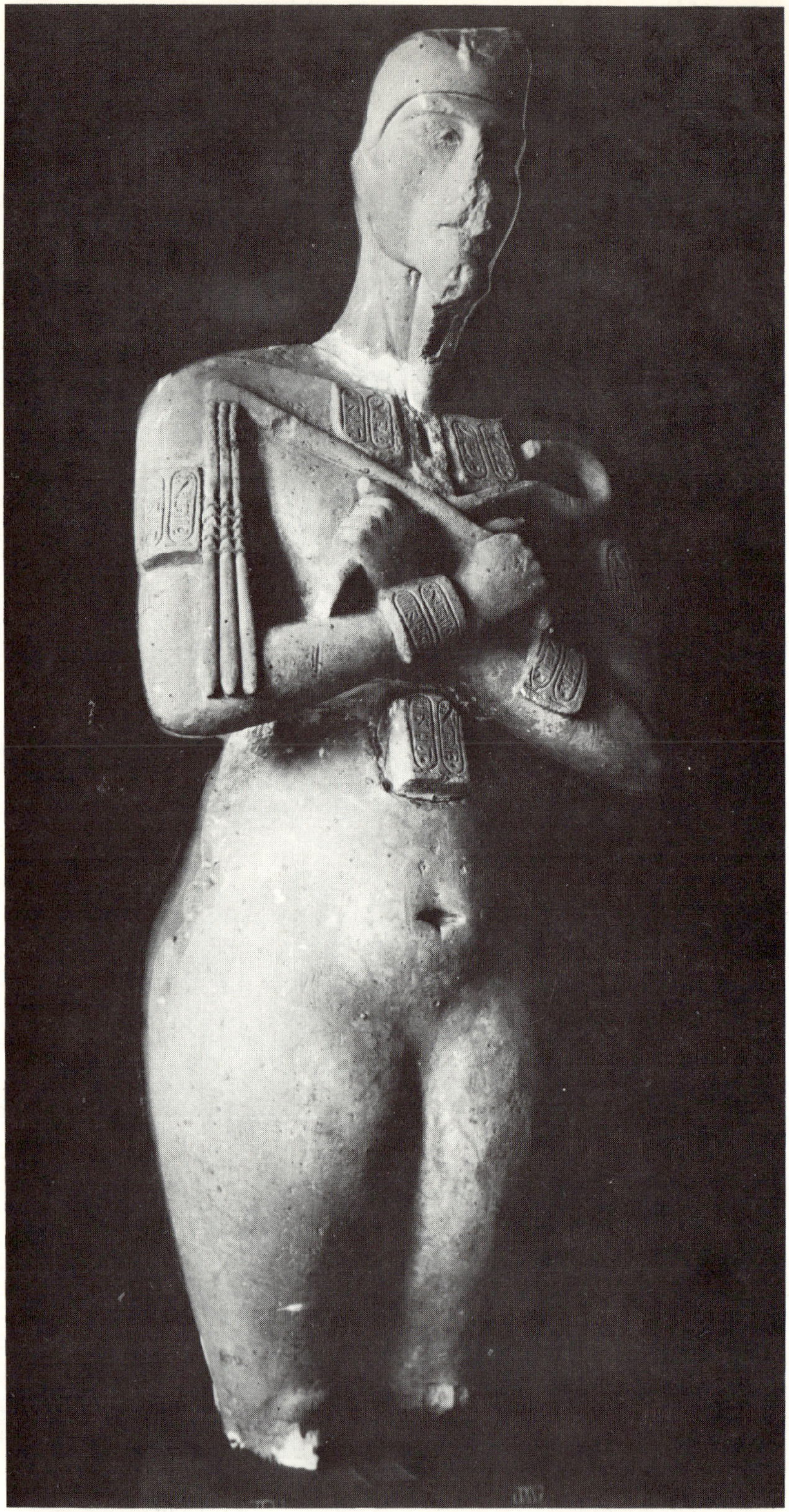

Man with a Lamb 1944 Bronze
Pablo Picasso
Philadelphia Museum of Art. Given by Sturgis and Marion B F Ingersoll
See page 25

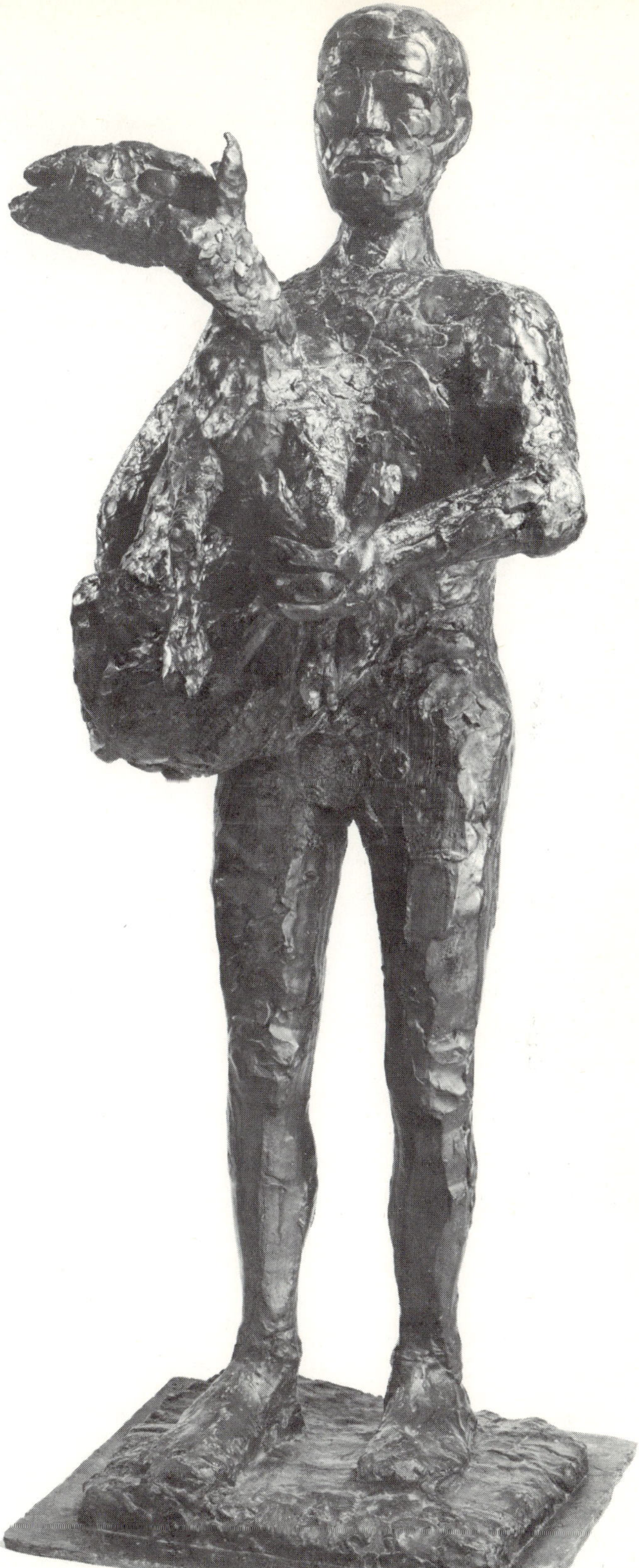

Detail

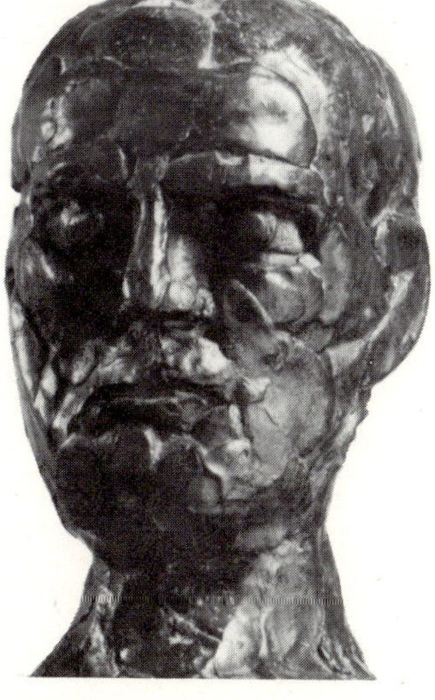

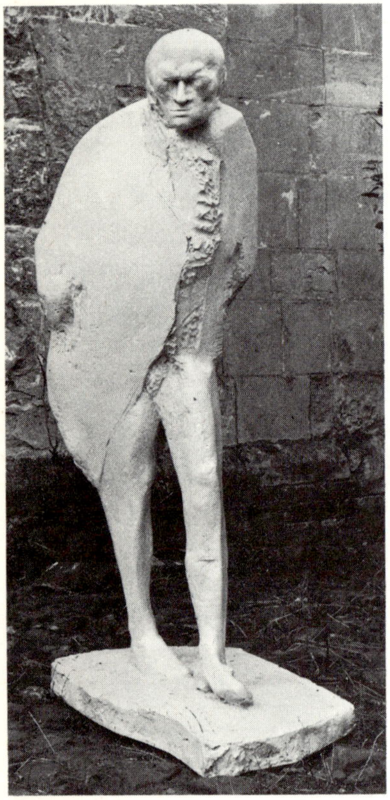

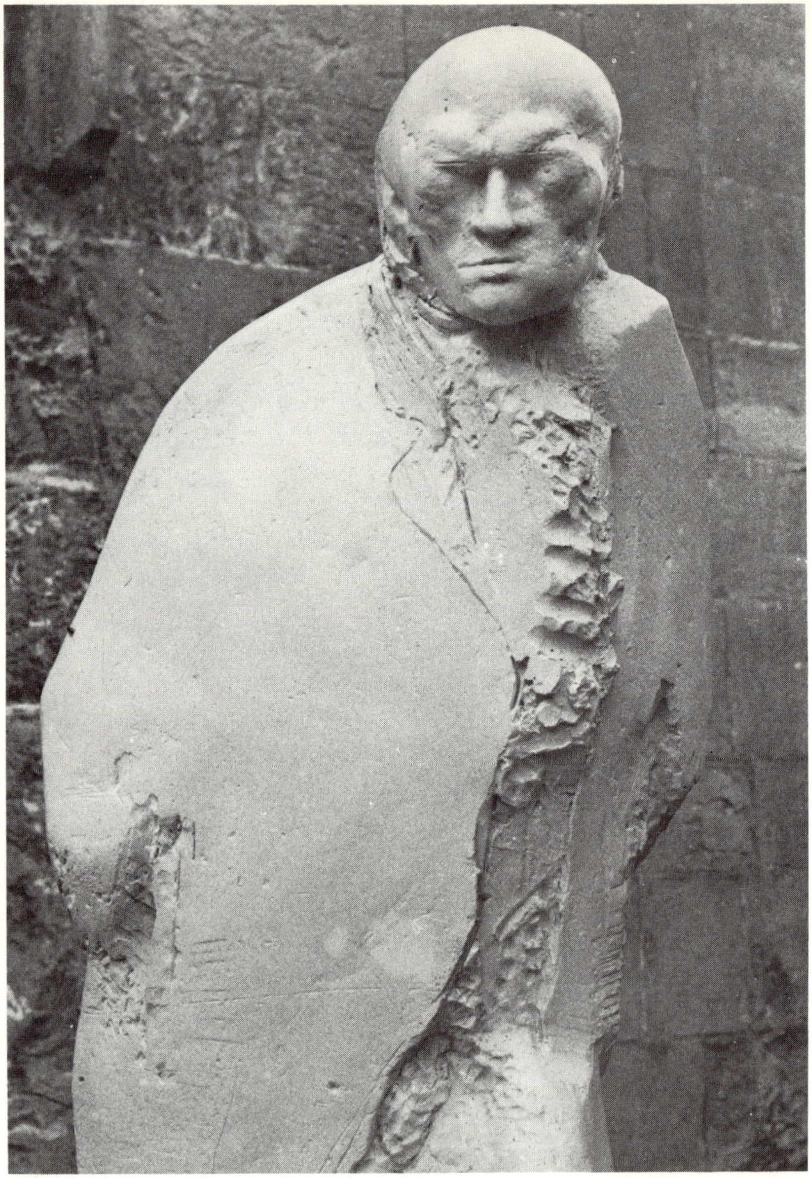

Study for William Blake GRP
John W Mills
photograph John W Mills

Detail

Memorial to William Blake
Aluminium and Bronze
John W Mills
William Blake House, London
photograph John W Mills

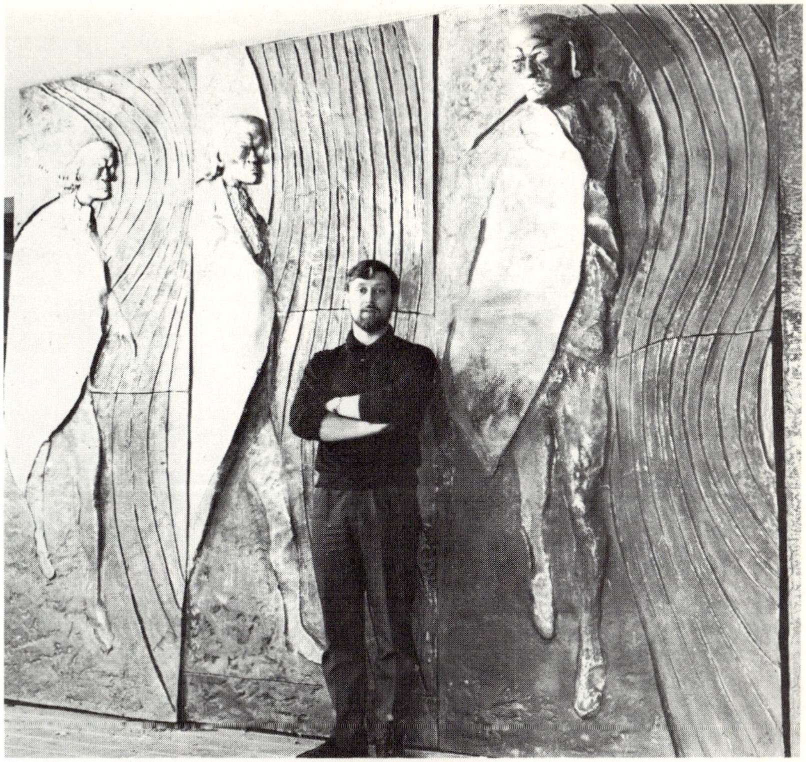

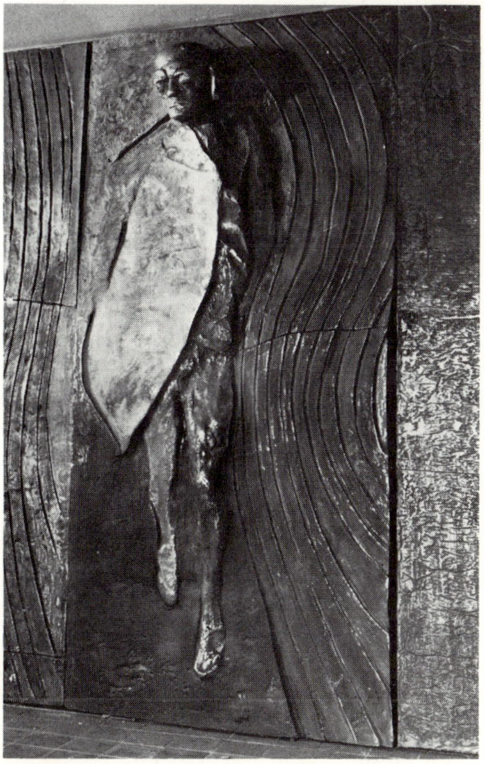

Detail of Bronze panel

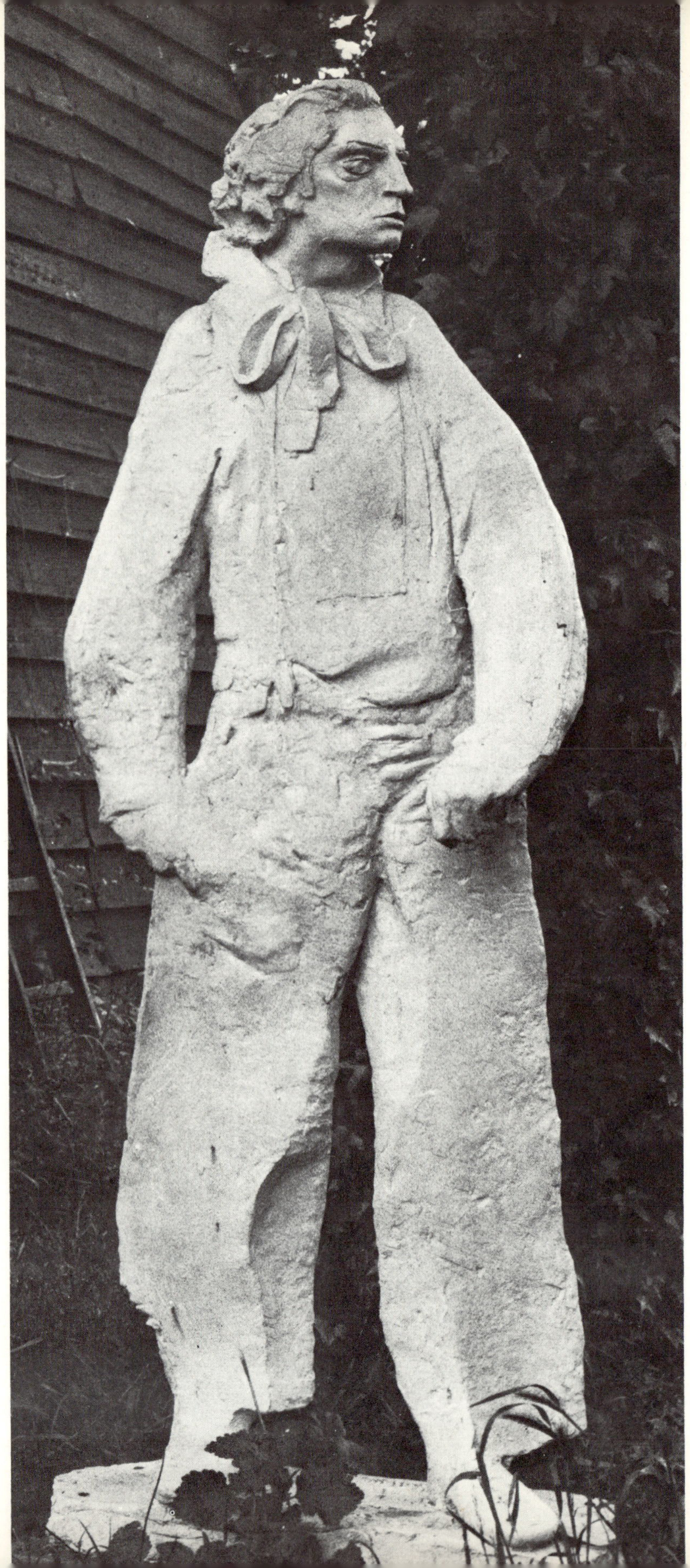

Buster Keaton Ciment fondu
John W Mills
photograph John W Mills

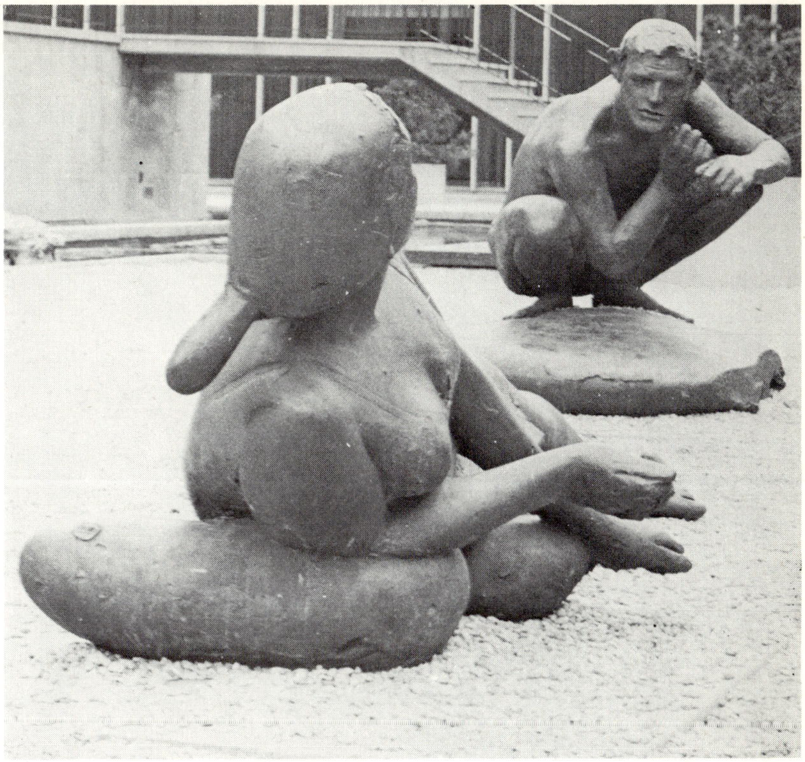

Detail

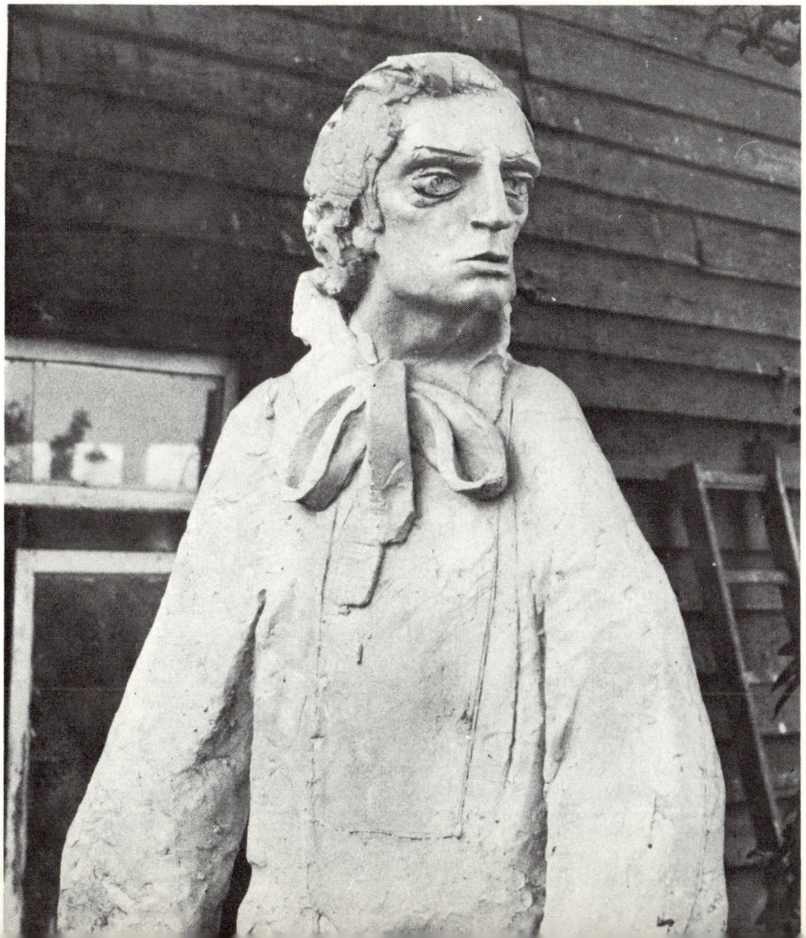

Sculpture group Bronze
Giacomo Manzù
Wayne State University, Detroit
photograph John W Mills

Station of the Cross 1950 Bronze
Giacomo Manzu
Open-air Museum, Middelheim, Antwerp

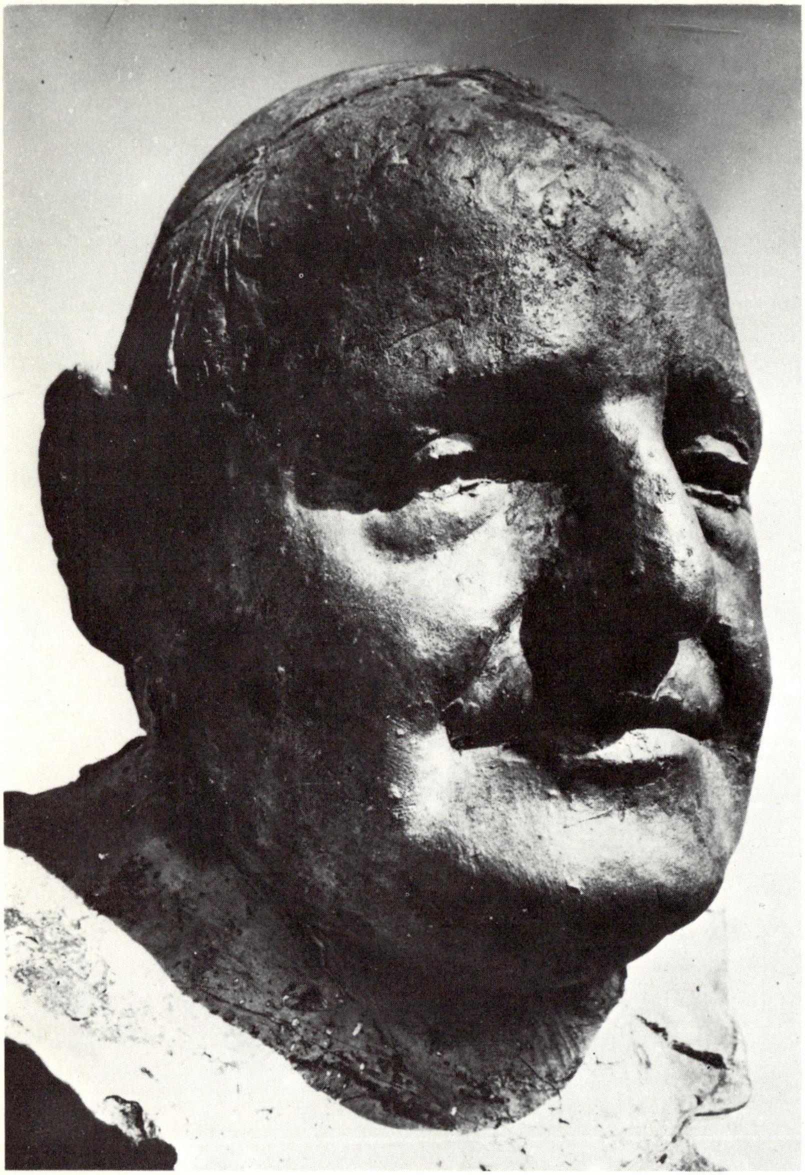

Pope John XXIII 1963 Bronze
Giacomo Manzu
Collection of Bishop Capovilla
See page 25

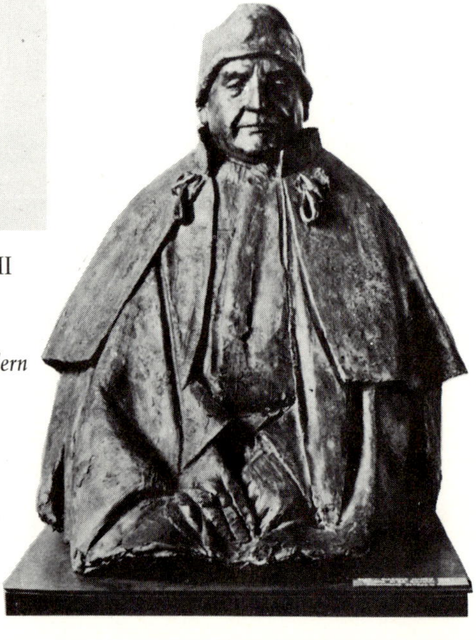

Portrait bust of Pope John XXIII
1963 Bronze
Giacomo Manzu
Vatican Museums. Collection of Modern Religious Art
See page 28

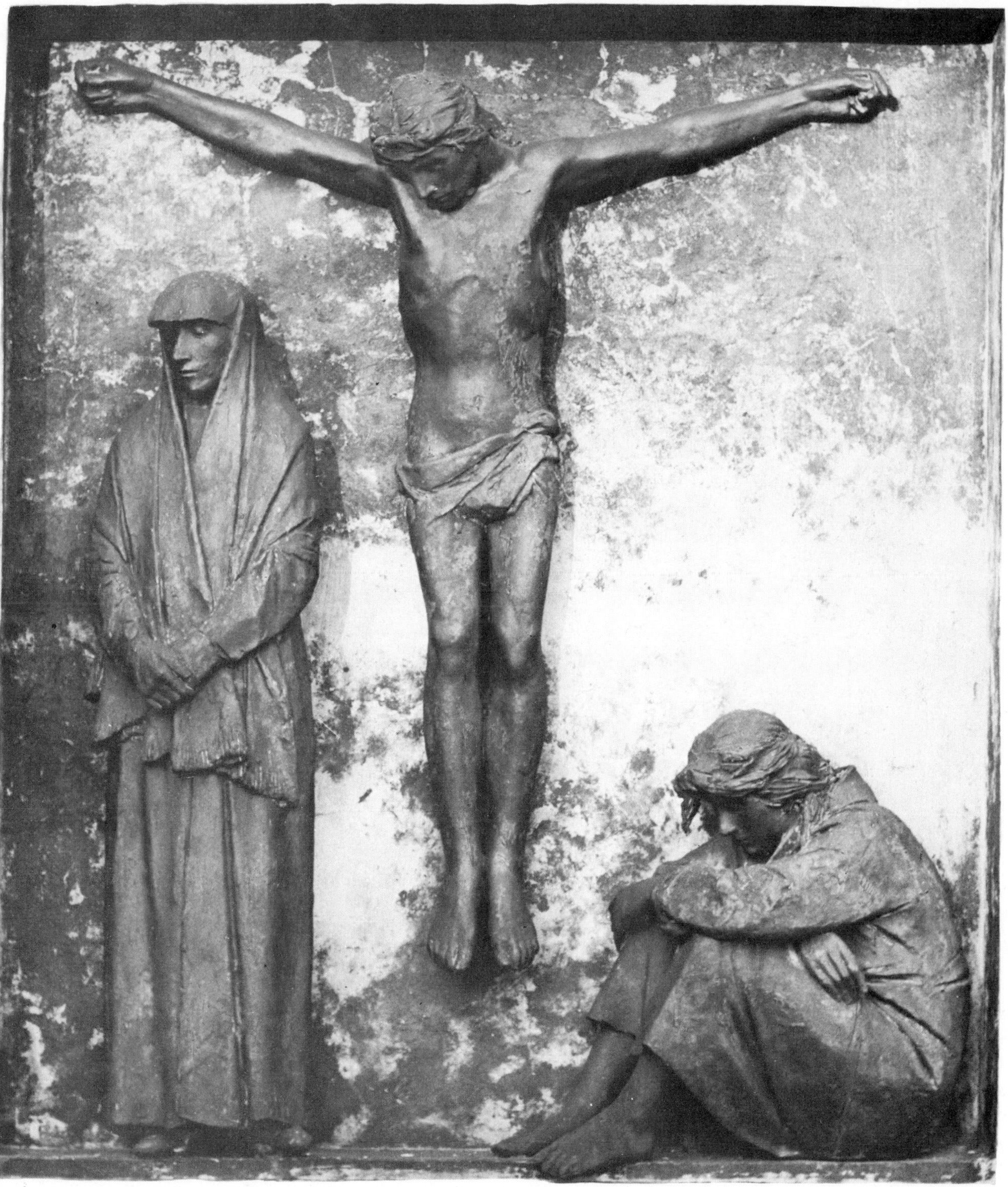

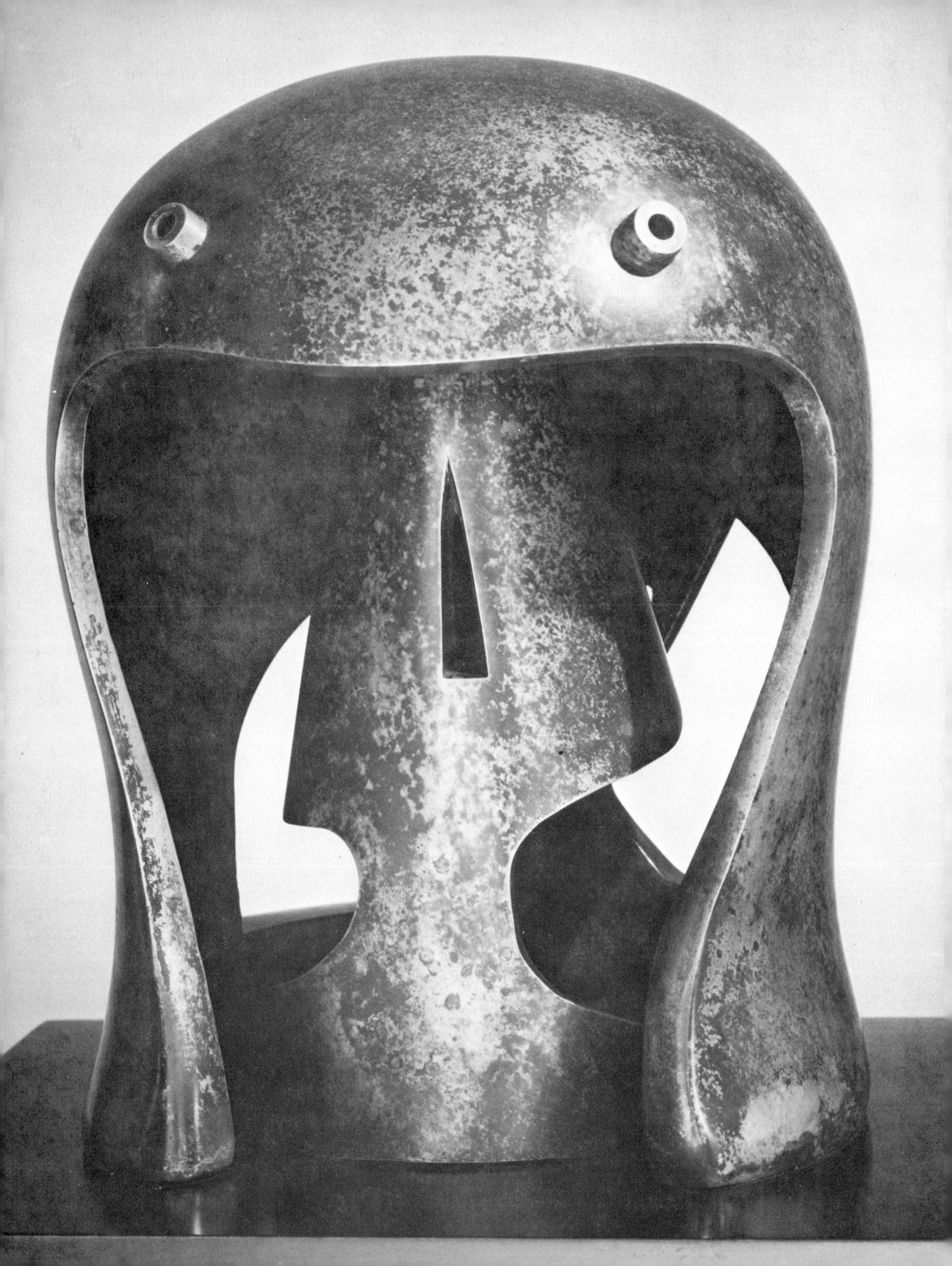

2 Modelling materials

The modelling materials commonly used to make the kind of sculpture briefly discussed already are; clay both natural and synthetic, wax, pâpier mâché and plaster of paris. My book *The Technique of Sculpture* deals explicitly with sculpture media in depth, and will provide a useful corollary to this work, aimed at specific application.

Modelling media is basically of two different characters, that which is soft and malleable, and that which starts as a liquid, gradually to solidify and become hard.

Clay

Clay is probably the most common modelling medium and is usually to be found in a sculptor's studio. It is moist, stiff tenacious earth that can be shaped and fashioned with comparative ease. Any clay can be used, of course, but the end result aimed for will effect to some degree the choice of clay. If for instance the image is to be made in terracotta (fired clay), then clean and well prepared clay must be used, and the relative thickness of sections controlled to facilitate baking by allowing for even shrinkage. Clay used simply as a medium with which to create a form that will subsequently be cast, need not be so clean nor so precisely prepared. It should however be free of grit, or grog, as this may inhibit the casting process of moulding.

Common to both uses of clay are the methods of modelling. This is ideally an additive process so that in the course of construction the form grows. The volume being smaller than that finally required, until the very last moments. This additive procedure is the distinguishing difference to carving, a subtractive process. The cutting away of one and the adding to of the other, determines to a large extent the different nature and qualities of sculptural form. Unless the cut quality of clay is particularly needed for a texture or specific form, it is best avoided. These apparent rules however are as open to use and abuse as any other.

Helmet Head No. 1 Bronze
Henry Moore
The Tate Gallery, London

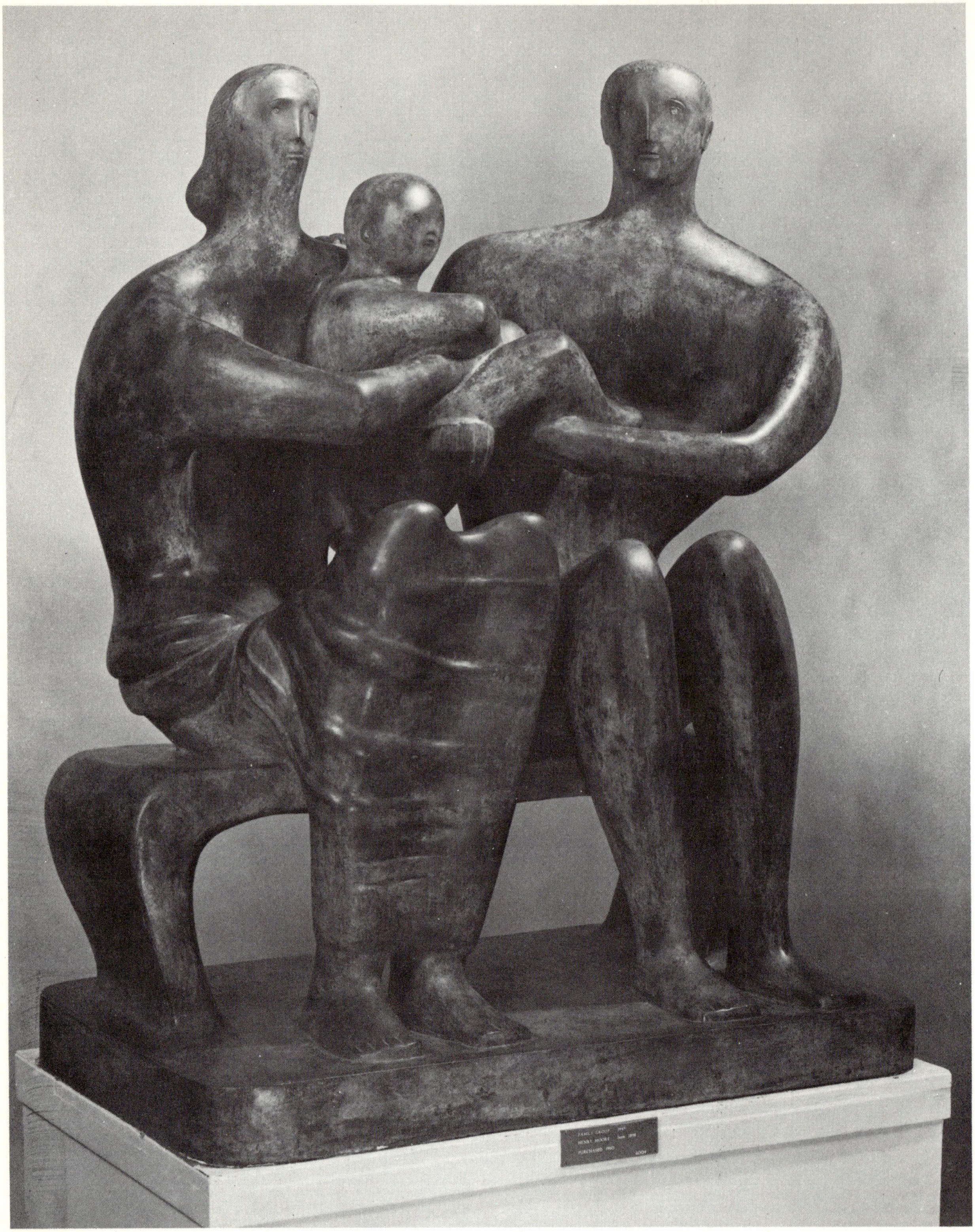

Broken rules that help achieve a successful image are justified by that success. Knowing the rules as recognised by purists, is a necessary discipline, it is also as necessary not to be inhibited by them. Sculptors whose background training favoured carving, tend to expose this factor in their mature work. Their modelled forms are usually made in a rigid and over controlled manner, indicating an inhibited attitude to the material, leading to uneasy compromise.

The reverse, of course, may be true of sculptors with a dominant modelling background. Their carvings are often soft and lacking control, and with too great a use of the rasp and file. These two examples can be studied in some of the work of Henry Moore who represents the former, and some sculptures of Auguste Rodin who is typical of the latter.

TOOLS

The tools usually found in a modeller's studio are important to know about, so that useful items can be found and useful tools purchased whenever the opportunity arises. I use the term *useful* because so many poor quality and badly designed modelling tools are marketed today, especially in kits sold for recreational modelling. Wooden modelling tools are usually made from box wood, and although their shapes and sizes are many, the best are always smooth, curved to fit the hand comfortably, and to ride smoothly over the clay. At first it is best to work with two basic wooden spatulas, and to acquire others as experience dictates. Home-made tools should be made from close grained hardwood, the best being old box wood rules. Well designed and well used tools are often beautiful, combining admirably both function and design. They should be maintained well, kept free from clay when not in use for long periods, and should never be left standing in water, they should be oiled occassionally. Well treated they will last a life time. Wooden mallets of various kinds, and with patterned striking faces are useful for texturing and for consolidating clay on large works. Knives and scrapers have obvious usage, both with clay and plaster, having a predominantly cutting job to do. Cheese cutting wires too serve this purpose and should be available.

Clay can be added in pellets of uniform or random size, to build a volume. It can be pushed with the full force of the hands and arms, or with the finger tips, or with the edges of the palms. It can be punched and bullied or coerced with these natural modelling tools. Wooden mallets and wooden spatulas can be used in addition to the fingers and palms, but ideally as extensions to them and not instead of them like palette knives. Steel spatulas are useful to make cuts, thin lines and fine marks. They give distinctly different effects to marks made with wooden tools, but the clay

Family Group Bronze
Henry Moore
The Tate Gallery, London

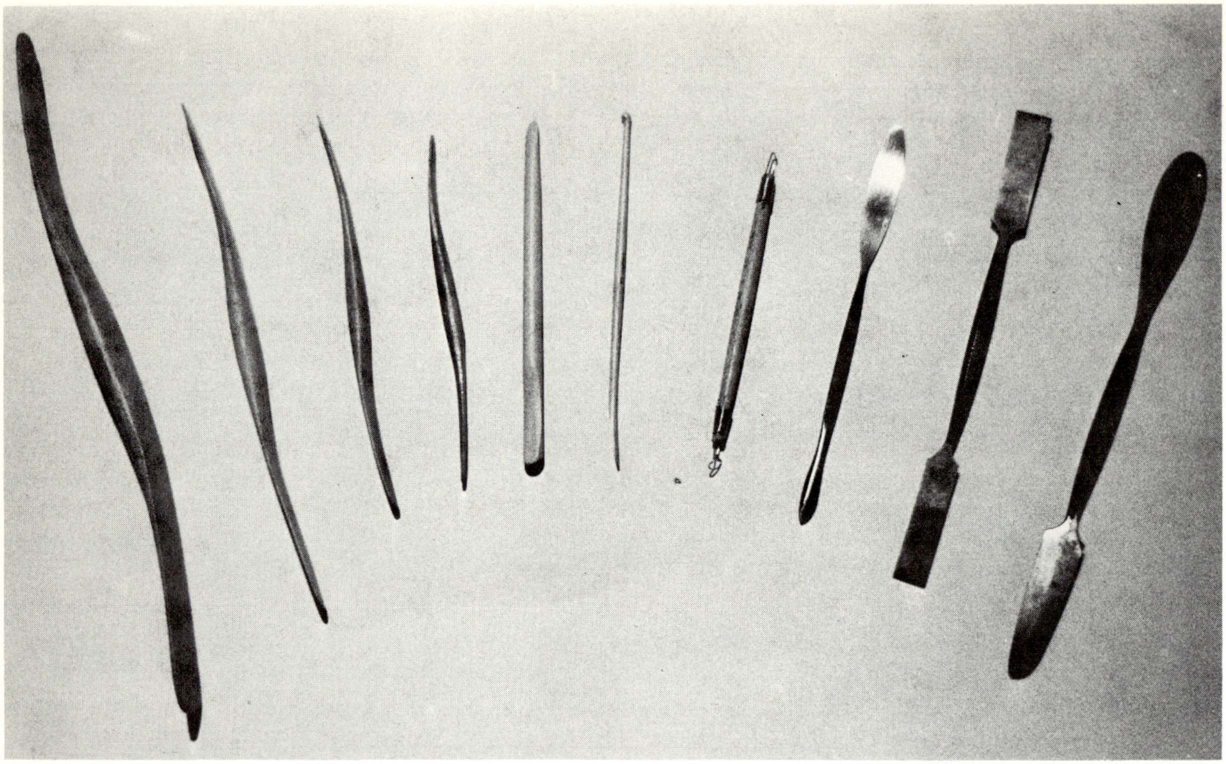

Selection of wooden and steel spatulas, suitable for modelling clay and plaster of paris
phoograph John W Mills

sticks easily to metal, and large sections are often dragged out.

The wet condition of clay preferred by sculptors is very much a matter for personal preference. Very wet clay can be used to model on the surface, it is not useful to apply directly to an armature, or to build hollow forms to be fired. Combinations of clay of varying hardness will prove to be most agreeable, quite what variety will depend on personal experiment. Leather hard clay can be burnished to achieve fine tight surfaces, and this used in combination to softer clay enables interesting complementary hard and soft shapes to be exploited. An ideal studio will have bins of clay in differing states of hardness, so that work can carry on freely according to the needs of the moment. This material has little or no tensile strength especially when wet. It will not retain a long form without support, it has only compressive strength (See diagram). Forms can be made by piling clay upon clay, so without support clay facilitates bulky forms and ponderous images. To test these different qualities try making a hollow form as high as you can at one attempt. The clay will tend to collapse when the weight and softness are not compatible to the wall thickness. Complex forms, and slender forms therefore are made around an armature, or support (these are described in chapter 4) or if fired made in separate sections glued or joined together at a later stage.

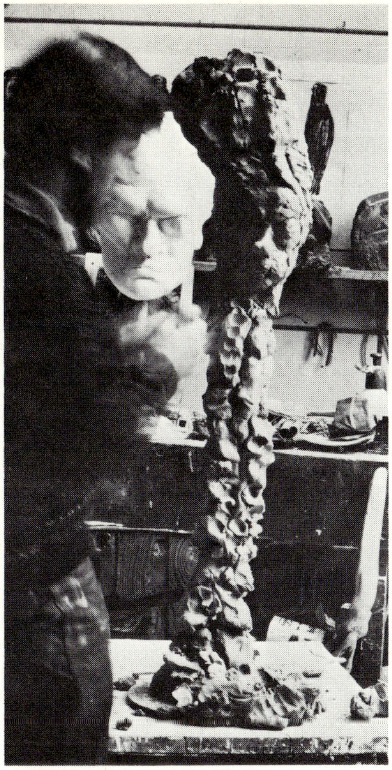
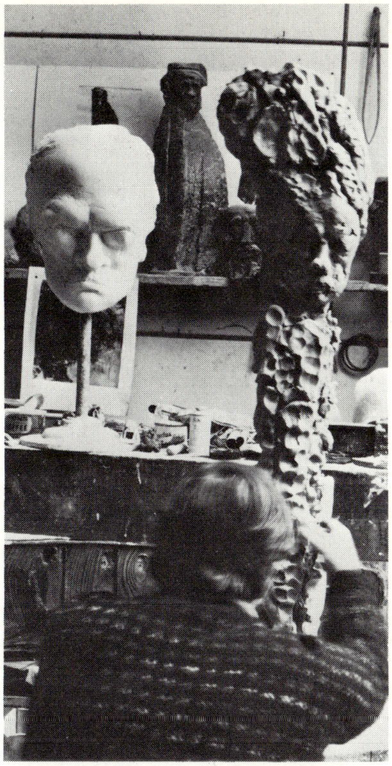
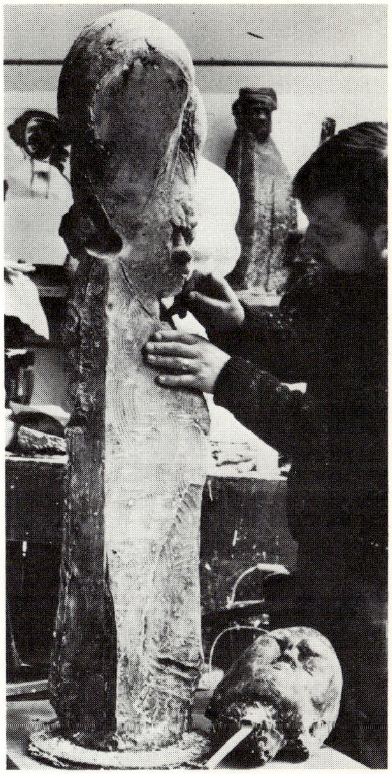

Stages in modelling of a sculpture entitled *Rembrandt Turban*
John W Mills
photographs by John W Mills

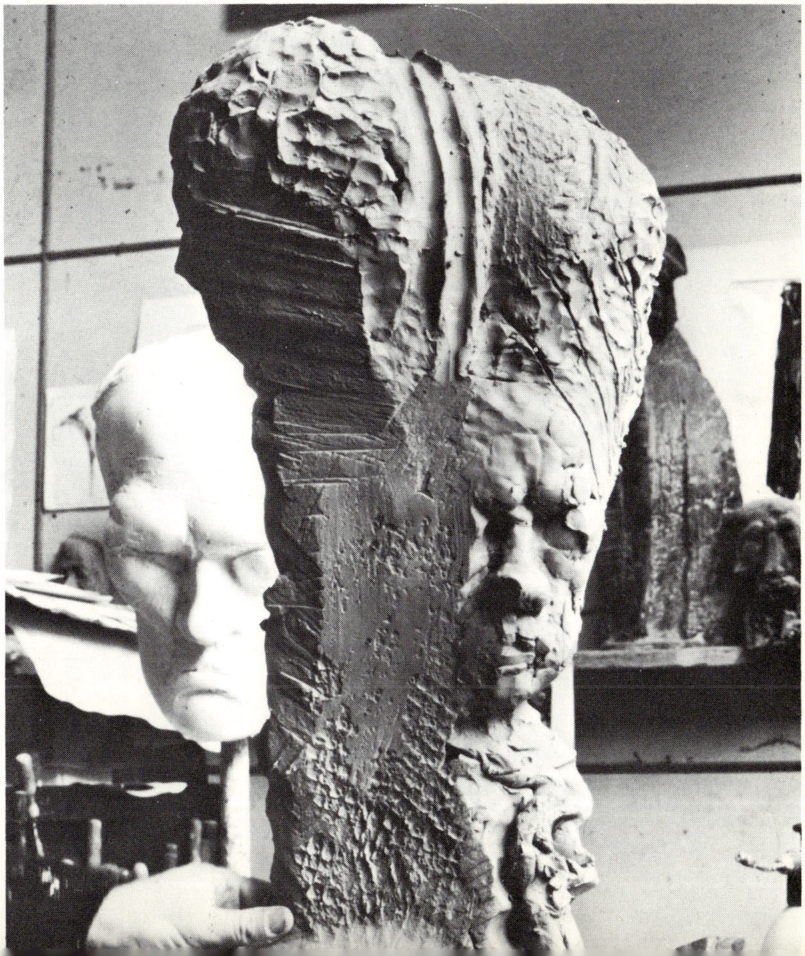

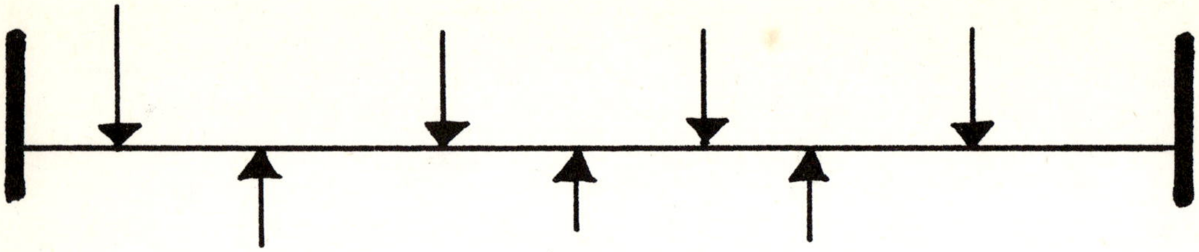

A

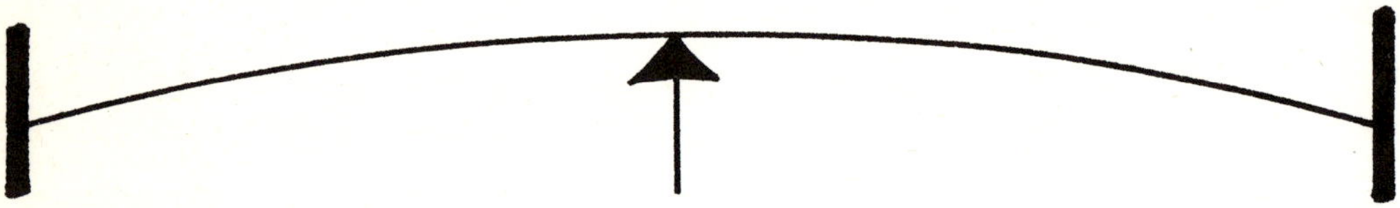

B

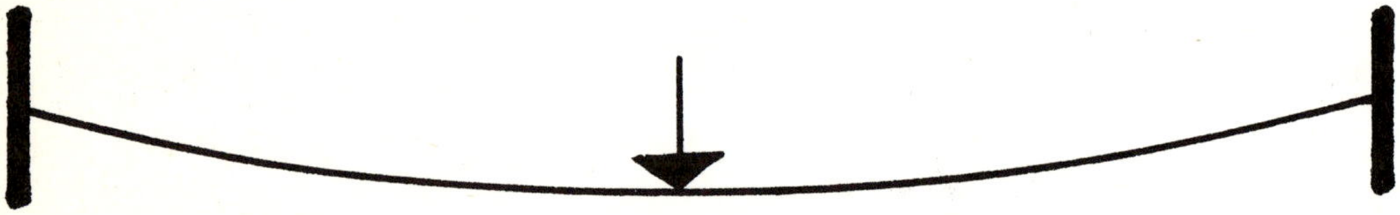

C

These diagrams illustrate the principles of tensile and compressive stress. *A* represents a long form held in equilibrium because all forces along its length are equal. *B* illustrates the arch of a bridge structure and its potential strength, which is the reverse of the sag demonstrated by *C,* in which greater forces exerted from above cannot be supported
D and *E* illustrate the nature of compressive forces and the kinds of structure necessary to resist them, large column and pyramidal forms

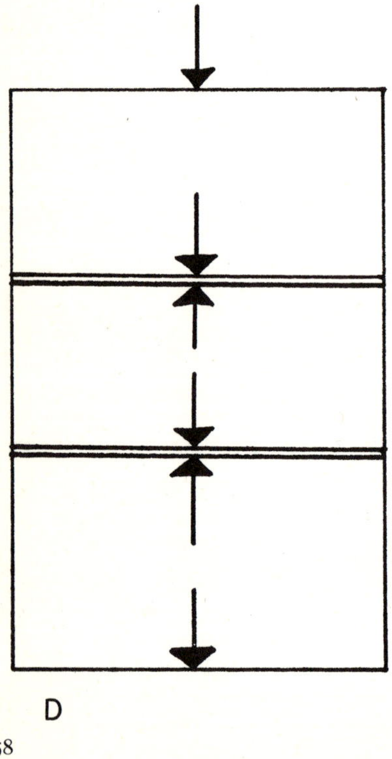

D

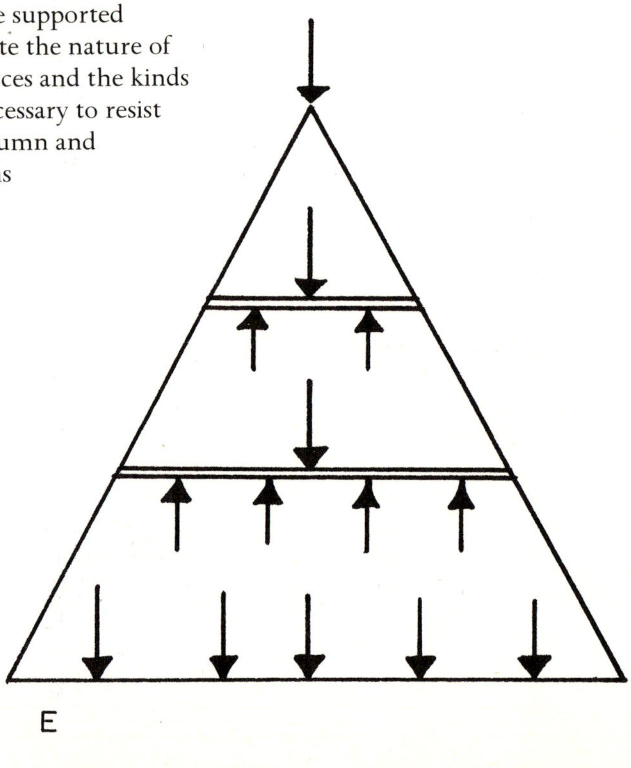

E

Fashioning sculpture for firing, by building up sections, requires skill and patience, plus clay free of foreign matter that might cause havoc when baked. To make baking possible the figure or head must be hollow in section and of an even thickness. Very small items can be fired solid successfully with great care, but it is never a sound proposition. The simplest method for making hollow forms is first to build them solid and leave them nearly completed to harden and become firm. This time will vary in duration according to the studio temperature; central heating of course hardens clay quicker, sometimes too quickly. When the clay is firm the form can be cut with a cheese cutting wire and the sections hollowed out leaving an even wall thickness of about 6 mm ($\frac{1}{4}$ in.). The hollowed sections when ready are then glued together using liquid clay, slip, and the join modelled over to complete the work on the surface.

Building a hollow form by coiling and sticking ropes of clay together is equally simple, but limiting in the variety of form possible. Small hollow shapes can be made by modelling the clay around a rod and paper. See diagram. Tubes made like this can be assembled to make figures, or can be used in combination with larger coiled or built forms.

A section through a clay build up, with a layer of plaster and jute reinforcing. The saw cut indicated is the means of opening the plaster to remove the clay, to make a hollow form

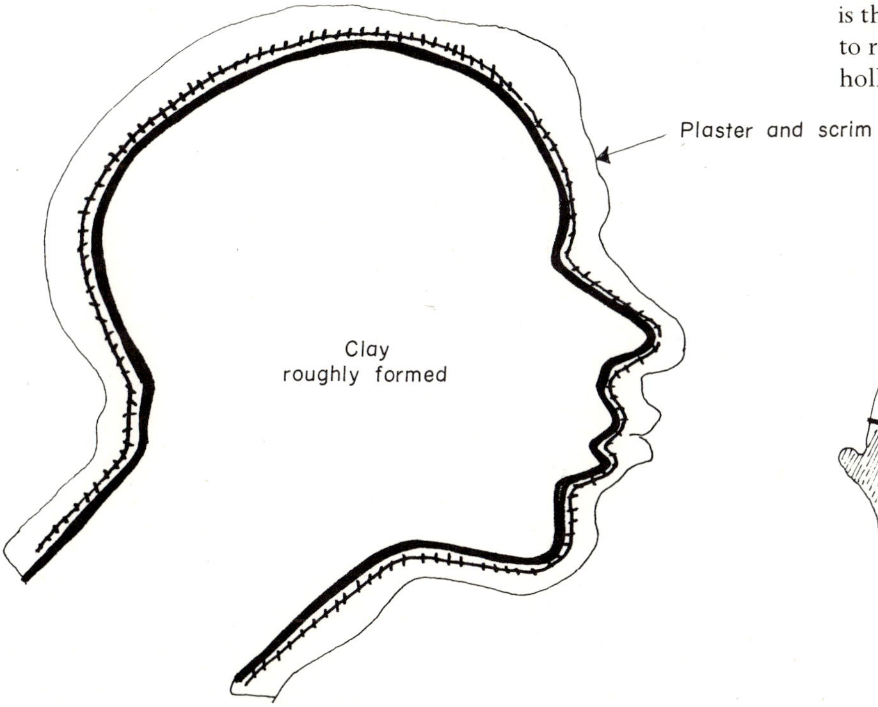

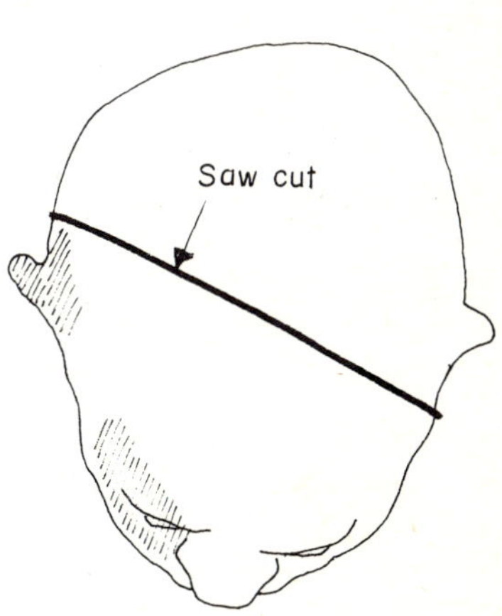

The malleable nature of clay should be retained and be identifiable in the final work. The image should be a result of handling clay as much as it is a result of observation. The tactile qualities of a modelled sculpture come directly from its malleable nature and the hands of the sculptor. The hands therefore are the ideal modelling tools, allowing the finest surfaces and forms, and such skills should be nurtured as much as possible.

Clay should be kept in reasonable condition according to its use. Clay for modelling only, should be returned clean, to a waterproof bin after use; make sure no pieces of plaster are left in the used clay. Spray the clay in the bin with water to achieve the required softness or cover the clay with wet cloths. Clay on the armature should also be kept wet to facilitate modelling, but I have already mentioned the kind of consistencies that specific kinds of modelling requires. After each session of work, wrap the clay sculpture in wet or damp cloth and cover this with plastic sheet. Wrap the plastic sheet to exclude air, in this way it should keep for as long as needed in good condition. Terracotta clay must be kept clean at all times and separate from modelling clay. Its damp, therefore soft condition, is maintained according to preference. If allowed to dry it should be immersed in water to make a slurry, then layed out on plaster bats to become firm, and then it is kneaded to an even consistency ready for use, this can be done by using a pugmill, an item of equipment necessary when great quantities of clay are needed. This process applies only to clay that has dried out completely, soft clay can be simply wedged and kneaded into a workable condition.

Diagrams to illustrate the use of paper around a wooden dowel, a paper coil, to make hollow clay shapes

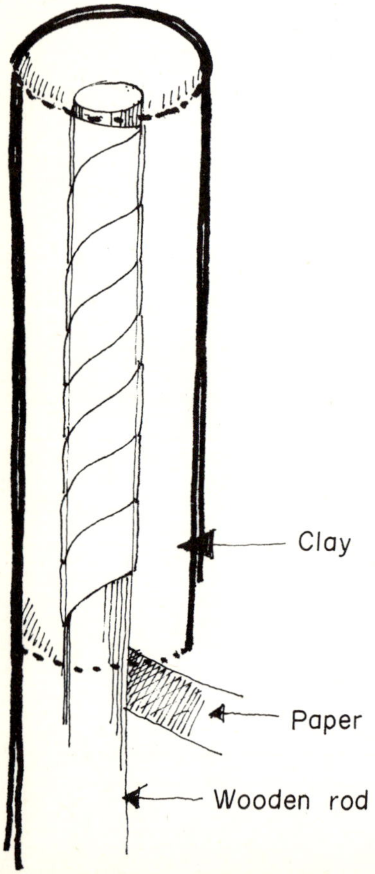

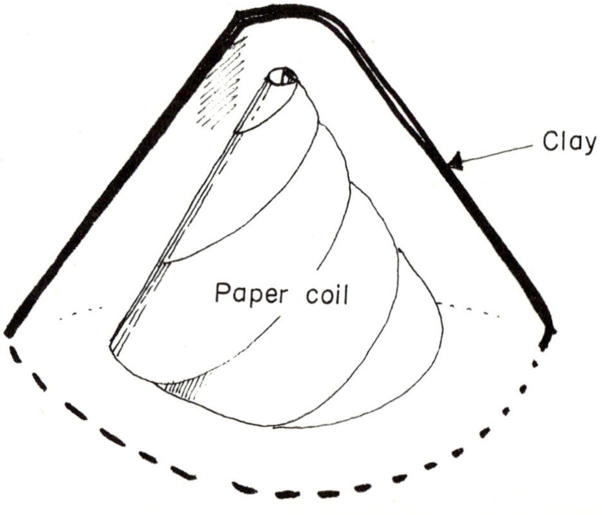

Rembrandt Terracotta
John W Mills
photograph John W Mills

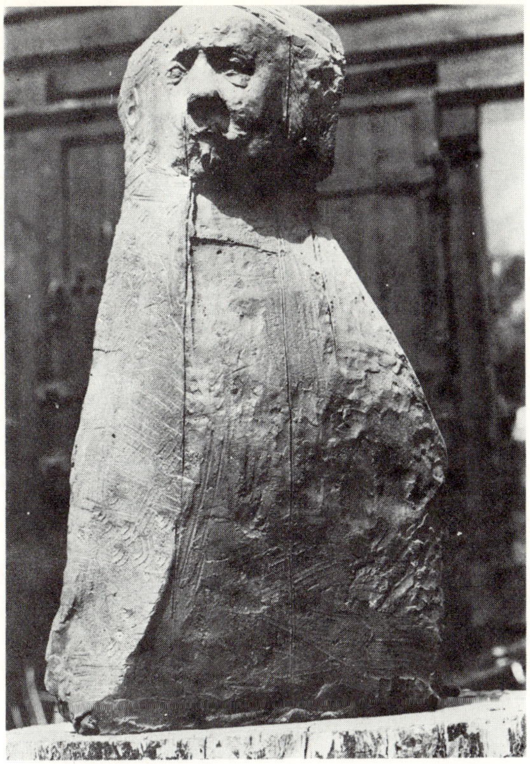

Detail

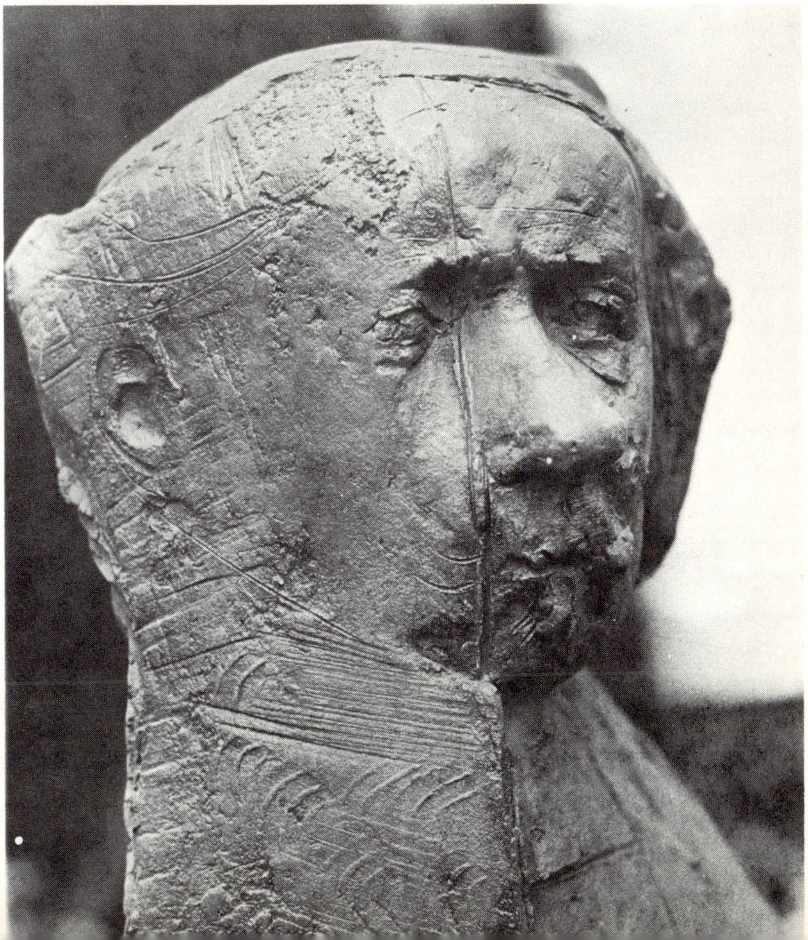

Synthetic clays

Synthetic clays: plasticine, clayola, plastalina, etc., all bear to a greater or lesser degree similar properties to natural clay. Some are oily, some are dry. Some harden to a permanent material by exposure to air or by heating. All synthetic clays require experiment. Plasticine for instance although oily and somewhat disagreeable to use, comes in many colours and can be put to excellent use were small coloured images are required. It doesn't shrink quickly, so can be modelled about an armature if necessary and left. This makes it a useful material for maquettes, and three dimensional studies. Plastalina is usually grey and does not dry, remaining like well-pugged clay. Its shortcoming therefore is due to its inability to harden and permit hard modelling and burnished surfaces. Clayola is a non-toxic, non-greasy synthetic clay, similar to plasticine and useful in the same way, especially in classes for the very young. These materials can be easily moulded from to make castings. Most fine art material manufacturers market self-hardening clay of one kind or another, they differ from country to country and should be explored personally to find that which suits best.

Wax

Wax is an interesting medium because it falls somewhere between natural and synthetic clay in modelling quality, when warm, but with the advantage of being self supporting; having greater tensile strength than clay. Smoothness and softness are additional qualities that suit particular kinds of form and surface, and can therefore contribute to certain images. The wax most widely used is micro-crystalline, a by-product of oil refining. It can be purchased from suppliers in varying hardnesses. By adding to the hot wax clean oil or petroleum jelly it can be softened, and by adding rosin it can be hardened. Beeswax can be added to give a fine modelling consistency. Experiment with small samples will help to arrive at a personal preference to suit personal techniques. Colouring agents too can be obtained from manufacturers together with instructions for mixing. These dyes are usually colour fast.

TOOLS

The tools necessary for working with wax should be metal; spatulas, knives, etc., of a range of shape and size. These need to be heated by means of gas or spirit flame, and therefore should not be high quality tempered steel. Useful small shapes can be easily made from 3 mm ($\frac{1}{8}$ in.) welding rod flattened at the tip to a

Diagrams of aids to modelling with wax. *A* is a spirit lamp made by piercing the lid of a small glass jar, through which a string is inserted to rest in spirit in the jar, to make a wick. *B* is a typical proprietory butane gas lamp. *C* illustrates a modified electric soldering iron, the heads can be varied to suit particular needs. *D* shows small spatulas made from welding rod, and *E* is a needle in a holder used, heated, to cut wax

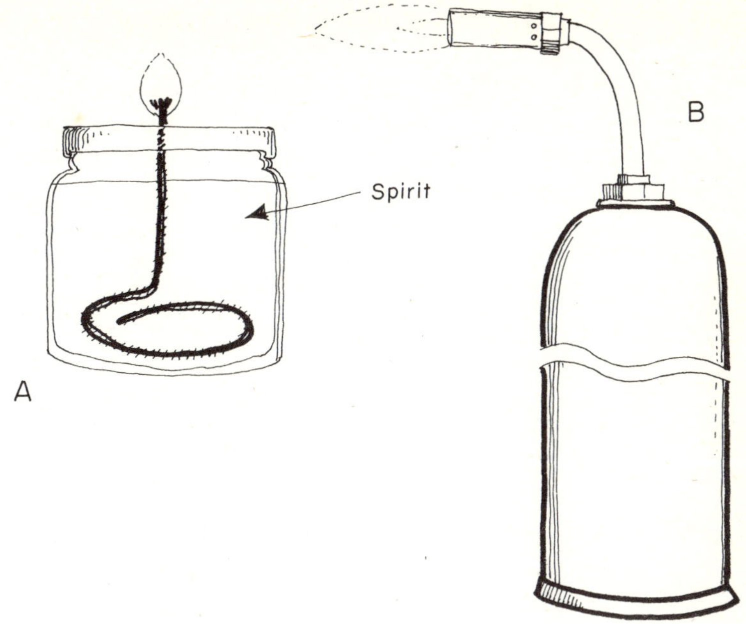

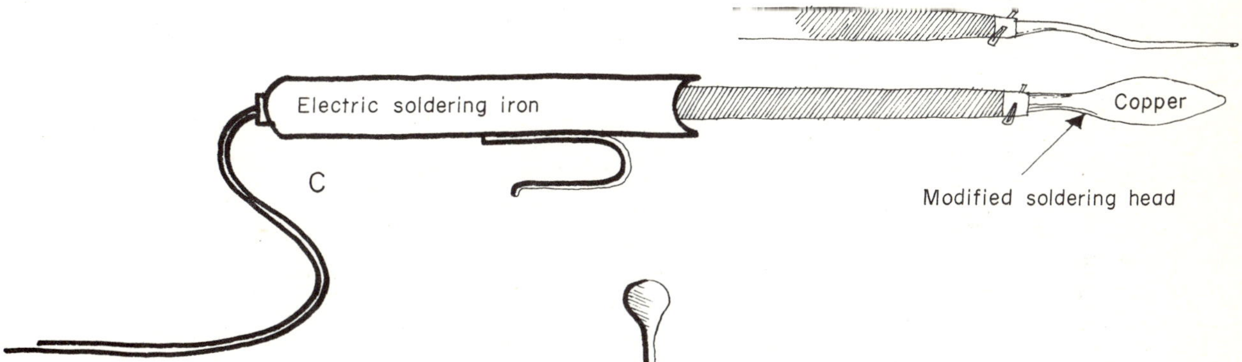

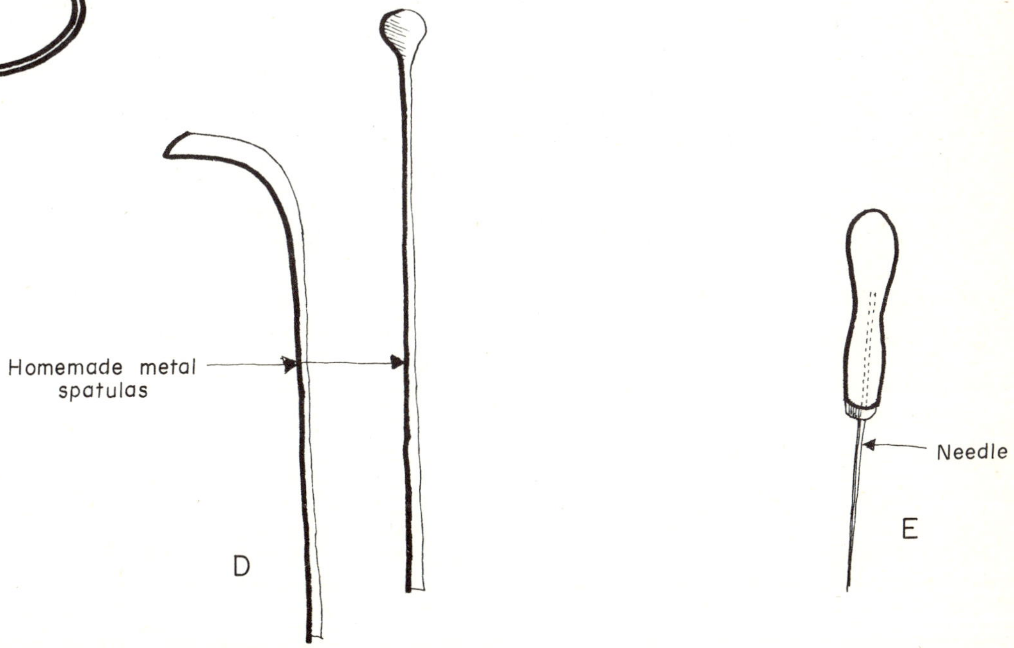

suitable shape. The heated metal modelling tool allows free working of the wax, facilitating modelling and the adding of wax to wax. A modified electric soldering iron is a very useful tool, modified as in the diagram on page 63. The wax can be kept molten in thermostatically controlled boilers, various items of kitchen equipment can be put to this use, and should be looked for wherever such second-hand equipment is sold. A porringer arrangement made as shown in the diagram will provide a safer melter for the wax. Sheets of wax made by pouring the molten liquid on to a wet stone or cement slab, will provide useful beginnings to modelling. Lengths cut from these wax sheets can be used to build up self supporting structures, permitting fine and slender shapes. Wax rods made from a plaster mould giving sticks of various diameter, will prove to be useful in the same way. The mould must be wet when the wax is poured or else the rods cannot be taken out. See diagram page 65.

An interesting technique is to dip the model, in progress, into a bath of hot wax now and again. This treatment smooths the surface and helps pull fairly free and expressive modelling together. Clay roughly shaped and dipped in wax is another useful technique. The clay will remain soft inside the wax, so that the shape of the volume can be changed. If the wax is sufficiently thick and controlled to approx. 5 mm ($\frac{3}{16}$ in.) a hollow wax can be made suitable for lost wax bronze casting. Cutting the wax allows the clay to be removed and cleaned with a soft brush and water,

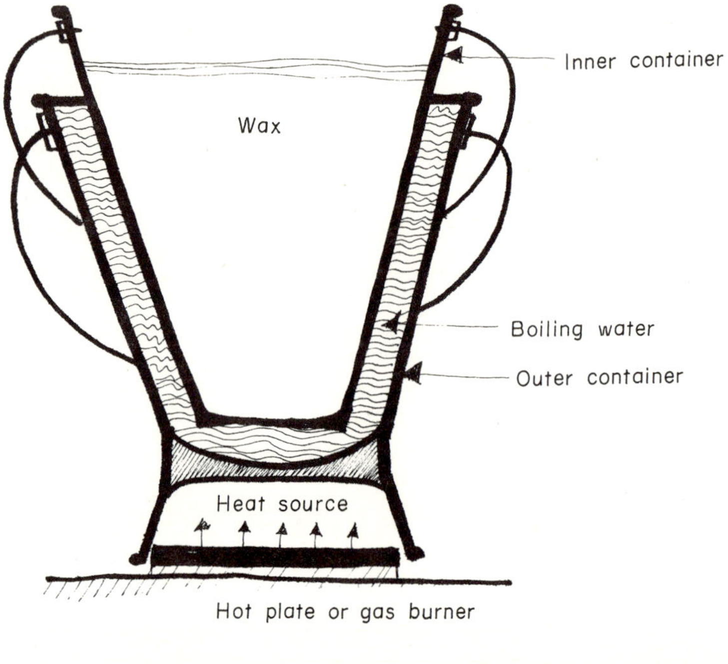

Diagram of a porringer, made from two metal galvanised pails, used to heat and melt wax safely

the prepared dry sections can then be put together and modelled over to make the final wax form. To gain interesting surface qualities, gentle applications of heat from a gas torch is another useful aid to modelling the wax. Experiment is again the sensible advice one can give to the student, and working with wax in particular requires personal research. Because it is often used in its molten state, care must be taken with hot wax. For instance hard wax in a boiler other than a porringer, must always be covered during melting to protect against splashing. Pressure can build up unevenly causing hot wax to burst through the softening surface as it melts, this is an avoidable hazard. Hot wax can be painful on the skin so great care should be taken. Despite the small element of risk however wax can be an enjoyable material with which to work.

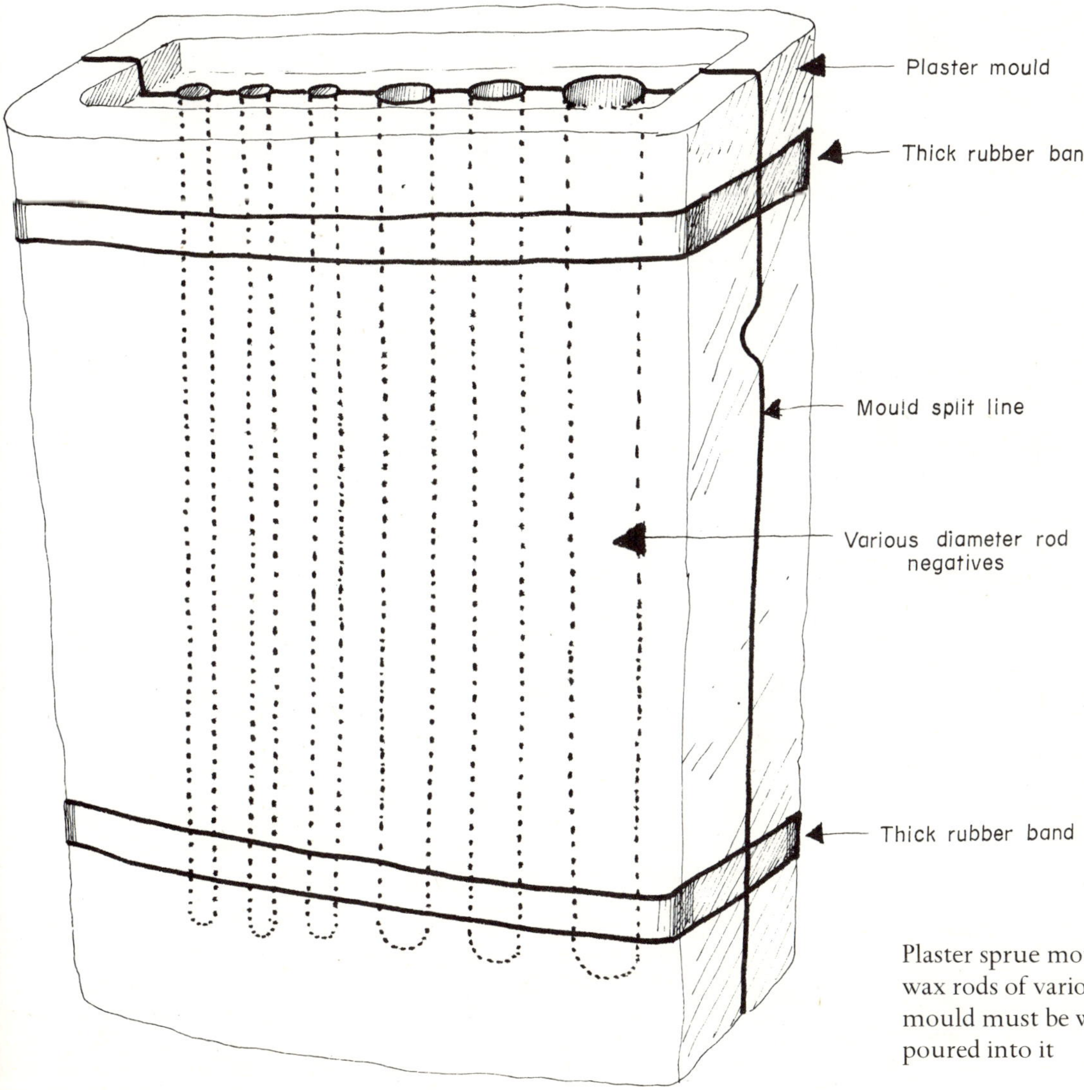

Plaster sprue mould, used to cast wax rods of various thickness. The mould must be wet when wax is poured into it

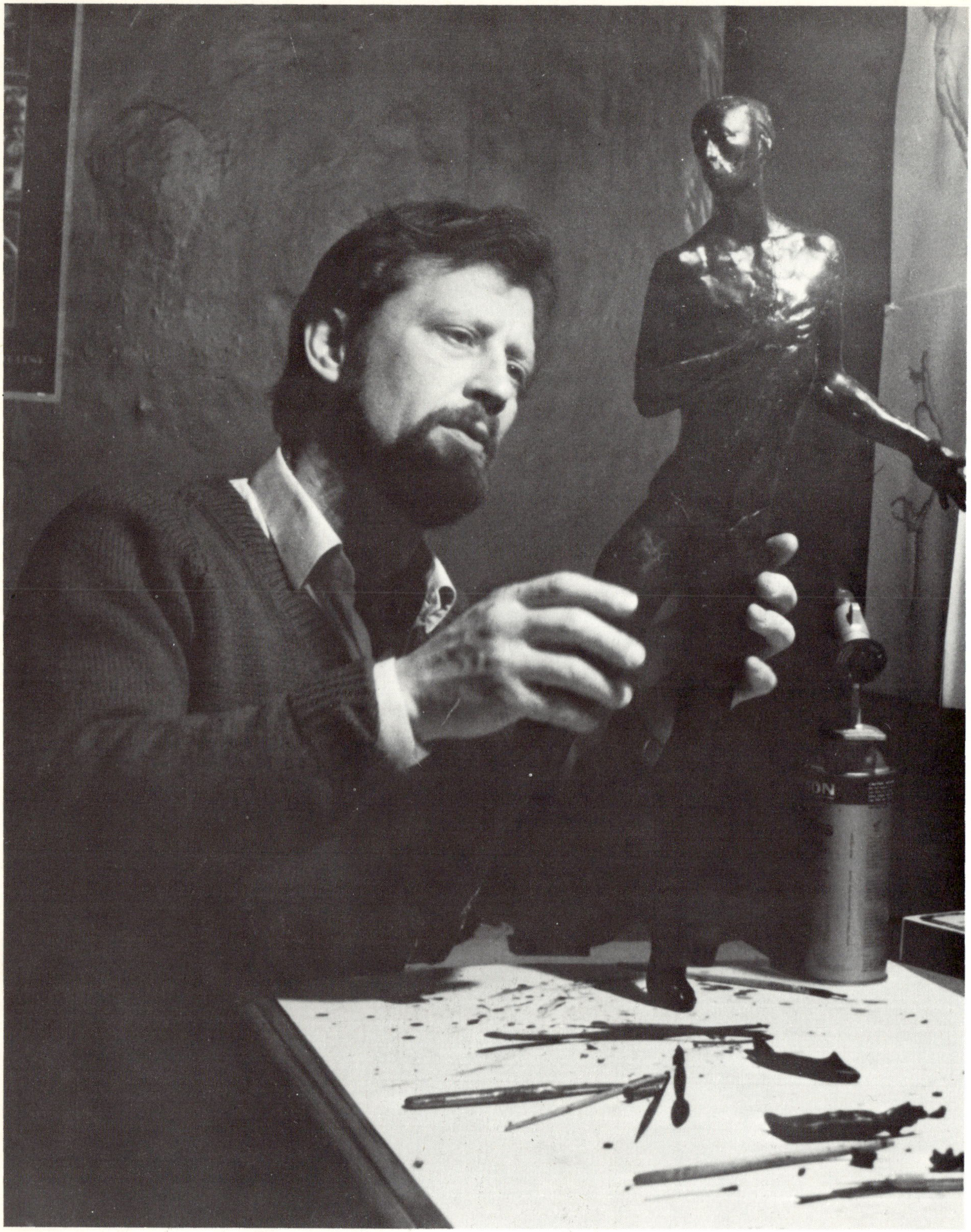

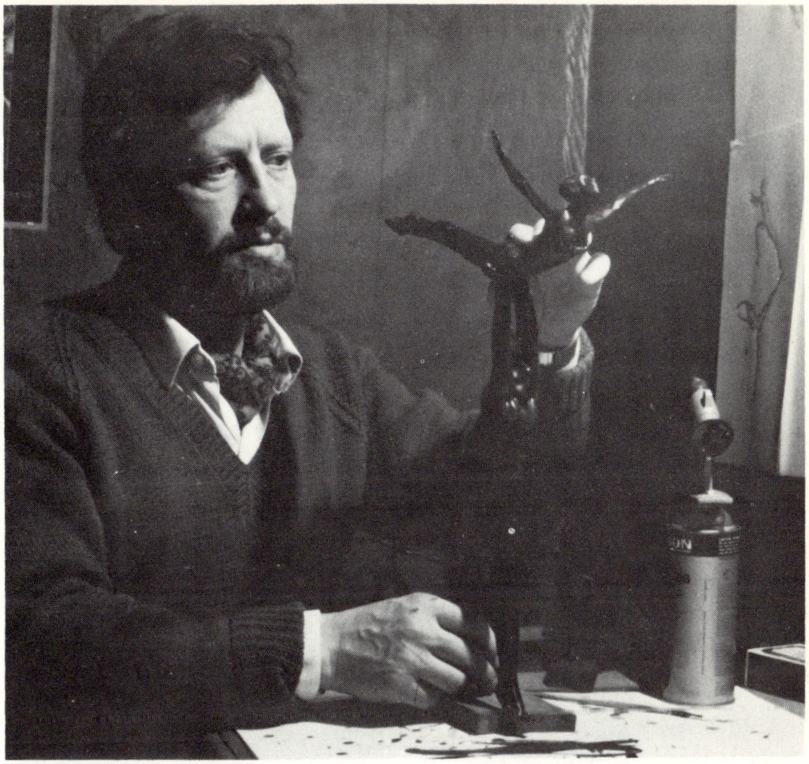

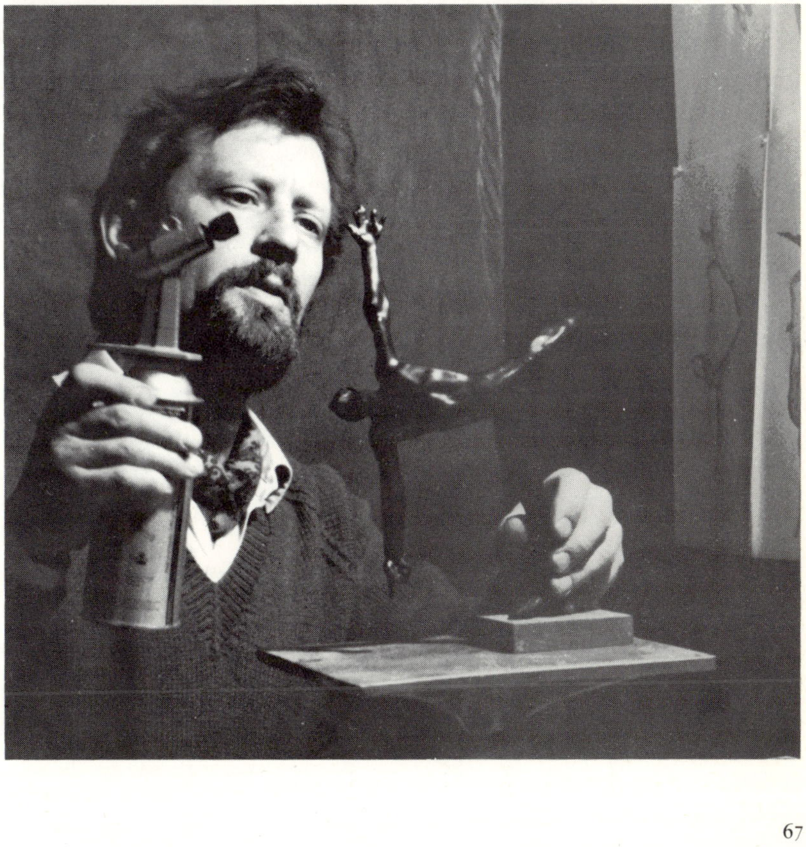

The author modelling wax figures
photograph Josephine Mills

Plaster of paris

Plaster of paris together with clay is the work horse material of the average sculpture studio. It is made from ground and heated gypsum and is named after the Monmartre area of Paris, where it was first quarried, manufactured and marketed in its modern form. It is a very old substance in fact, and it can be traced back to use in sculptor's studios of Ancient Egypt. It has many applications in the studio generally, but in this book its use as a modelling medium is the preoccupation.

When mixed with water the powdered plaster goes through the process of rehydration, changing from a liquid to a solid. The proportion of powder to water being equal parts of each. It is important that the mixture is not less than this, any error should be in favour of more powder; too thin a mixture makes a very weak solid. Although various containers and devices are used to transfer the plaster to the water, the method most widely adopted is that of filtering the powder through the fingers onto the water, allowing it to dissolve gradually without becoming lumpy. First stir the powder in the bin or sack so that the particles are separated to permit easy dissolving in the water. The plaster is added to the water until a small mound appears above the water level. See diagram. The mixture can be left to stand (it can be left quite safely for up to ten minutes) and then it is thoroughly mixed. The setting action will then take place at a speed related to the nature of the plaster, its kind and quality. Manufacturers produce a wide range, varying in hardness, expansion rate and speed of setting. As the plaster sets it will heat up, this exothermic heat is caused by the molecular change from liquid to solid and is nothing to be alarmed at, in fact the heating up and cooling gives a good indication of the state the plaster is in. After cooling it is safe to remove a casting from a mould and it is safe to carry on working on a direct build up.

Diagram of plaster of paris added to water, the pile of plaster appearing above the water surface is sufficient indication of the correct proportion (50:50)

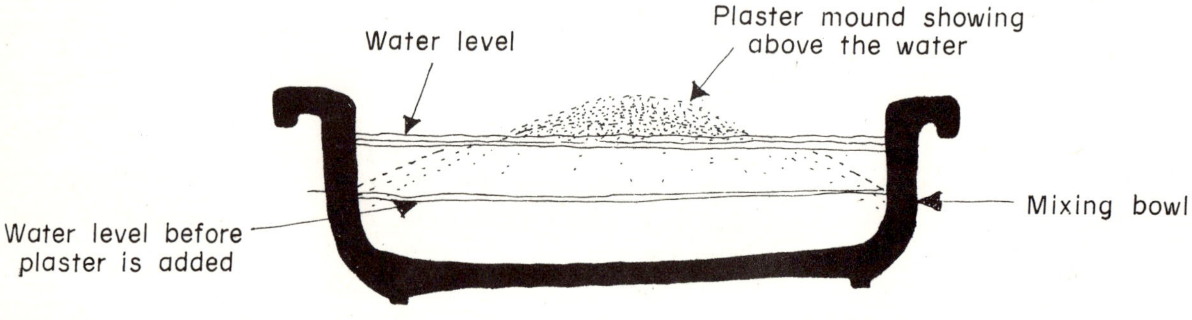

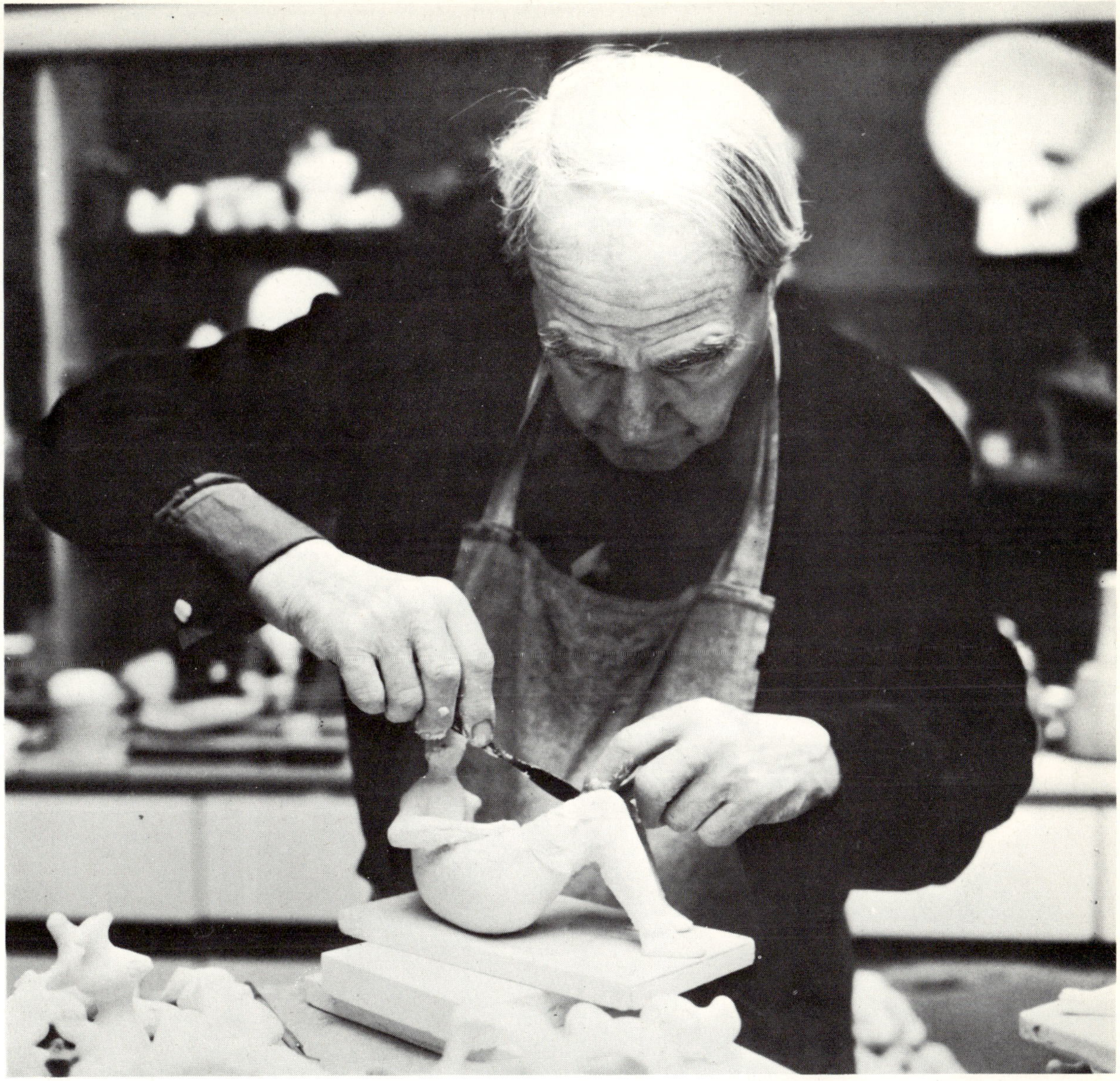

Henry Moore working on plaster maquette
photograph Errol Jackson

Modelling or making forms directly in plaster of paris is done by exploiting the gradual change in consistency to a solid state, which is so characteristic of the material. Steel spatulas or old flexible table knives are the tools used during the modelling stage. When hard the plaster can be carved, rasped and smoothed. Carving or chipping is best done using small hand axes or modified hammers, or indeed hammers made to suit a particular job. See diagram. Rasping is best done using special plaster rasps designed not to clog (See diagram), cheese graters especially of stainless steel are good substitutes for the proprietary rasps.

Home made picking hammers for working on plaster of paris, these tools can be made from metal tubing, welded and shaped according to the job in hand

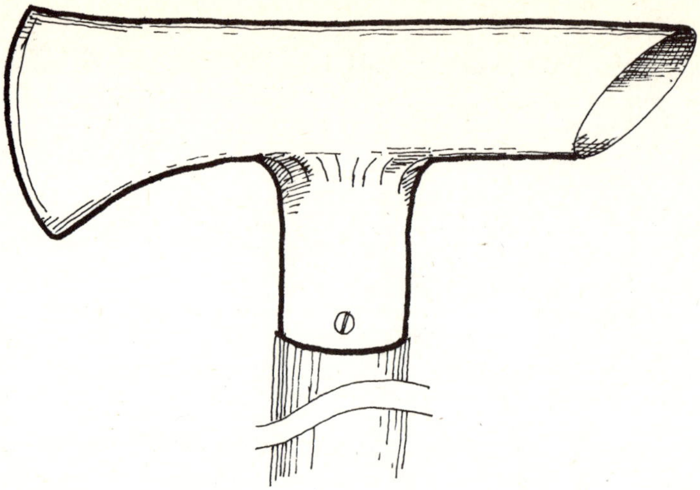

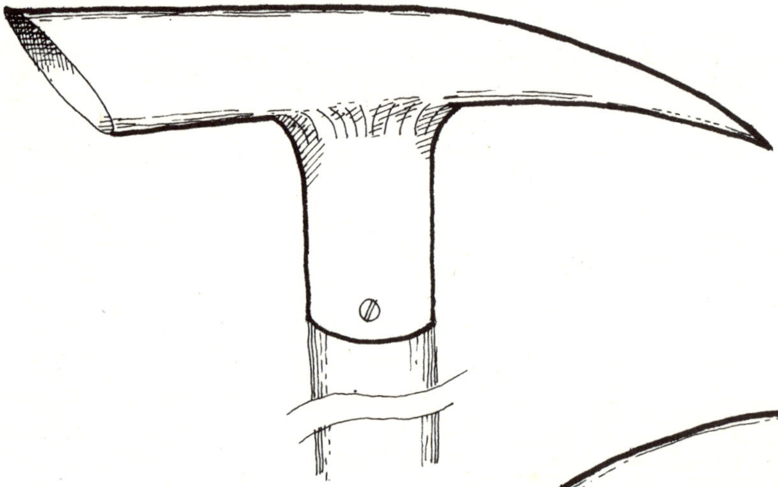

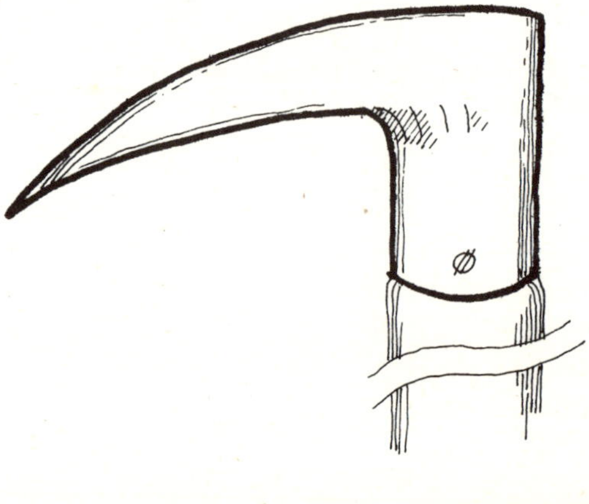

Smoothing the surface is achieved easily on very dry hard plaster with glass paper of various grades or with steel wool, but when wet a woven wire mesh is best, which can be easily cleaned and unclogged. This is an old victorian device and is still the most useful on wet plaster, it allows smooth forms to be made at a sensible stage in the development of the sculpture. It should be remembered that plaster needs to be wet to receive more plaster. If a fresh mix is added to dry plaster it will be killed by the suction of water from the fresh application. Treated properly and with care the additive process of modelling can be achieved, with the bonus of subtracting, as in carving, on the hard plaster to create a wider range of form and texture than is possible with clay or wax.

Plaster of paris is a brittle substance and requires fibrous reinforcing, given by using hemp or jute scrim; cotton scrim can be used too but only for fine work. These fibres are used also to attach the plaster to a constructed armature, but too much will prevent easy working on the plaster. Use only enough to fix the plaster to the armature and to give tensile strength, there is nothing more irritating than to have whiskers protruding from the plaster as you work.

Large hollow forms can be made by first making a rough clay shape without detail, then this is covered with plaster reinforced with fibre and the detail and texture modelled on the surface of the plaster. The volume of the clay must be less than the volume of the completed form by as much as the plaster thickness.

Expanded polystyrene or polyurethane can be used in the same way and the hollow form is made by removing the core of clay or foam. This can be done by sawing through an enclosed shape or by digging the clay from underneath an open form. The expanded foam can be removed with a solvent.

Wood wool, sawdust or laths of wood can be used as additives in the plaster build up. These additives make it possible to extend a form quickly and because they can be cut easily do not inhibit work on the surface. The various expanded foams can be used in this way too, of course, but do not give as much strength to the plaster, so require some thought before inclusion. Experiment is the key word with these materials, as with all.

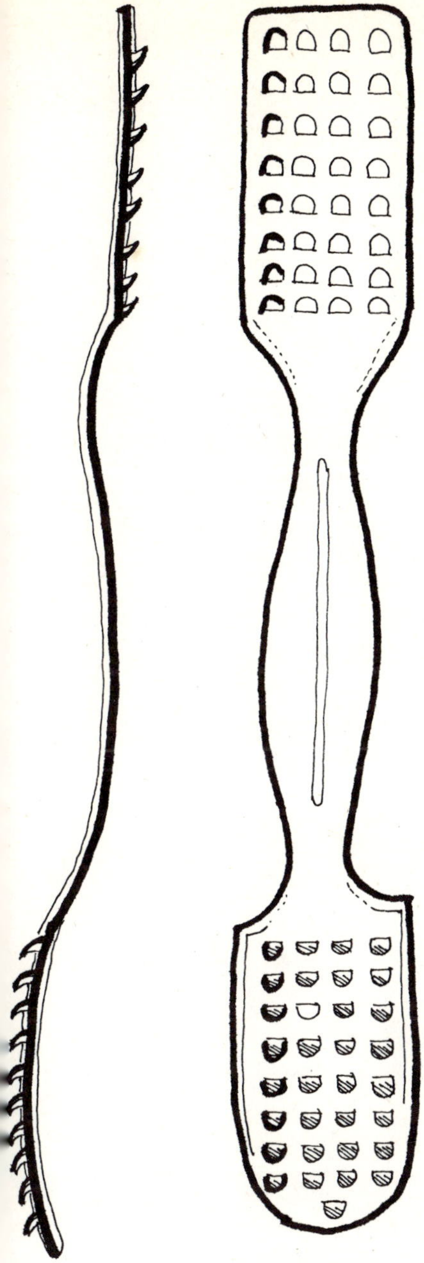

Plaster rasp, designed to allow plaster to pass through the holes in the rasping face, and not clog. These rasps are sold in a range of sizes

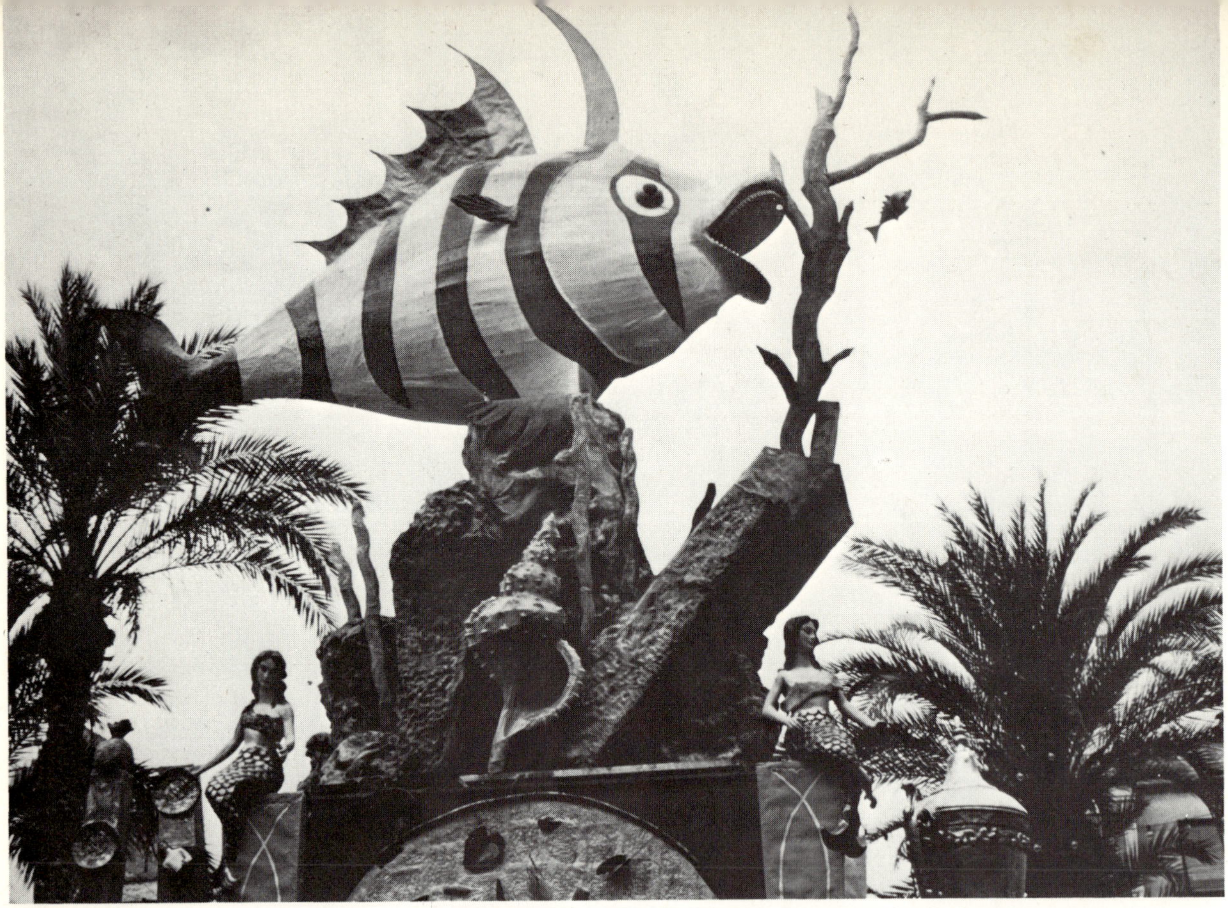

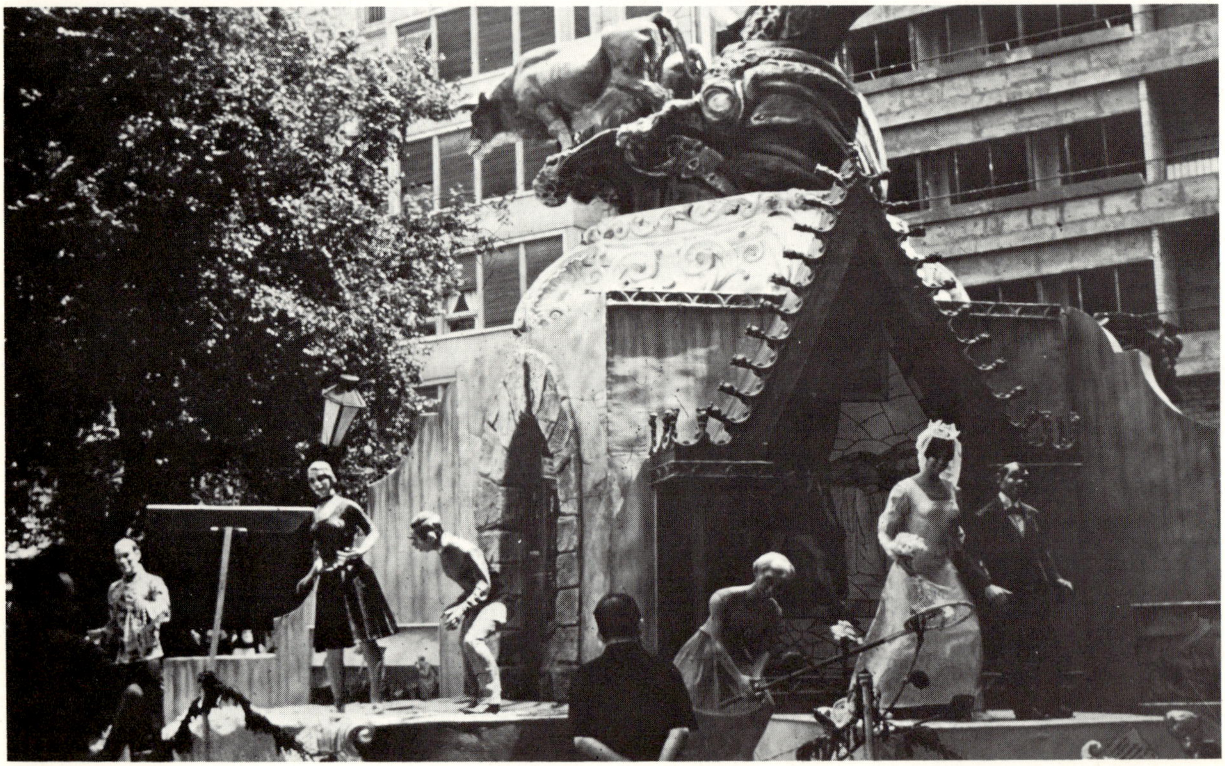

Festival Floats Papier mâché
Alicante, Spain
photograph T A Jones

Papier mâché

This is a medium often used in schools because it is usually cold and can be used with comparative safety. Its most common form is made up of strips of paper soaked in a water-soluble glue then built up in laminates, allowing each layer to dry before applying the next. Papier mâché for modelling however is slightly different. There are many formulae according to the available glue and paper, these being the most important ingredients. Any paper can be used but tissue paper is the most acceptable to the purists. Packaging made from compressed paper pulp, used sometimes for marketing eggs or fruit is a product of modern industry useful in this respect. A useful formula is as follows: Soak the paper or pulp until it becomes soft and doughy in consistency, boiling slowly will quicken the process. To this dough water-soluble glue is added and a preservative. A small quantity of carbolic acid or formaldehyde will help preserve the mixture. Plaster of paris added to the mixture will give the final result greater strength, but it will speed up the hardening so should be added to small amounts of papier mâché. Pumice powder or any available inert powder will give added bulk to gain a suitable modelling consistency and act as a fire retardent.

The act of modelling with the resulting rather sticky material is one of patient build up. It is necessary to build up in modest layers allowing each to dry before proceeding with the next: dry meaning firm throughout. This allows the material to harden as the glue hardens. Too thick a build-up keeps the glue from hardening right through. The simple papier mâché technique of soaking strips of paper in glue and laying them onto a chicken wire construction, or over a clay form, leaving this to harden provides a good base on which to model. This technique will also allow the construction of large pieces slowly but surely, with the advantage of being able to pick up the work at any time and continue.

The advantages of this material are few from the facile modelling point of view. Apart from the continuing modelling process it allows, it is the final state of the material that endears it most. When hard papier mâché is lightweight, it can be coloured easily and is very strong relative to its weight. So in relation to the conditions under which it is used it can be a very useful medium indeed. The control of its toxicity make it a desirable teaching aid, supplemented by its facility for extended working over long and possibly infrequent periods.

Overleaf
Students at work in the sculpture studio at Hertfordshire College of Art and Design. The masks on the shelves are in papier mâché
photograph John W Mills

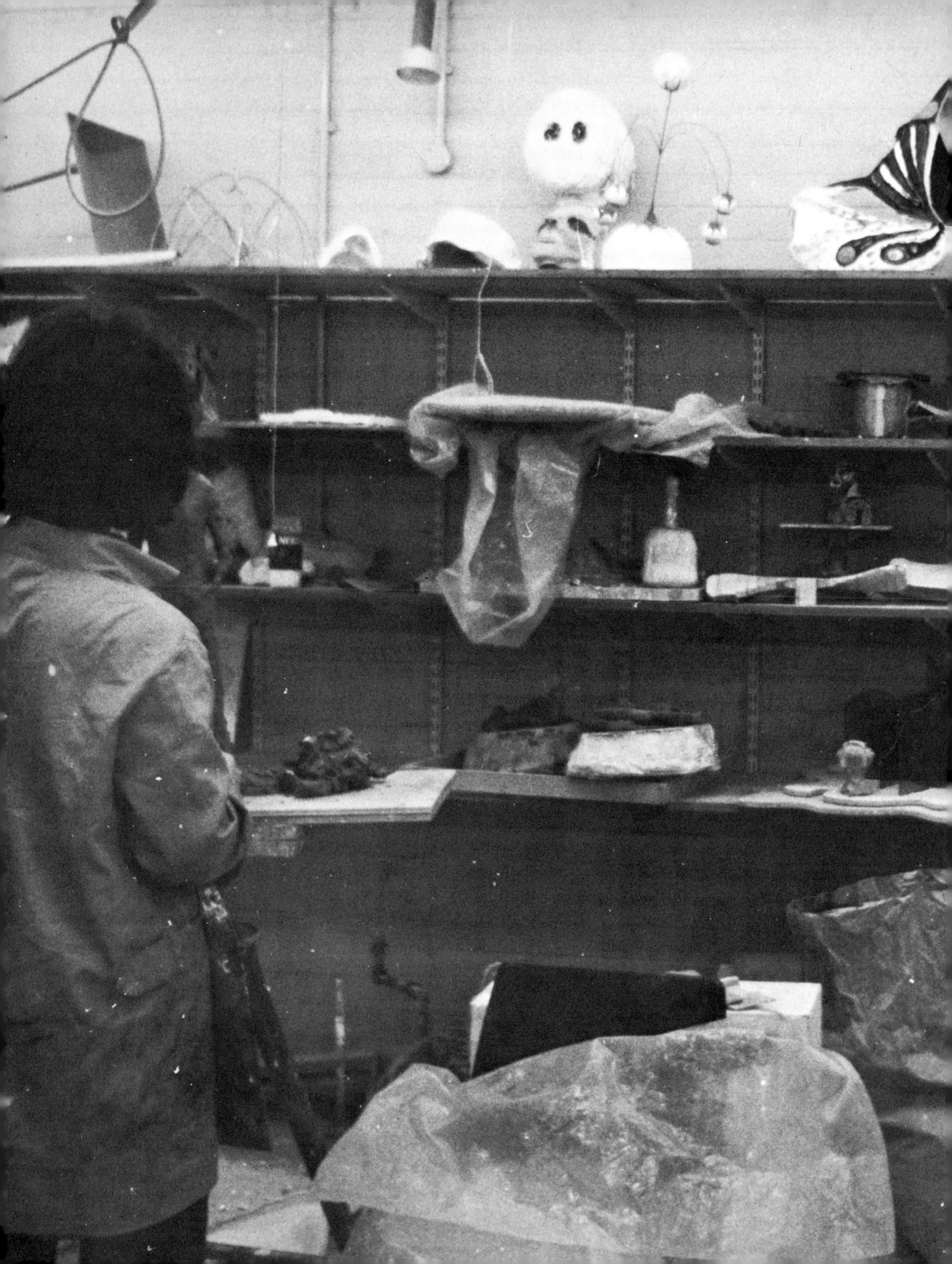

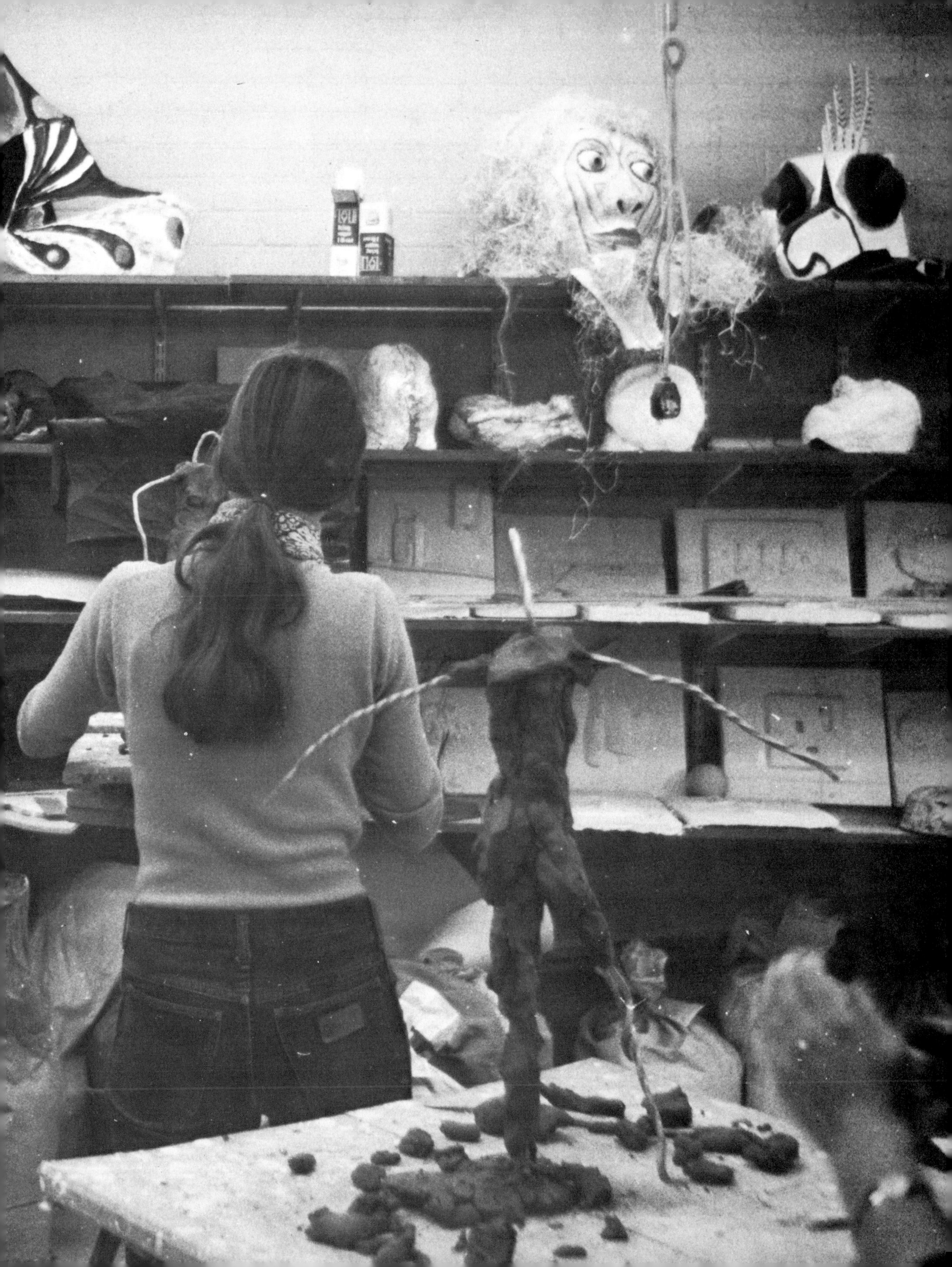

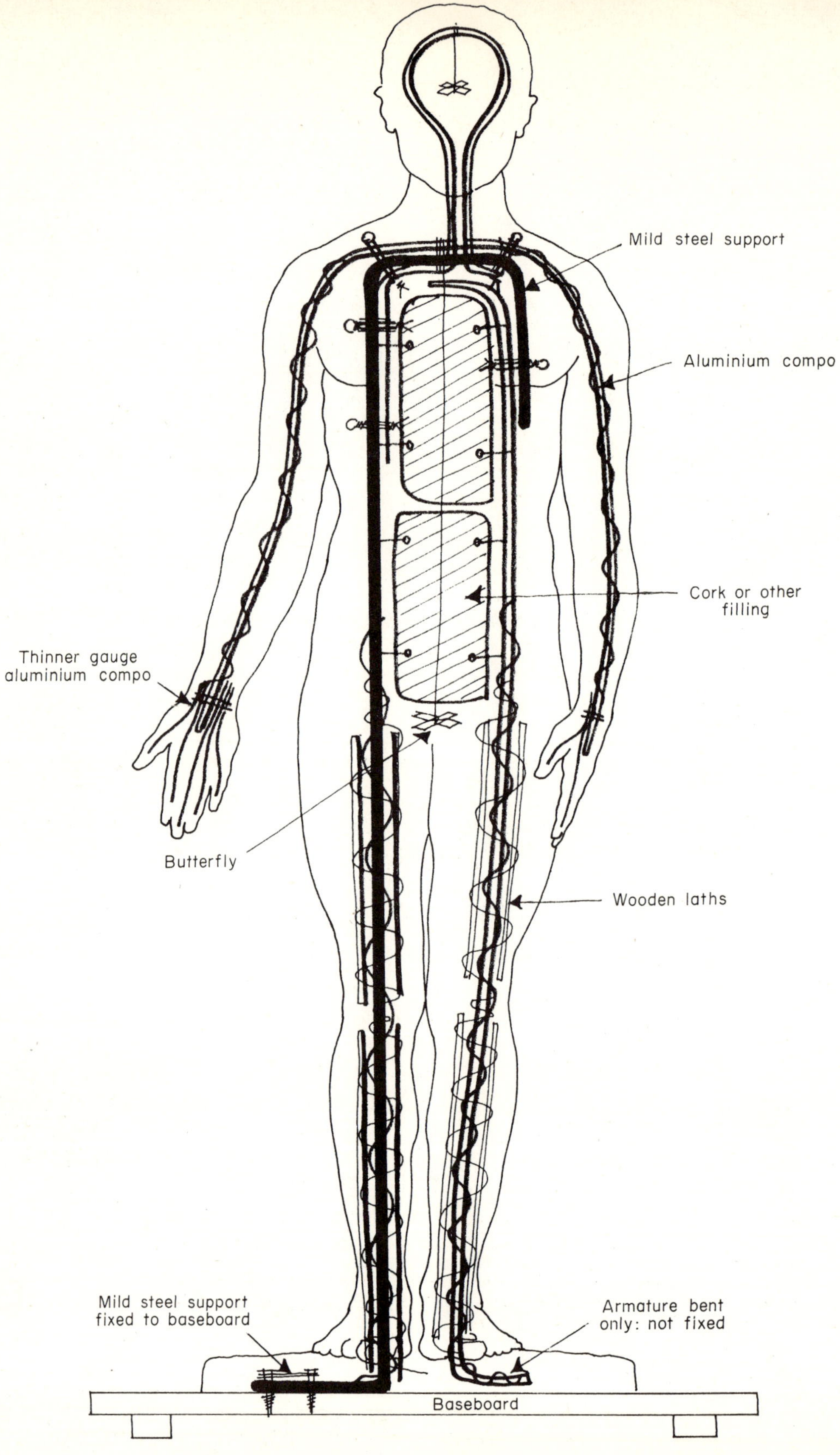
Mild steel support
Aluminium compo
Cork or other filling
Thinner gauge aluminium compo
Butterfly
Wooden laths
Mild steel support fixed to baseboard
Armature bent only: not fixed
Baseboard

3 Armatures

This subject is of prime importance to the modeller of the figure and head. The armature is the internal support that makes it possible to model complex shapes with comparative freedom. This support needs to be secure and strong. The human skeleton is a useful model on which to base the design of an armature, in so far as it provides the natural equivalent. The skeleton supports the soft amorphous forms of flesh in the most finite and articulate manner. The engineering principles embodied in the human skeleton are of the highest and most complex order and their study can only be of great use. It is of course more complicated than the support required from a sculpture armature, but it embodies the rule that most forms are only as strong as their internal support, a factor that indicates the importance of a sensibly designed armature.

For clay

The fact that clay has no tensile strength means that it cannot be modelled to any height or length without a sensible armature. This structure must be capable of supporting solid clay forms, and allow free working for as long as necessary. Figures are often kept in their clay state for weeks, months or even years before completion. Clay being a very dense material weighs a great deal, a factor that must be borne in mind when making an armature to support it. This support must be secure and must not whip or move loosely, or else the proper balance of forms one against another will not easily be made. A loose armature will not permit free modelling and is as impractical as an unsteady banker or modelling stand. The armature must be made from materials strong enough to support the clay, and can be made from a suitable gauge mild steel rod. By suitable gauge I mean thick enough for the size figure being made. This mild steel is easily shaped cold in an engineer's vice, heavy gauge rod will need heating to red heat to bend easily, and this can be supplied by means of a forge or a gas torch. The strong basic structure supports additional skeletal shapes made from more flexible materials. In the past, lead piping was used for these additional items, and still may be used when available, but a cheaper, lighter and longer-lasting material is aluminium composition wire. This is usually square in section and can be purchased in coils by the pound or kilogramme, and in size from 3 mm to 25 mm ($\frac{1}{8}$ in. to 1 in.). Round section wire will require hammering to provide a good fixing where one piece of wire is to be attached to another. This composition is very pliable but has the disadvantage of low tensile strength, by twisting the wire along its length, the surface tension can be increased thereby gaining an increased tensile strength, without losing too much pliability.

The bulk of a form can be taken up by binding to the armature lightweight substances, wood, cork or expanded plastic foam of one kind or another. Provided these are kept well inside the proposed final volume, they will help to lessen the load taken on the support. Binding lengths of wood lath to the metal gives extra rigidity too, the wood swells with the moisture taken from the clay and so tightens the structure. The laths also provide a key for the clay to cling to which thus preventing it slipping down the armature. Other methods for making this key are to bind wire around the main supports, twist the square aluminium wire or to attach thin strips of wood at intervals along the length of the rod. Remember the clay can be sliced easily, so its weight in relation to the thickness of the rod must be considered. Another very useful device for supporting large volumes of clay on an armature is a butterfly. See diagram. This butterfly prevents the clay slipping too and is useful for forms that cannot be packed

A

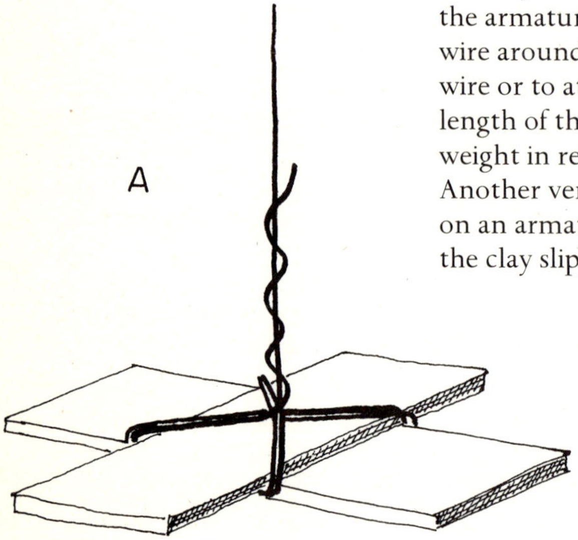

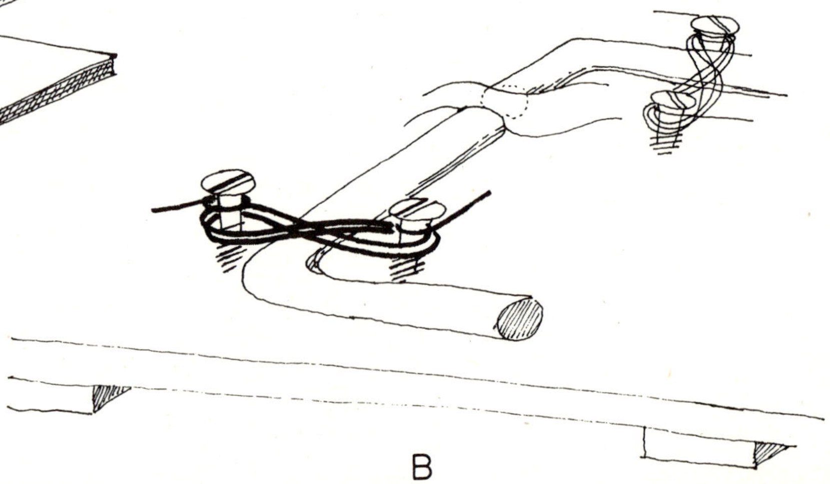

B

A is an illustration of a butterfly, made from wired crossed wooden lath. Used to support large clay forms. *B* shows the best method for fixing metal armatures to a baseboard, using wood screws and wire

with another filling, and to support solid bulky forms.

The mild steel support may be located in the centre of the supporting limbs, making a free-standing armature. This is most useful but fairly difficult to make, so an external support, known as a *back iron* has been invented. This is an angled iron support that has projections from which flexible skeletal structures can be hung to make the figure. The kind of armature you use depends upon your skill in making them, and upon the kind of figure you wish to achieve. See diagram. A standard armature permanently fixed is a useful expedient, but most sculptors prefer an armature without projections into the sculpture. Back irons no matter how well designed affect the easy comprehension of the figure in progress. It has the advantage of allowing a firm armature to be made quickly however and should therefore always be considered.

The support made inside the figure is ideal, and although it takes more time to make, it will prove to be worth the effort. The armature illustrated in the diagram enables the support to a free standing figure to be adjustable, because only one leg is fixed. A number of armatures made in this way will allow a group of figures to be made simply, each with a separate base board, giving a maximum flexibility not possible with external supports. It is always an advantage to be able to move large forms during modelling so that a total freedom is achieved. Protrusion of odd items of armature is best avoided so that a clear view and comprehension of the form in progress is possible.

This information applies to armatures at any size. I have emphasised the requirements of large figures, but small figures require similar support at their relative scale and therefore similar considerations. Much of the support for bulk is not necessary, but a stable structure for clay should always be the brief to which to work.

Useful examples of internally supported armatures I have either devised or seen in use in other studios are many and various but the most practical and of the most universal application is as follows: steel piping threaded at one end and screwed into a base plate, attached securely with bolts or screws to a suitable wooden base board, provides a sound and variable basic support. This can be utilised to make a head armature or a figure armature. See diagram. A range of sizes can be made in advance, giving a practical variety of supports ready to hand. The examples illustrated are items that I have found useful, but of course all are open to personal modification according to the image being made.

The armature for a clay figure must be easily demountable. This enables the clay and support to be removed from the plaster mould without difficulty. Therefore a welded armature is to be

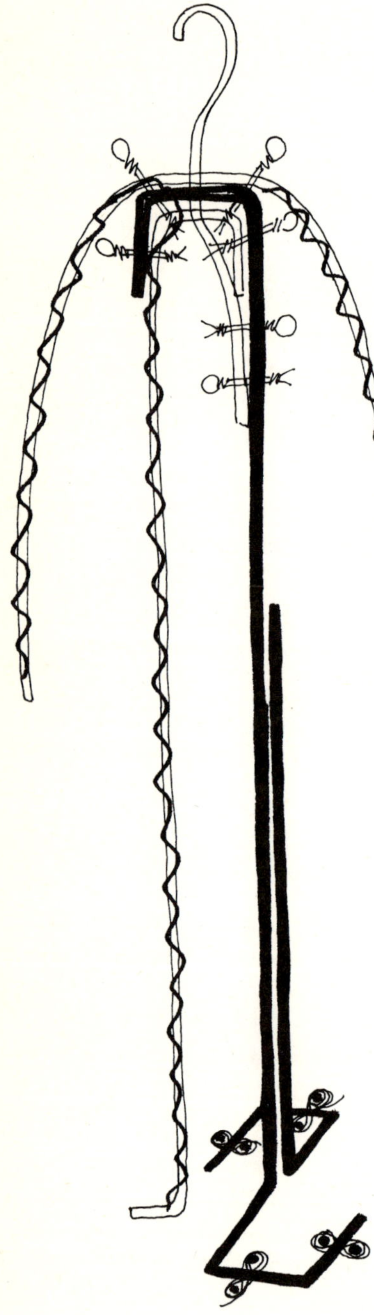

A

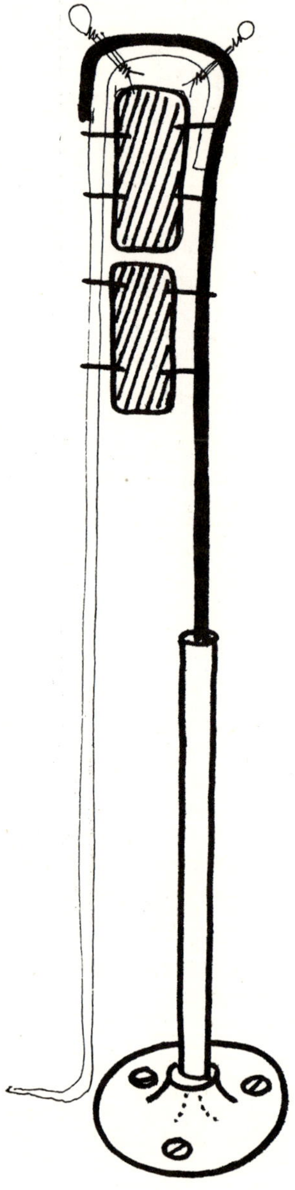

B

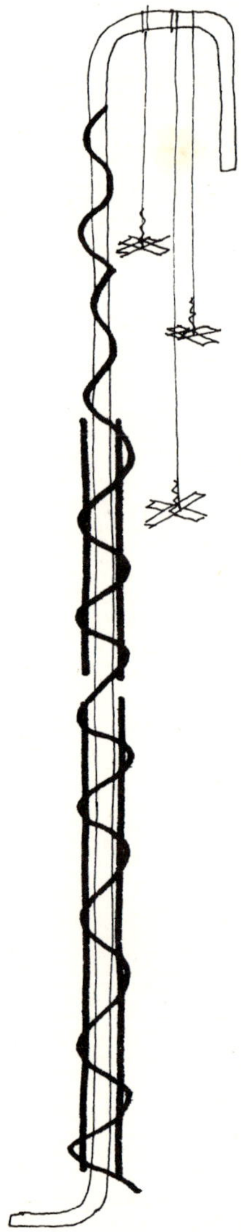

C

avoided because it will inhibit removal from the mould. Various items of skeletal support should be bound together with galvanised binding wire tourniquets as shown in the diagram below. The armature should be fixed to a base board (page 83) which also allows easy dismantling. These techniques make it possible to mould from clay figures with comparative ease, and the kind of forethought mentioned here will save time on the somewhat tedious processes of moulding and casting.

Illustrations of armatures made with an internal support. *A* shows the configuration of mild steel that affords the best support. *B* illustrates a similar armature utilising a galvanised tube and base plate. *C* is a detail of the malleable part of the armature with binding wire loosely bound about it, holding also wooden laths to give extra rigidity in the right places

This is illustrated further, in relating the armature to the figure. *D* illustrates a simple wire tourniquet, used for attaching pieces of armature.

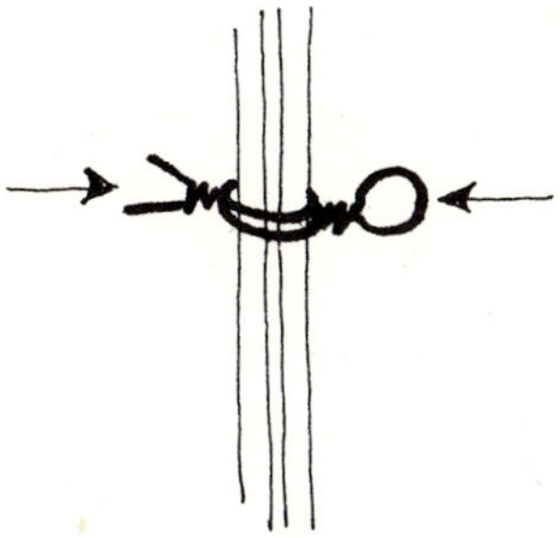

D

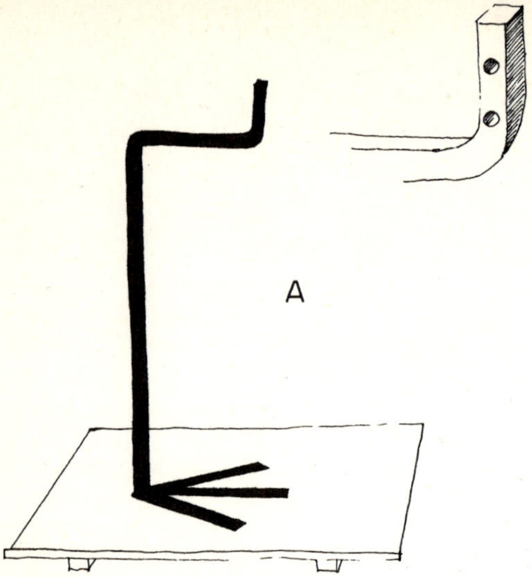

A

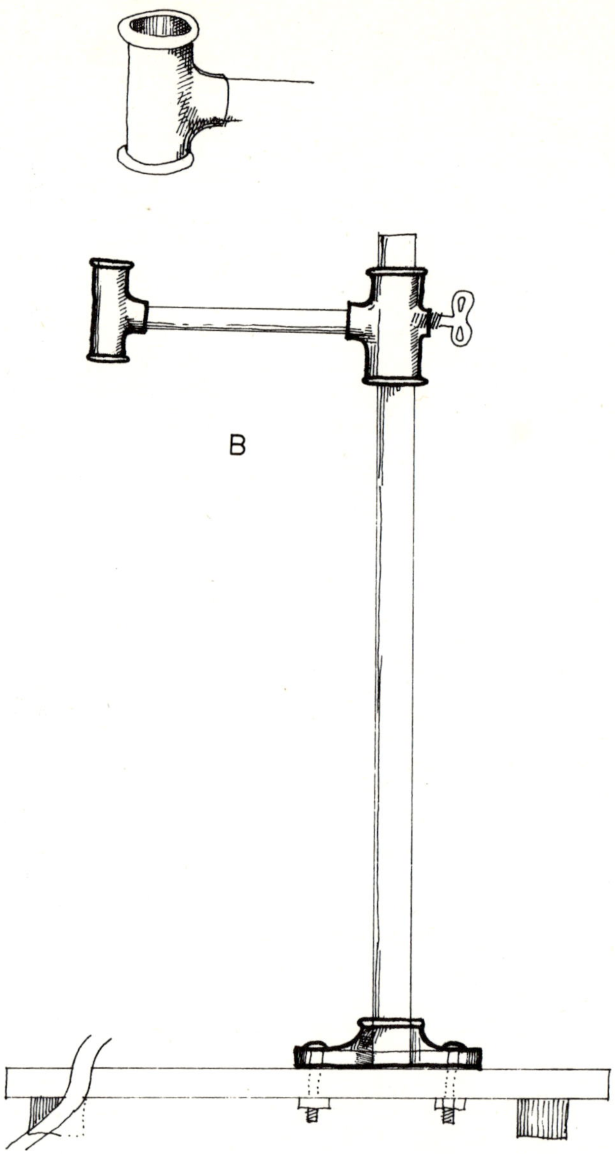

B

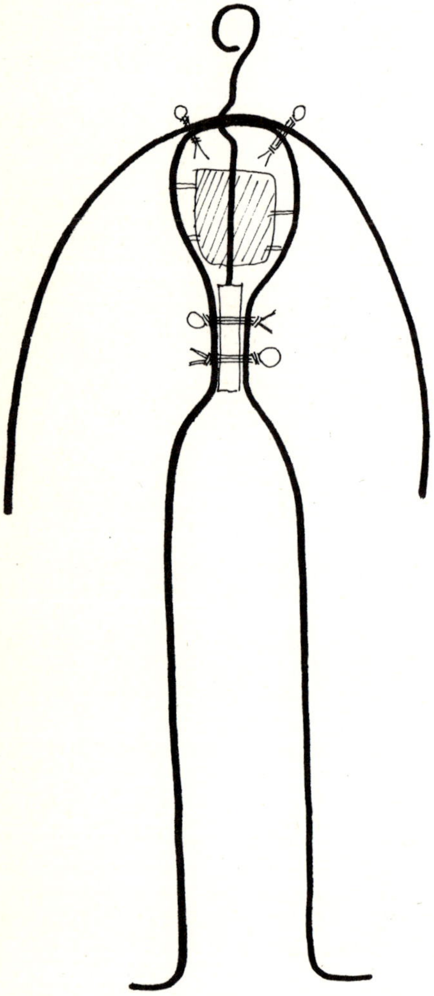

C

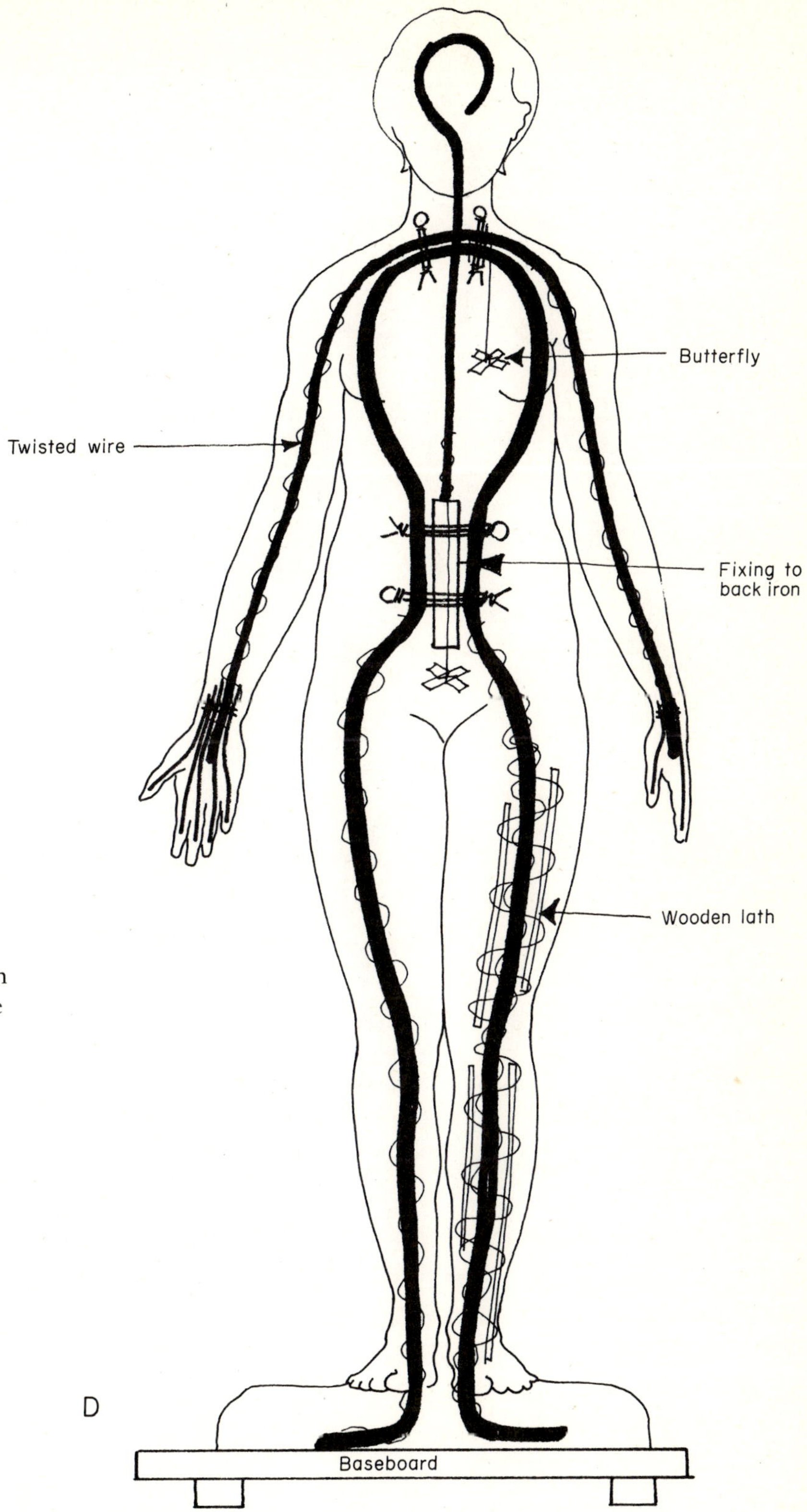

These are diagrams of external supports for figure armatures (back irons). *A* is the traditional back iron, available at all sizes up to life size, the detail is of the fixing arrangement. *B* illustrates an adjustable back iron made from galvanised tubing, as shown in the detail. This can be made to accommodate any size figure. *C* is an illustration of the armature used in conjunction with a back iron. *D* shows the same kind of armature in the figure. Note the allowance necessary to model, by adding, the final volume of the figure

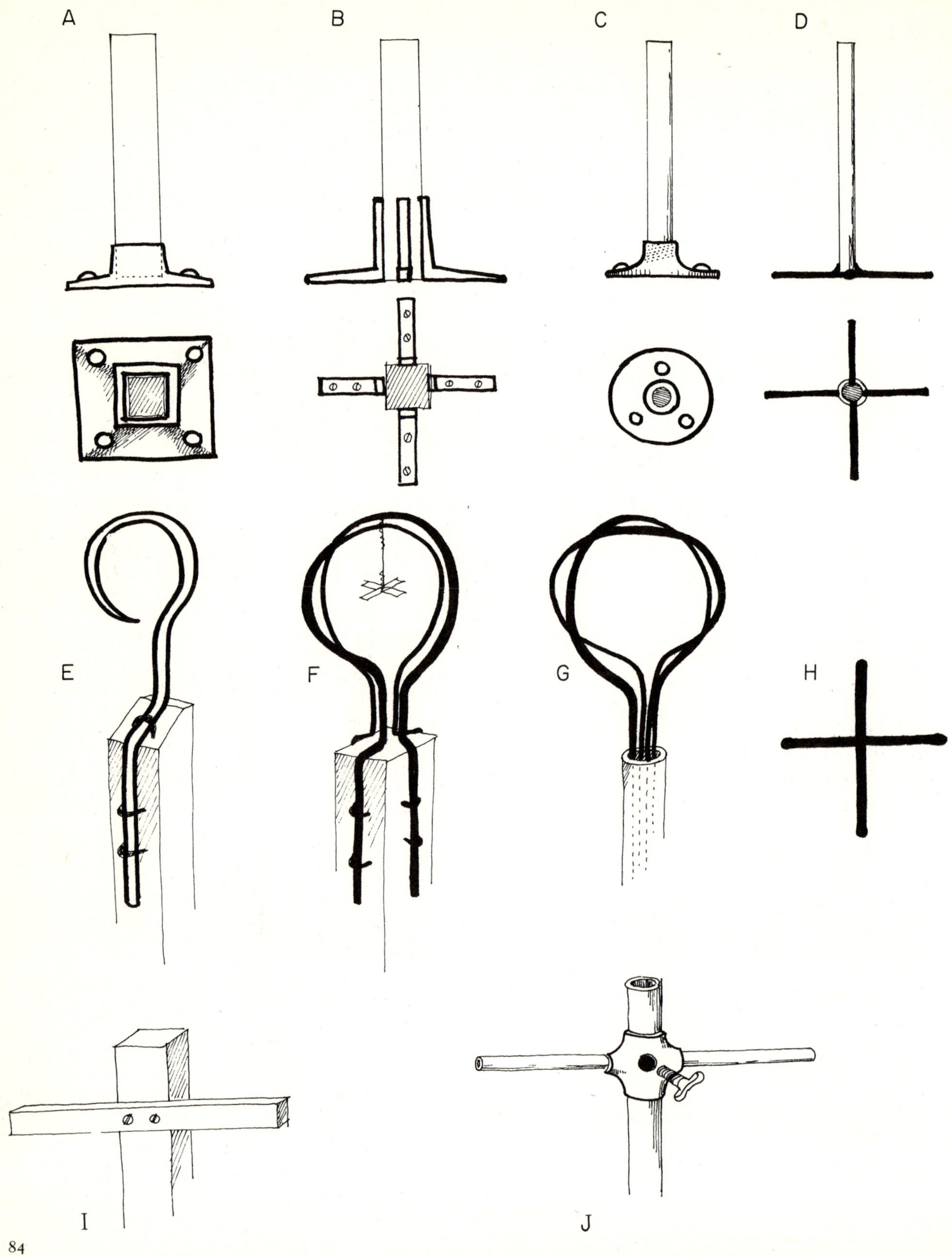
A
B
C
D
E
F
G
H
I
J

Diagrams illustrating the various types of head peg, to support the armature on which the head is modelled. *A* and *B* are wooden pegs supported by metal brackets. *C* and *D* are made from galvanised tube; *C* is supported by means of a base plate whilst *D* is supported by means of welded rods in the form of a cross. *E, F, G* and *H* illustrate the alternative forms and fixings of the armature. *I* and *H* are diagrams of the additions required to supply support for shoulders

Modelling a sculpture maquette entitled *Rembrandt Regardant* Illustrated is the sequence from forming the head armature to the completed modelling prior to moulding. The final material will be bronze
photographs by John W Mills

Shaping the loops of armature to make the head peg

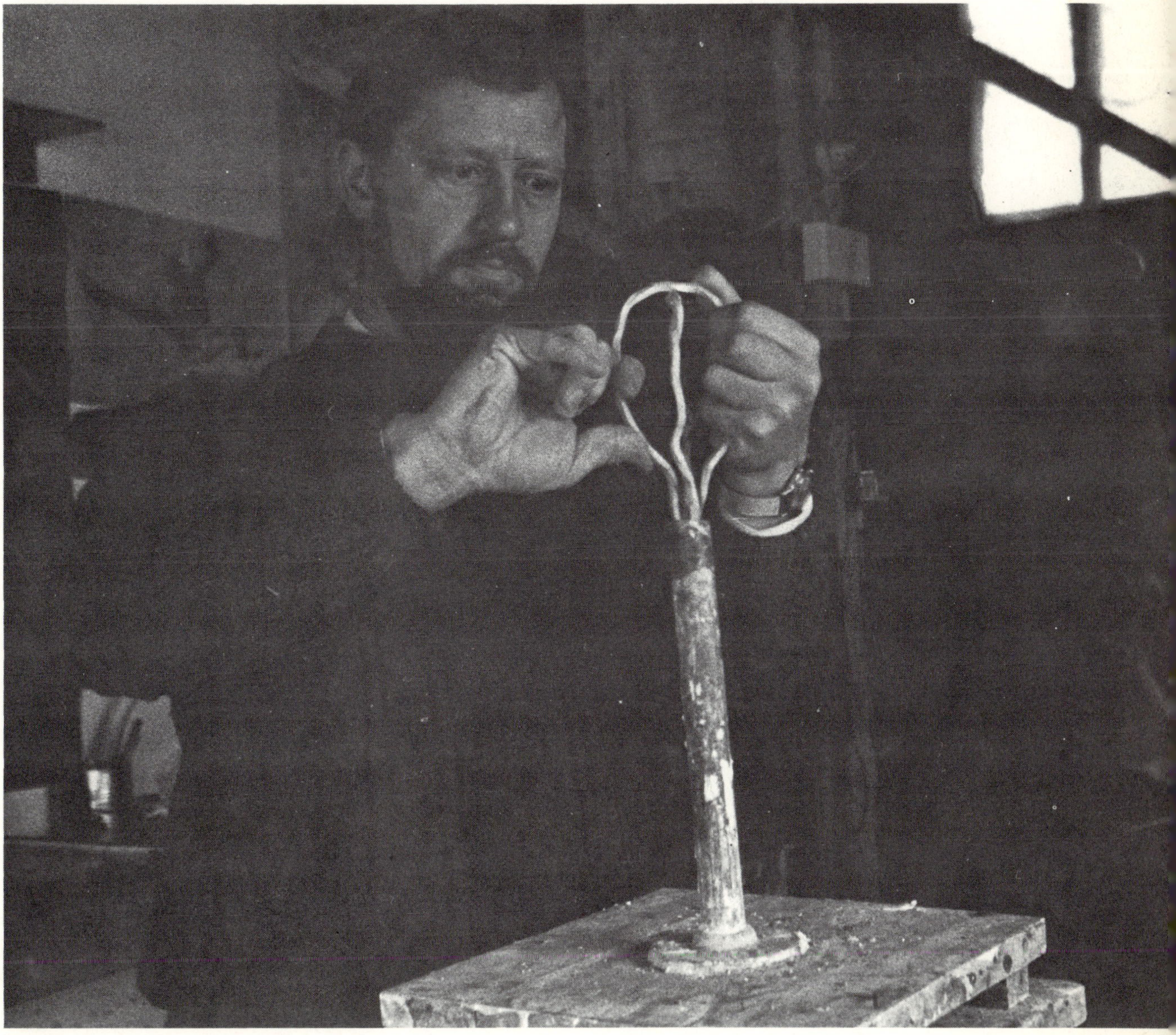

Clay being packed between the loops of the armature to begin the build up

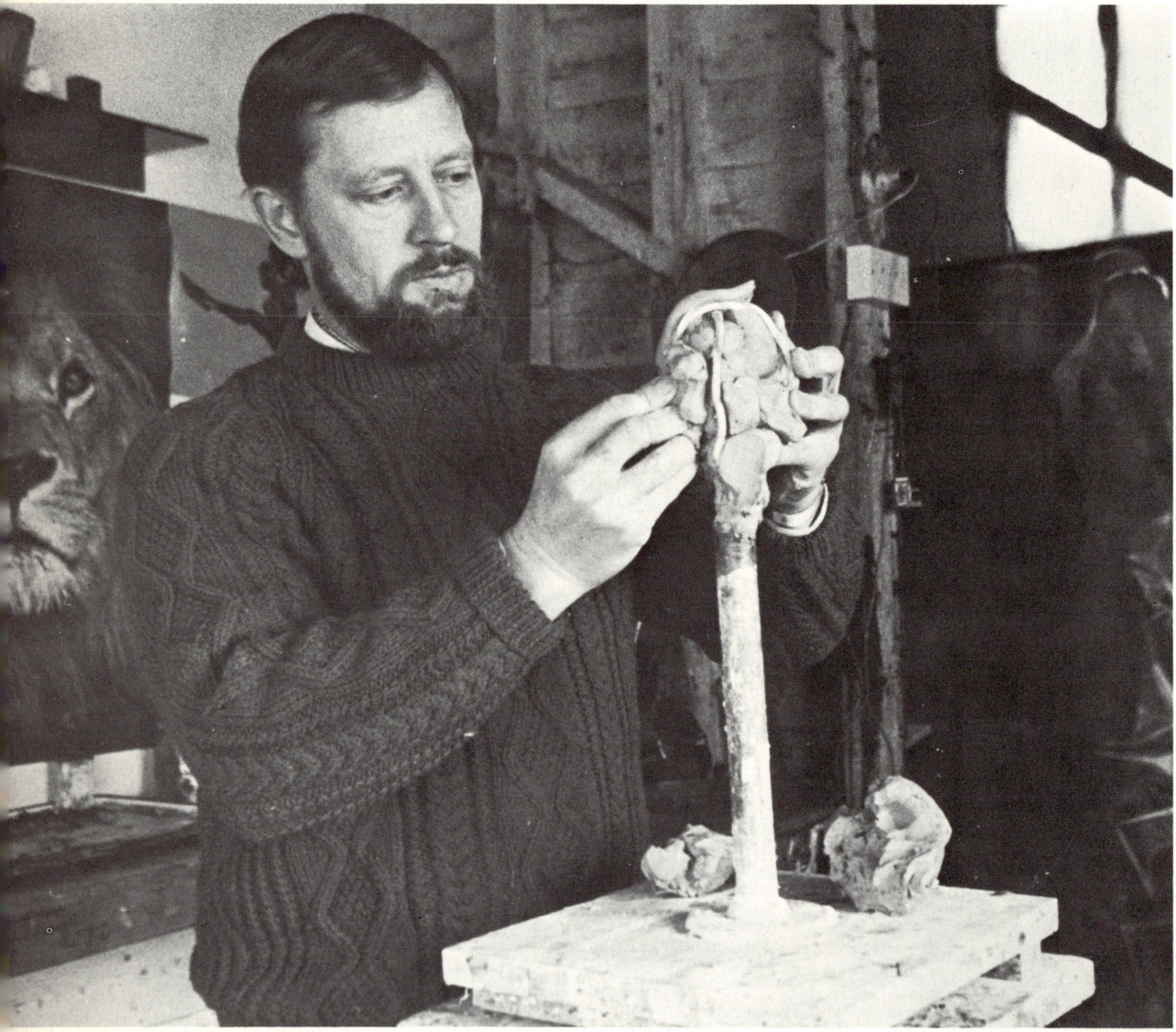

The head taking shape
Depressions being formed to make the eye sockets. The character is established as soon as possible

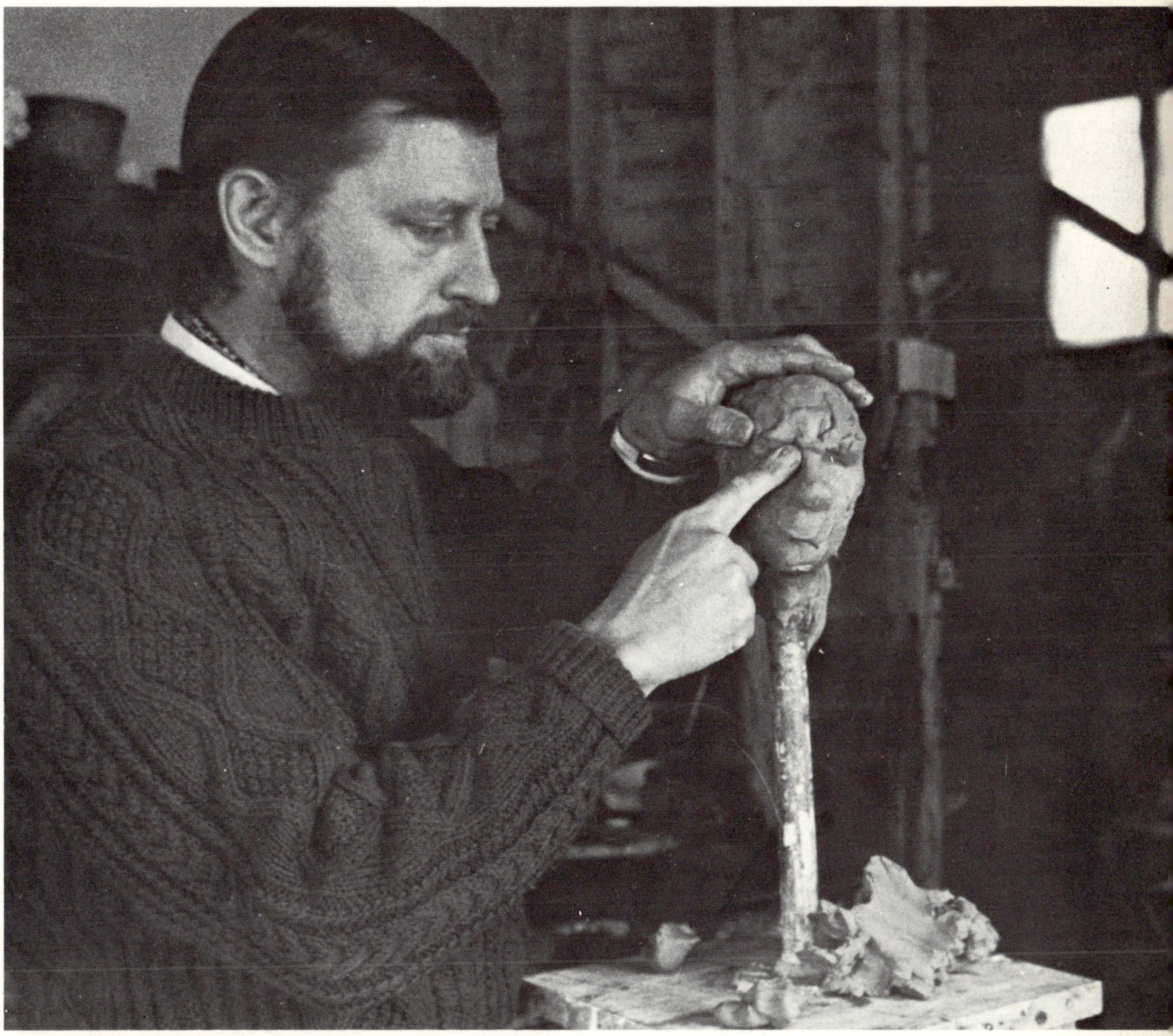

Profiles and silhouette are emphasised, the thrust of the neck livens the character

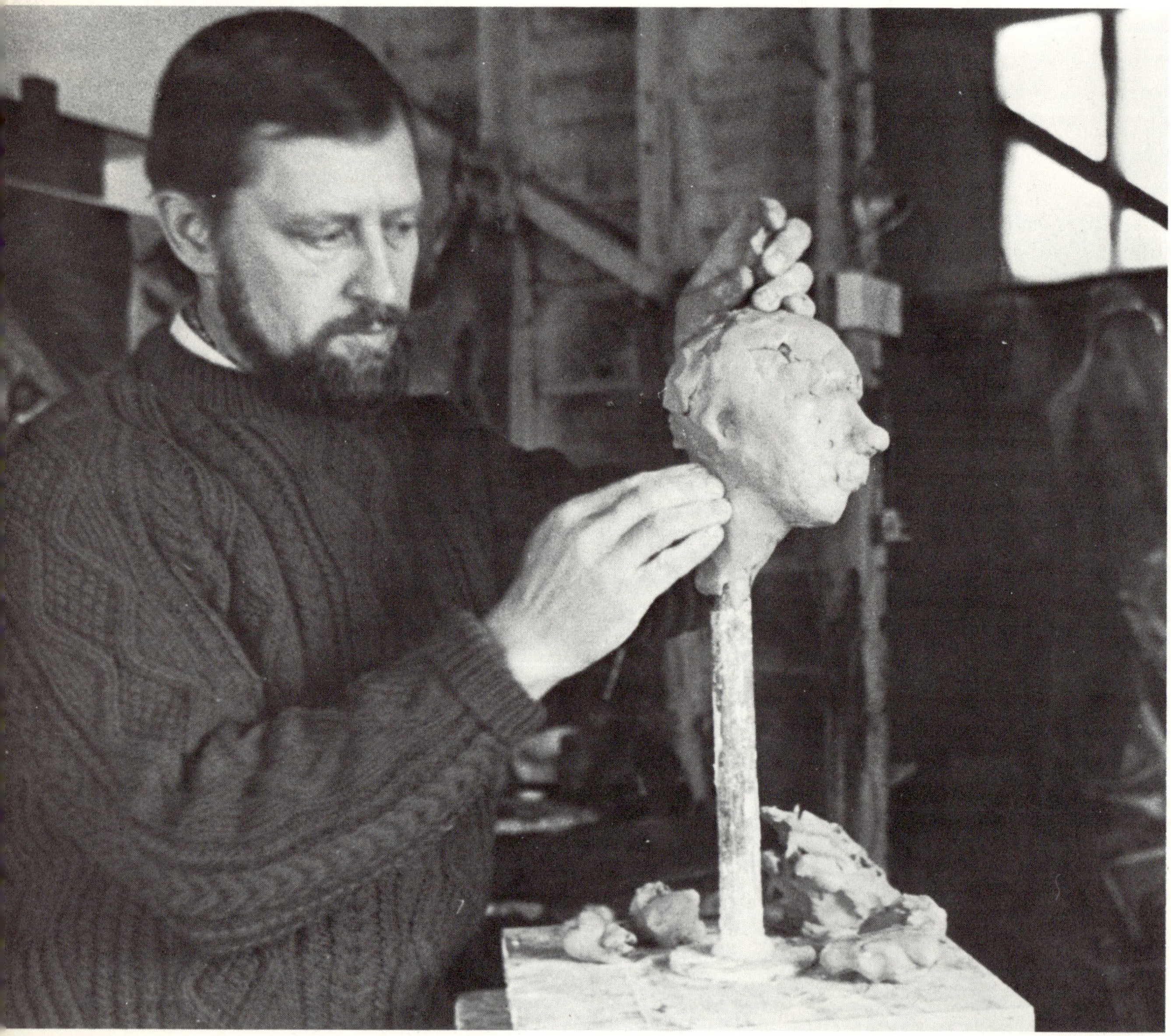

Clay being added boldly

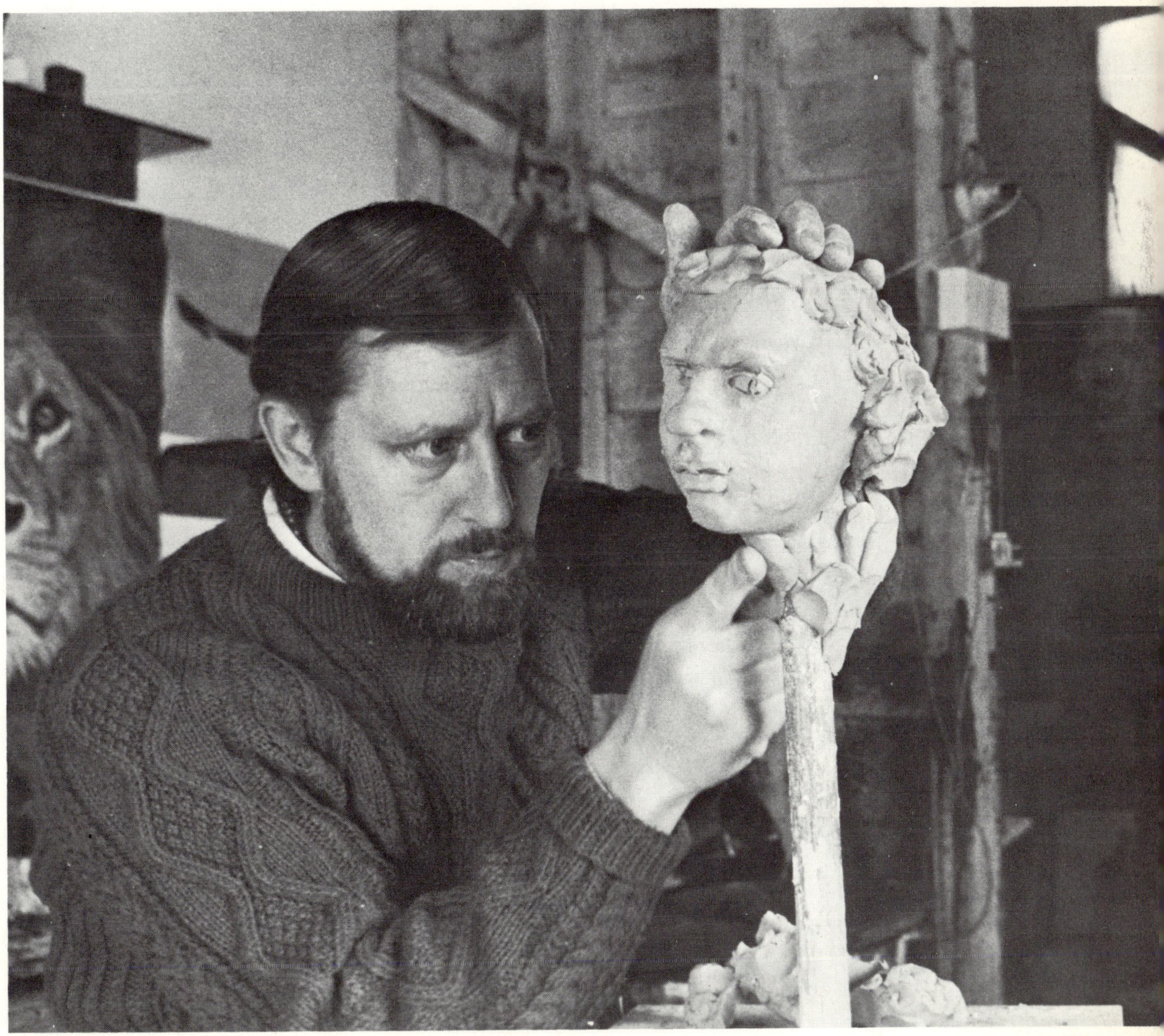

Modelling tool being used to draw form and features more clearly

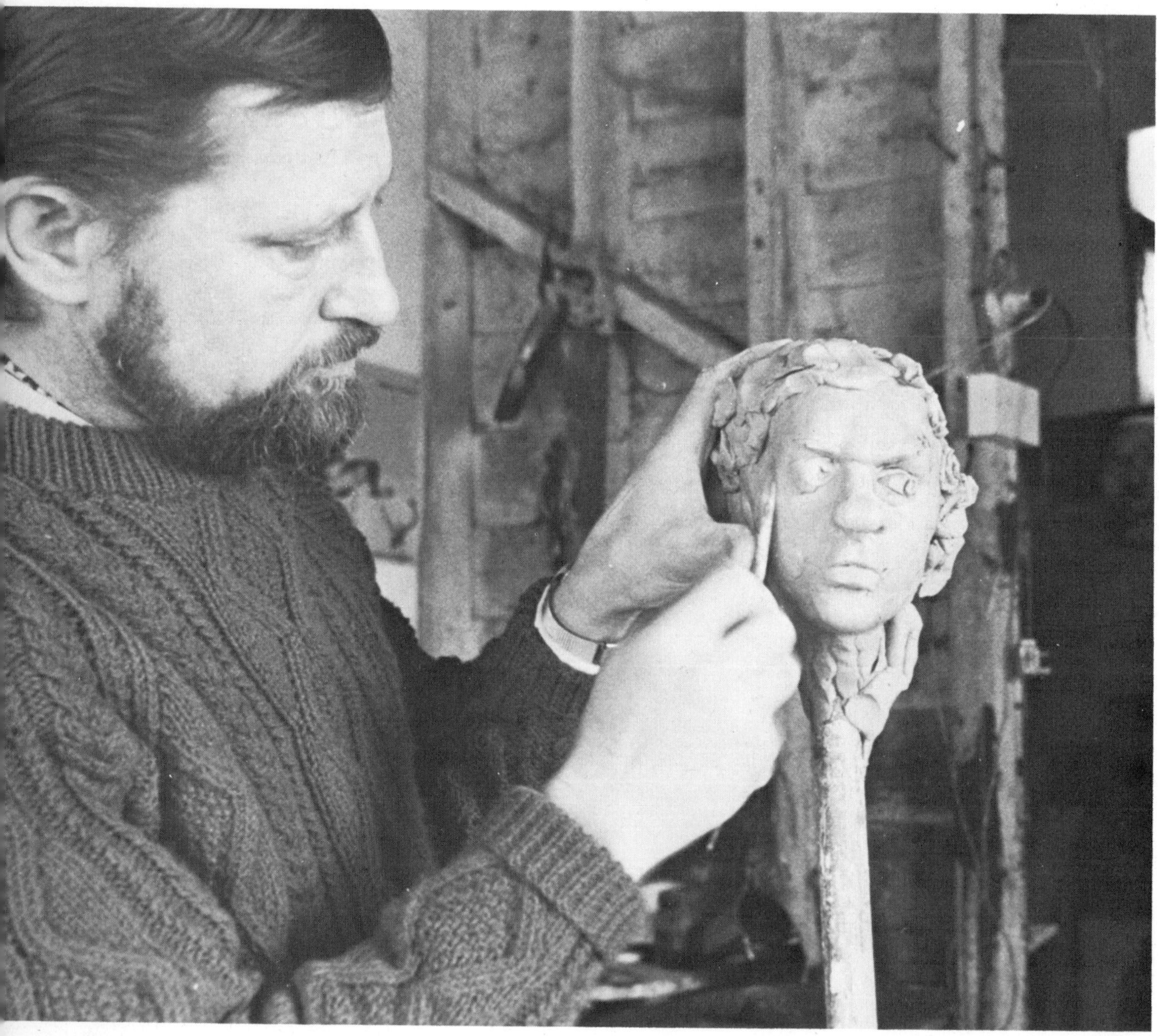

The final touches prior to moulding
photographs by John W Mills

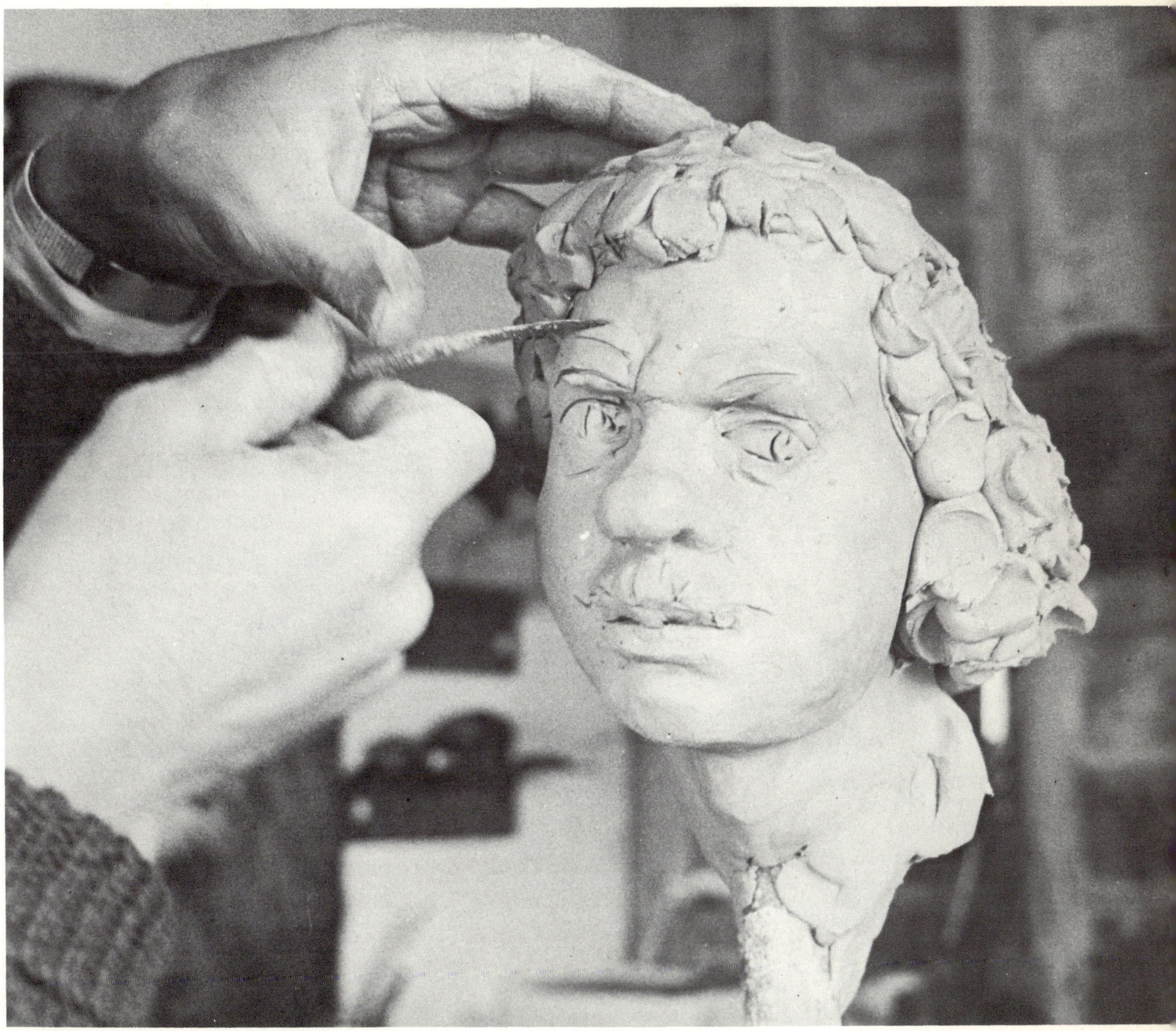

For relief modelling

An armature for relief modelling is best made by first attaching to a suitable flat board a frame as shown in the diagram. This is of a pre-determined depth and shape and is attached by means of screws put in from the top. This will allow the frame to be removed without damaging the clay modelling when preparing it for moulding. The frame is filled with clay and a straight edge drawn across to make a flat surface. If the area of clay is large it will need supporting, which can be given by hammering large headed galvanised nails into the board. Wire or string threaded about these nails will give additional support on very large areas, and by nailing wooden battens to the board as well, a greater build out of clay can be made, a random shaped relief can be made in the same way but without the restriction of the frame. Support to the clay will be necessary for reliefs of 195 sq cm (5 sq ft) or over.

Wax reliefs are unusual, normally being prepared from moulds to cast in metal via the lost wax process. Should experiment lead to the manufacture of large forms of wax in relief that demand extra support it will be found effective to use thin wooden laths dipped in wax and attached to the main body of the work by means of hot metal spatulas. Cotton scrim wax covered and added to cover the wooden reinforcing will give greater security. Small figures can be modelled around thin wooden or lead rods, if the ambient temperature proves to be too warm for the wax to remain firm and keep its shape. The lead and wood will burn out of the mould, if bronze castings are made from such reinforced wax figures. There may well be other methods and materials that will give support, indeed any of the armatures already described in this chapter can be used for wax modelling, but only those that burn and carbonise at 600°C or under can be used if the wax is modelled direct for the lost wax bronze casting process.

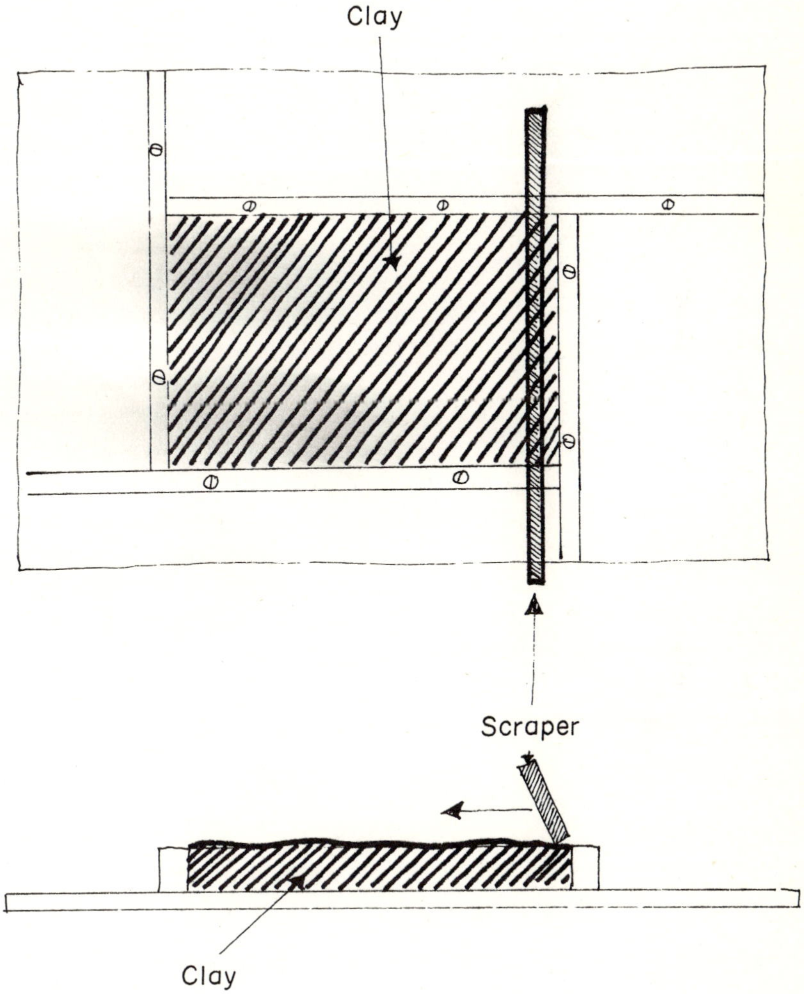

This diagram shows the frame used to make a flat clay surface on which to model a relief sculpture

For plaster of paris

Plaster of paris modelling requires slightly different armatures to those described above. The main difference being that no allowance need be made for removal when moulding. Armatures for plaster can therefore be welded, unless it is to be cut later to make patterns for sand casting. A rigid secure armature is of course required, as for any other material, but for plaster it must allow for chipping and cutting that will go on during the modelling/carving process. The consideration for weight is less, because the forms can be built hollow in the various ways already mentioned. The plaster is heaviest when wet. The plaster built over chicken wire, attached to the main support can be hollow, built up with jute scrim (burlap). Expanded polystyrene attached to the main support will enable bulky forms to be made quickly too. An external support is not helpful to modelling in plaster. Base boards can in some cases be dispensed with, because the armature can be set in plaster. A shuttering or mould can be constructed from clay or wood in which the armature is placed and propped up in the correct position, this mould is then filled with plaster and fibre reinforcing. See diagram. When this has set and the shuttering removed the armature will be held securely.

The mild steel used in plaster of paris needs to be painted to prevent rusting, which would show through at the surface. The iron can be painted with cold galvanising paint, with brunswick black or with a mixture of wax and rosin. These will effectively seal the iron and prevent oxidisation.

The armatures described for plaster of paris are suitable for papier mâché too. These require strength and need to be lightweight.

Sculptors develop a sixth sense that enables them to understand structure in relation to specific materials, being able to detect weak points in armatures, etc., an instinct that comes from familiarity with various materials, experiment and experience. Getting to know the relative characteristics, strengths, weights, and processes involved in working modelling media, develops confidence and freedom to shape any image.

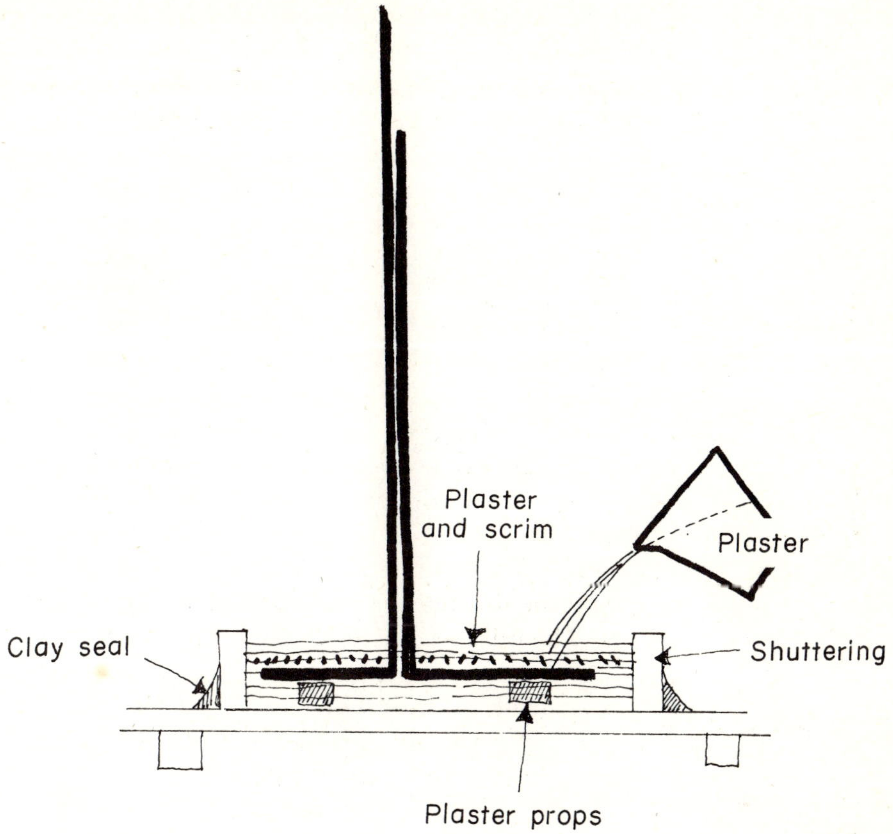

This illustrates the method for casting a plaster base for a fixed armature, used especially for direct plaster build-ups

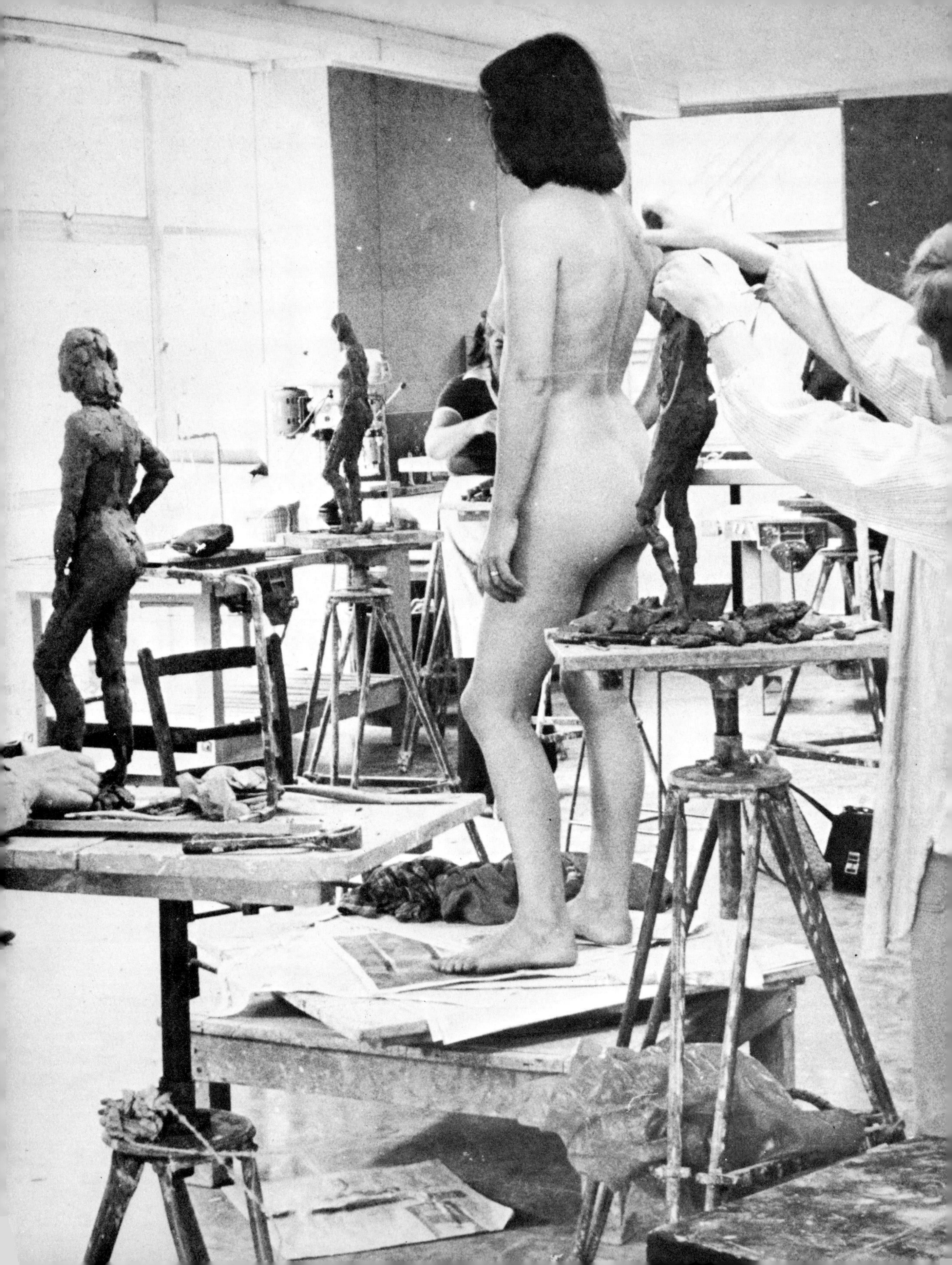

4 Modelling techniques

A sketch provides the sculptor with the opportunity to try an image in as many variations as observation, memory or imagination will allow. A three-dimensional note permits the artist the freedom to explore balance, implied movement, proportion, visual character and expression, factors that need to be understood to a certain degree before embarking on a large scale project.

The important factor of visual memory, that is the ability to recall an image observed so as to make a statement corresponding to it, can be tested and trained by making quick studies at a reasonable size. The visual memory cannot be over stressed in importance. After all, no matter how laboriously you look at each and every detail, the moment you turn from the subject to the sculpture being made, memory is being used. It is therefore good sense to train the memory so that it provides a reliable and constant source of information related to observation. An exercise that will prove useful in this respect, is to practise making small studies of characters encountered or observed on the way to the studio; seeking in these small sculptures to recall the visual impact of complete shape and not details. Not the least interesting point in favour of training, by means of such exercises, is that the memory provides the necessary filter to observed phenomena, that makes the remembered facts personal and unique to the individual but directly related to the subject. These facts assist the manufacture of personal imagery derived from common subjects, without the desperate search for originality so often detected in inferior work. Too close adherence to direct study in front of the model can often inhibit personal recall and obscure individual potential.

The quickly made sketch often contains a freshness of touch and spontaneity, which if understood and exploited can endow the enlarged sculpture with life and vitality. Detail is of little importance at this stage, and so forms are made that correspond to the size of the sculptors fingers, the nature of the modelling media and the dexterity with which it is used. Shapes that may be complex in origin can be summarised, so that a volume of the

Life modelling class
Hertfordshire College of Art and Design
photograph John W Mills

correct general character is created and made to relate to neighbouring forms, giving the sculpture its particular identity.

Sculptures viewed from a distance concern the spectator with silhouette, overall configuration, scale relationship of masses, and with balance. Such considerations if properly controlled create and sustain interest in the work. Successful sculptures contain these features maintaining the interest of the viewer as he approaches the work and walks around it, until by touch and close attention he can comprehend the scale and relationship of smaller forms and surface detail. Of course these factors are present in living forms, particularly in human beings, animals and birds. The three-dimensional note can be the means of establishing power and attraction, related to a particular study and image.

The exercise of making small studies of characters observed on the way to and from the studio, should give the kind of experience necessary to make good use of the life modelling situation, no matter where it is practised. It is just as useful to make quick three-dimensional notes from the life model, and many of them, before embarking on a large ambitious work. By making such quick notes in the round, bearing in mind the importance of the silhouette and the proper relation and balance of masses, the character of the model will be more easily understood. Repeated modelling of forms, adjusting stance and gesture, balance and poise, will prepare the eye for larger work. Large sculptures demand a large proportion of physical effort, and will entail the sculptor in up to 90% labouring activity. This effort needs to be controlled as much as possible to make it a productive effort. Time taken making repeated studies will assist in gaining this control.

From two to three dimensions

Making the awkward transition from drawing on a flat surface to drawing forms in the round, from two- to three-dimensional statements is a serious problem for the student. A method that I have found useful in aiding this transition and understanding the difference, involves both means of expression, one leading to the other. This method is as follows: make up a tablet of clay as for a relief sculpture. See chapter 4. Using a pencil or pointed tool, draw your subject, either from life or imagination, on the clay. Having made this essentially two-dimensional image, add clay between the lines drawn on the tablet in an effort to express the nature of the form between the lines. Consider the distance in depth between forms, ie the distance in depth of an arm and torso, across the torso to the other arm, etc. Try to build the image as high in relief as possible. The difficulties encountered will be similar to those that occur when modelling in the round, but without the complication of the armature. The difficulties of understanding a limb are simplified when seen in foreshortening and in juxtaposition to its partner. This lesson when accomplished will provide a springboard into three-dimensional expression; it will also be an aid to painting, and can be extended to any pictorial image. This technique is in part embodied in the development of perspective during the Italian Renaissance. The exercise of transition can of course be used to make notes, and can be developed to make elaborate and complete relief sculpture, which to most sculptors is considered the consummate test of drawing ability.

The problem of becoming accustomed to expressing ideas in the round is the all important one to resolve. The greater part of our learning practices are done two-dimensionally, by reading and writing. Scholastic three-dimensional activity is usually limited to games or physical training, geared to engender health and relaxation, but seldom taught as a means of self-expression and awareness. The awareness of a personal physical presence and its interaction with others, cannot be emphasised too much. Physical empathy, projected to understand fully a particular contemplated image, is a faculty that develops in harness with self-awareness. Such empathy makes it possible to understand a pose or a gesture, as it is mirrored in ones own being, during the drawing, two- or three-dimensionally.

Drawing, which is deemed to be the basic of all visual expression, in sculpture means a fully explained volume. So that drawing in the round demands expression fully articulated, of all parts totally resolved. The spectator must be presented with visual explanations, derived from the observed phenomenom, filtered by the artist and expressed so that what is on view is what was intended to be seen. Drawing therefore can mean the resolution of intention.

Study of work by the masters

The study of work by the masters of fine art, leads one to the conclusion that often they were men who developed few ideas. Few themes are followed, and what seems to be endless repetition occurs in their work. The exception that proves the rule is da Vinci, who although concerned with invention and innovation in engineering on a wide scale produced few paintings and sculptures, and all within a relatively narrow subject range. The reason can be seen to be the preoccupation with clearer statements, and the exploitation of alternative images, plus the exploration of minor differences. This latter point being the most interesting.

Head of a Woman Bronze
Pablo Picasso
Chicago Institute of Fine Art
photograph John W Mills

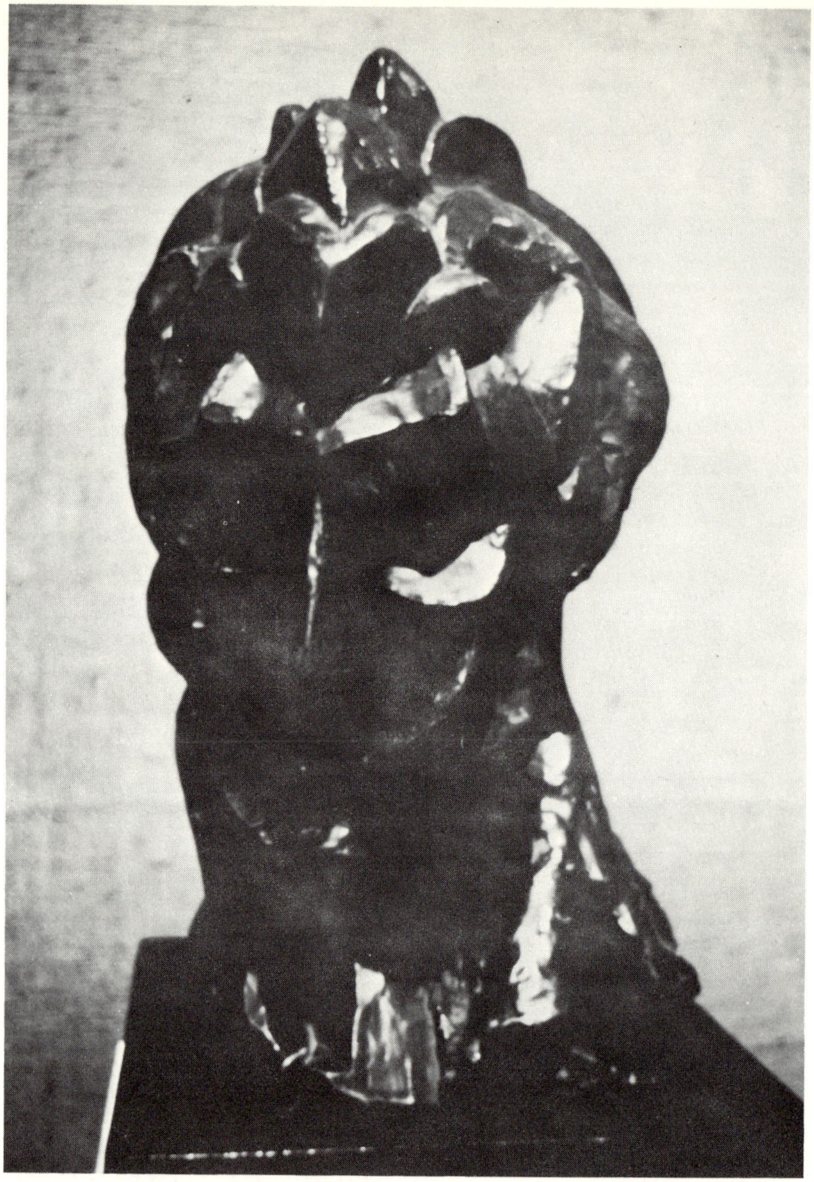

A subject that impresses itself upon the artist's sensibilities cannot be easily resolved in a single work. As work progresses on a subject, an alternative solution comes to mind, a different gesture, a different arrangement of forms, a different detail. Each alternative represents another possible sculpture. Corrections to an image or adjustments in relation to a specific goal. Some of the corrections or adjustments justify another sculpture. This puts the sculptor in the position of being able to select the best resolution of the image, being able to compare his various alternatives. If he decides to keep only one he is more confident that it is the best selection from his point of view. A decision he could not easily make if he had simply made corrections on the one sculpture, and produced finally a compromised image. The subject is only finished with when there no longer is an alternative image demanding to be made. This may mean indeed that another subject has usurped the old, but it also can mean that the old subject has been exhausted. The mistake that most beginners make is to look for a new subject everytime they come to the studio to work. Creative energy and imagination are reciprocally linked to physical effort, factors that make the daily search for new subjects a hopeless and unrewarding task. If demands upon creative energy and imagination are too great, the result is often total exhaustion and loss of confidence . The practice of making numerous sketches in the round, taken individually to various degrees of finish, detail, etc, is an admirable way of exploring a subject in its breadth and in its variety.

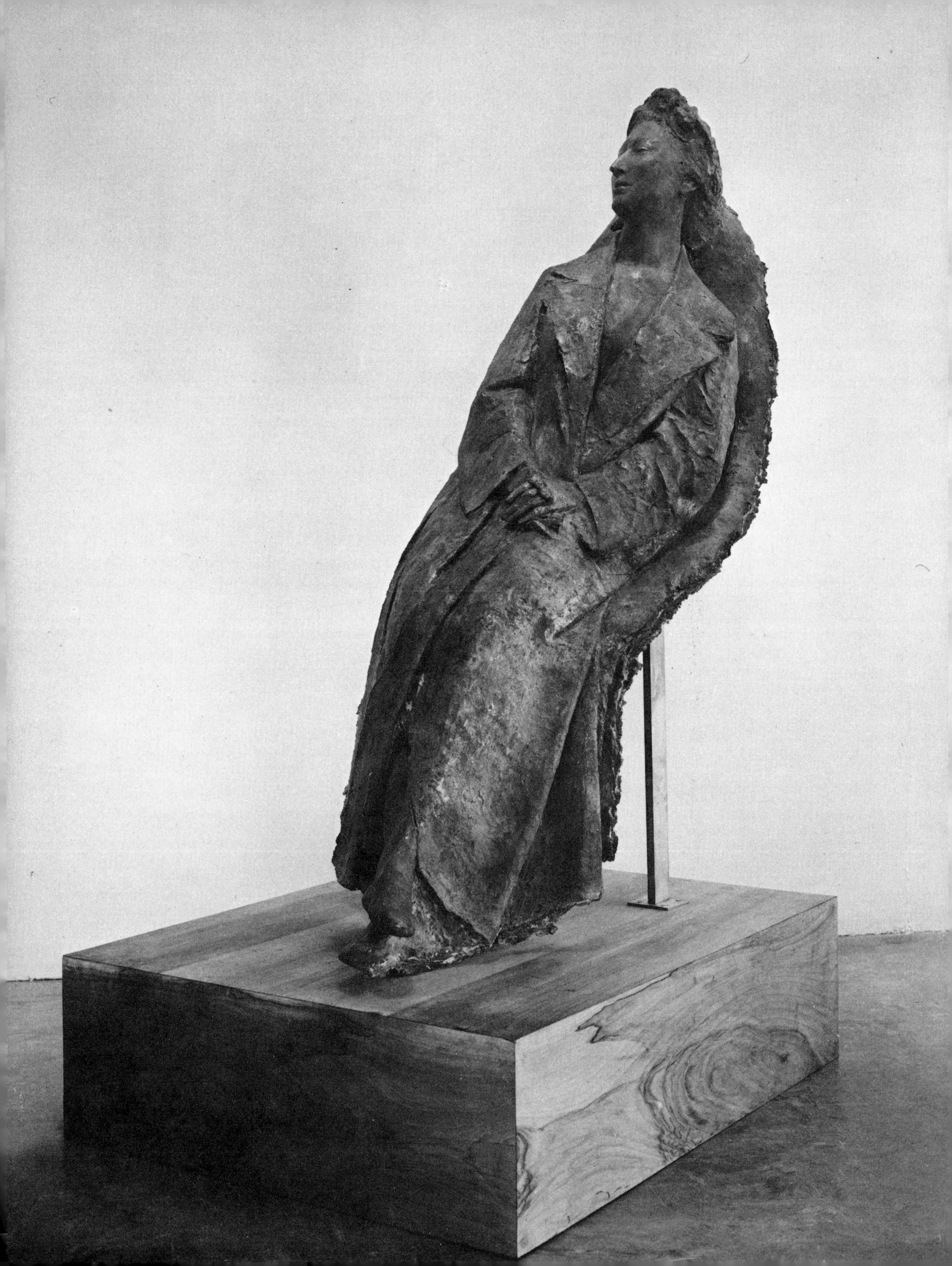

5 Life modelling: tradition and onwards

The basic traditional equipment in a life modelling studio is as follows: A revolving posing throne, modelling stands in a range of sizes; table top, lightweight sketch stands, and heavy duty studio stands: bankers with revolving tops and wheels. Tools include a range of calipers and portable water sprays, and as much space as you can make for yourself.

The traditional life modelling studio took a particular pattern, which is still favoured. The model poses on the posing throne, that makes it possible to turn the subject at will. The throne is usually in the centre of a large, well lit (top lighting), studio. Top light is important to clear definition of detail on the model. The students modelling stands are placed around the throne, as close as numbers will allow. To attempt to model at long distance from the model is of very little value, the change in visual scale complicates the issue too much. Keeping the model warm and comfortable is of prime importance as he or she will pose more willingly under these conditions. In art schools this usually means portable electric fires; in special cases banked stands of fires so that no part of the model need be cold.

The peripheries of the studio become the store of studies in progress, and usually sturdy shelves and benches house these works. In the past, elaborate waterproof containers or cages were constructed around the clay figures and heads to keep them moist and in a workable condition. Today plastic sheeting swathes the clay, once it has been covered with damp cloths. This double covering keeps the work in better condition, providing the job is well wrapped and the covering well pegged, to exclude air. Some art schools make elaborate damp cupboards, these are specially constructed with zinc trays at the bottom and cement rendered walls and shelves. The tray once filled with water and the walls sprayed and soaked will maintain a humid atmosphere in which to store clay work in progress. Such cupboards however are more useful for ceramics than for sculpture, where they are sometimes now equipped with electric humidifiers. Sculpture being of

Portrait of a Lady 1946 Bronze (cast 1955)
Giacomo Manzù
Collection, The Museum of Modern Art New York. A Conger, Goodyear Fund
See page 28

uncertain dimensions makes the planning of a damp cupboard very difficult, in the past this was made easier by the standardisation of examination life studies, in Great Britain particularly.

The private studio is of course a modification of this art school pattern whenever possible, but more usually it is a compromise between an ideal studio and what is available. Few sculptors can afford at the outset of their career, a custom-built studio, to accommodate comfortably naked models. Those sculptors primarily concerned with modelling from life eventually establish studios that reflect their particular methods of working and the nature of their work, the photographs on page 00 illustrate these two extremes.

Techniques

Modelling techniques associated with traditional life modelling studios are not so varied, and are useful to practise to become as accomplished and skilful as possible. I must emphasise however that no technique, no matter how elaborate, can be more than a means. I have already stressed the point that the subject studied must be understood before it can be reasonably interpreted. The visual and physical nature of the model must become as familiar as possible so that the forms modelled reflect the forms studied.

The first consideration is the pose. In a class of students this task of posing the model or models is usually performed for them by the tutor. If the subject is to be over a long period (we used to work on the one pose for anything up to 12 or 14 weeks) the model's comfort must be catered for. Standing poses are strenuous, and if required, periods of rest should be worked out and agreed with the model, to ensure the posers strength and interest are maintained. A normal timetable could be; the first hour without rest, then five minutes rest, with ten minutes rest in every hour after that, increasing the rest perod during the afternoon to fifteen minutes, over a working day of seven hours. This would be an average life class in an English art school. Private modelling is often worked in a similar manner, but of course is affected by who you can get to strip and for how long. Non-professional subjects are most rewarding to work from, and personal arrangements will affect rest periods. No more can be said really except that it seldom pays to bully a model. The problems are slightly relieved when the model is posing clothed.

The vexed question of stillness, allowing the model to move, is again a personal and varying factor. There are some schools of thought that believe the model must remain still at all times whilst posing. The slightest movement being enough to disturb concentration and thereby the study being made. Other schools of thought do not require the model to be still or take up a pose of any kind, because that would make the whole thing false. The answer, like so many, lies somewhere between these two extremes. Again reference must be made to the practices of Auguste Rodin, whose licentious reputation was in part due to the jealously regarded feature of his studio, that of numbers of naked models moving freely about, to be scrutinised and used by the sculptor. He did demand poses from them, but only after he had been attracted by a particular attitude or movement. Rodin's training included teaching by a master called Lecoq de Boisbauran, who included in his instruction drawing from the moving model, indoors and out, as well as from the antique and studio posed model. So in fact the two extremes mentioned above were embodied in Boisbauran's teaching and in the subsequent sculptures of Rodin.

It doesn't make sense to make the model keep still for extended periods, this is singularly unnatural, nor does it make sense to try to work from a model who is moving all the time uninhibitedly. This may be more natural but cannot aid study in depth. A useful practice that applies to both the figure and the head, clothed or unclothed, is to arrive at a pose that relates to the subject or the character of the sitter; a pose that can easily be remembered by the model and the artist. Once in the pose the model must be encouraged to relax, even if it is a strenuous and active position. A portrait sitter for instance relaxes better when talking or listening to music. The duration of the pose on a one to one basis, sculptor and sitter, can be arrived at by mutual agreement. 'If it hurts too much take a rest' is a maxim I use often. As a student I suffered the services of professional models, who although reliable, in general have a tendency to turn even the most extreme pose into a quasi classical standing position; weight on one leg, hand on hip, etc. This tendency encouraged a uniformity of pose and sculpture that became immediately identifiable as Art School, and in those in the UK this related to a specific examination. In the heyday of the life class, professional models turned up to work, with a variety of pose and costume which did endow the life studio activity with a certain excitement, albeit unrelated to life outside the art school environment.

The previous chapter on sketch models and the training of the visual memory applies to modelling in the life studio, as to any other, as I have already mentioned, because once the sculptor turns away from the model he is using his memory. Unlike the painter for instance, who can station himself and his work at fixed points in relation to the subject, so that by moving the eyes quickly between the two, they appear almost as one.This is a technique that enables the painter to make a reasonable comparison between the model and his work, but it is not very useful to the sculptor. The nearest a sculptor, working from life, gets to this is by positioning his work close enough to the model to be able to compare profiles and contours. The diagram illustrates the movement of the posing throne, designed to reveal profiles as the throne is turned, when modelling from the living model. This is based on the fact that forms have a central axis, this fact at first appears to be simple, but for instance, a gesture observed from the front, can only be comprehended fully by observing it again at an angle of 90° to the side. In this way the full projection of a limb or feature can be understood. By relating this principle in breadth and detail, to every varying profile, the complex human organic form may be better understood and modelled. The fact must be stressed, that the sculptor needs to work on his sculpture as close to the subject as possible, to permit close comparison of profiles etc. The further the distance from the model the more he works from memory, and the more the sculpture is likely to be a fantasy, drawing on imagination. The Picasso *Head of a Woman* is an example of multiple profiles retained in their basic form.

Page 100

The chapter on armatures likens the structural support to skeletal support, and this is a study that must now be given greater attention. When building up a figure or a portrait head, it is essential to recognise and use those parts of the skeletal structure evident on the surface of the flesh. Cheek bones, forehead, elbows, knees, ribcage, pelvis, shins, etc., often are features easily detectable no matter what the pose. Such features do not change in the way that flesh changes. A joint may articulate and move, but when it is flexed the same set of knobs press against the flesh. Because such characteristics are constant they become useful points of reference. So that the structure can be established based on these reference points, or as many as are discernible. The armature therefore is developed by adding clay, or some other modelling material, to realise the skeletal structure further, to provide a sound basis for modelling expressive features.

The mistake that most students make, when embarking on a study from life is the preoccupation with physical detail. The eyes, the mouth, cheeks, thighs, breasts, stomach, etc, are all features capable of movement around or contained by the structure. Anything that changes, according to its weight and to gravity, can only be used properly if the structure is right. Articulated parts move and affect surrounding area according to the articulation, stressing, flexing or relaxing attitudes. Too close attention to detail results in the lips or nose being drawn when the head is not

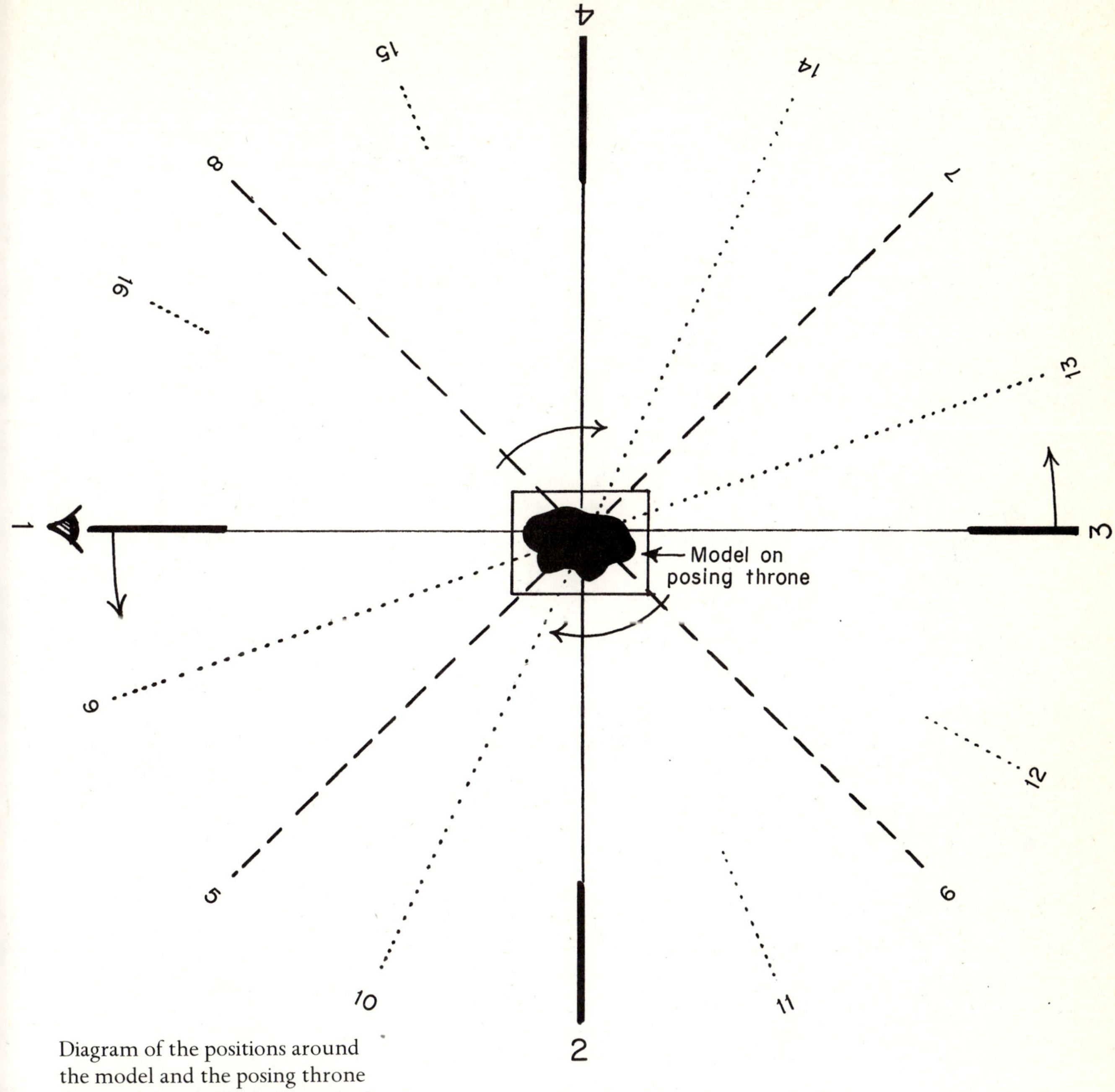

Diagram of the positions around the model and the posing throne that permits profiles to be studied and related. Read the diagram from number 1 onwards. The angle of view must be complimented on the opposite side of the model and by the two views at right angles left and right of the original view point

Overleaf
Life modelling studio
Hertfordshire College of Art and Design
photograph John W Mills

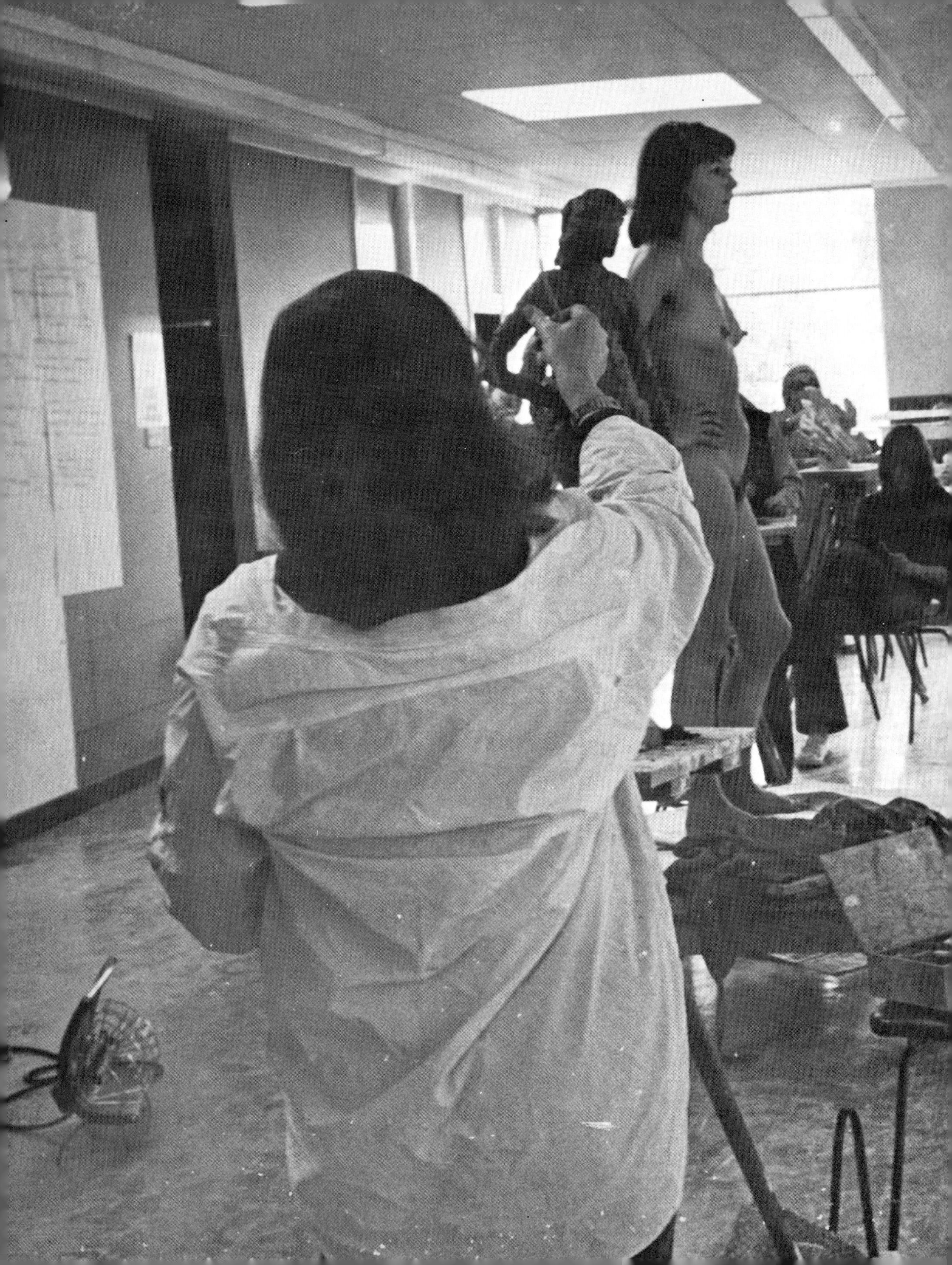

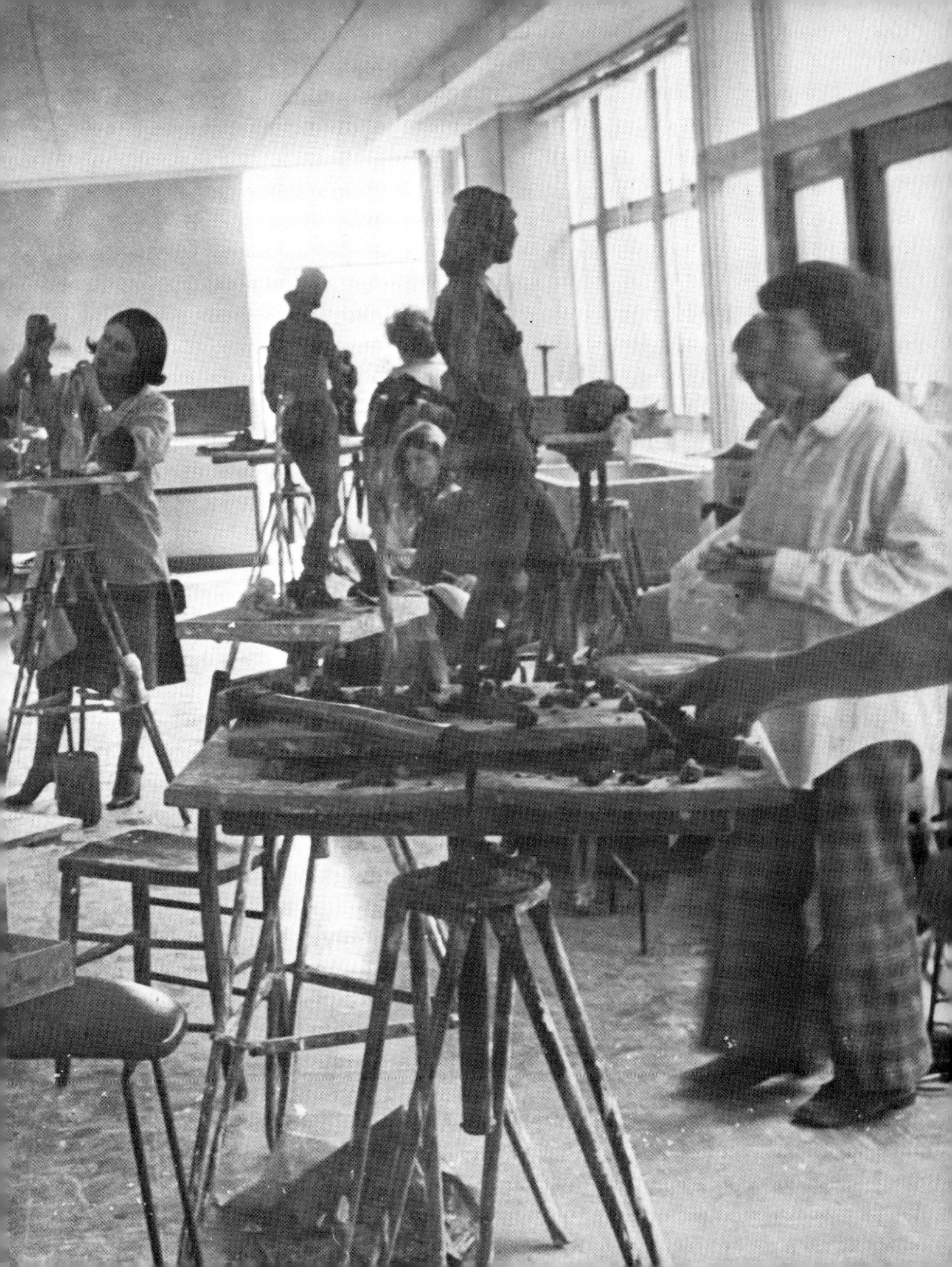

established in character, structure or disposition, and causes parts, usually breasts and buttocks, to be modelled out of proportion, and unrelated to the whole. These are indications usually of the students' keenness to get on with and into the problem of the portrait, but of course the objective is too often defeated by the lack of structure. Further energy expended will be wasted until the balance of structure, gesture and character is stated broadly, in advance of detail. It is an interesting phenomenon too, that when working from the unclothed model, it is usual for the hands, feet and face to be missed, or at least summarily stated. This is the reverse to everyday contact between people. The head and hands are the features of communication in common intercourse. Studio life study seems to reverse this fact so that anatomical features, not usually seen, are drawn, modelled or painted in detail. Perhaps it is a symptom of a general inhibition that can be released in the life studio, and in this sense it may be a useful therapy.

The clay, wax or other modelling material is built up bearing in mind all the relevant factors, so that the image grows. The volume of the form is always kept a little less than the original to allow for this growth. The rate at which this image develops varies from sculptor to sculptor of course, and to the size of the endeavour. If an error is made when at a fairly advanced stage in the modelling, the remedy is not necessarily to strike out a detail that has claimed great attention or maybe merely wrongly placed. This feature can be cut off with a fine wire and replaced in the correct position. In this way effort is conserved and the freshness of direct modelling retained. This method of correction is like using an eraser, it is wise always to preserve the marks to be corrected for as long as possible, to be certain that the correction is accurate. It is probable that the same mistake will be made again if the fault is erased before the correction is made.

A student will often ask 'how can I model an eye . . . an ear, or foot or head? Questions to which I give answers based on simple fact; formal fact rather than specific anatomical fact. For instance, an eye is a movable ball in a socket, the socket is the solid stucture and the two must be studied then modelled to convey this fact. Eyelids fit over the ball and are therefore movable; model the facts as in this simple diagrammatic manner. An ear is a hole in the head, with shell like spirals that catch the sound, model it to explain this. A nose is softish protruberance, with two shell like openings, model it as such. Lips cover the teeth and no matter how well the characteristics of particular lips are drawn, if the teeth are not stated the lips will be wrong. Toes are appendages on the ends of the feet that help maintain balance, model them to give this impression, fingers too should be tackled in a practical and diagrammatic way.

When modelling such facts it should be remembered that the scale of mark must be correct also. This applies as much to drawing and painting as to sculpture. A line occurs in the figure where two forms come together or overlap, ie fingers, toes, lips, etc. It is tempting to make a bold statement of these lines, but if this is done the scale of the mark will be larger than life size. These natural lines are in reality very fine and complex, and almost indistinguishable. Half close your eyes to see how clearly or not, they can be seen in the overall picture; you will be surprised. The same principle applies to all features, they must be modelled in the correct relative scale. By paying attention to the correct scale relationship, an exaggerated feature can be made to have greater impact and therefore more meaning in the total concept.

The size at which a figure is made, is often referred to by its relation to life size; half life size, a quarter life size, a third life size, etc. To be able to work out these proportions students were encouraged to know the simple geometry that could be employed to determine the enlargement or reduction of any measurement taken from the model. The life modelling studio usually carried the scars of graffitti geometry drawn on the walls by students to help each other. The diagrams clearly illustrate these geometric aids, giving examples for reducing to a quarter, a half, and two-thirds the scale most commonly used in the life class. It is important to remember, that the measurement taken from the model must be a sensible one. Calipers are used of course to make accurate measures, and if the model agrees, marks drawn on the skin will help determine specific points of reference. Like map reading, without these specific references the artist can easily get lost.

General proportions are useful guides, providing a datum against which discoveries can be assessed. For instance, the length of the index finger above the thumb in most people equals the distance from the chin to the nose, the nose to the brow and from the brow to the top of the forehead. The length of the arms outstretched is equal to the height, head to foot. Arms including the hands reach to the middle of the thigh. In a well proportioned man, the upper arm, the calf and neck are of an equal thickness. In a well-built person the measurement from head to crutch, is equal to that of the crutch to feet. The ear is usually situated at a height level with midway between nose and brow. The corners of the mouth in repose, are usually level with the centre of the eyes. The length of the foot is equal to that of the hand, which is equal to the length of the face. The distance from ear to ear equals the

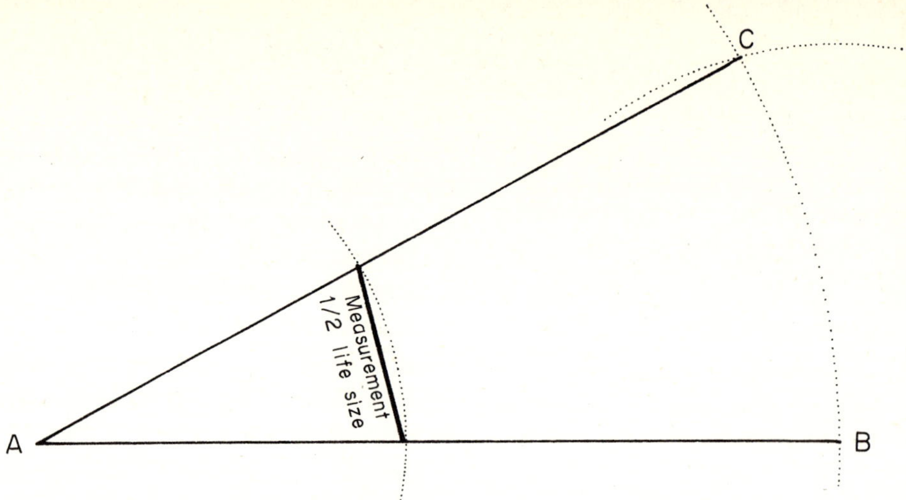

Height of model

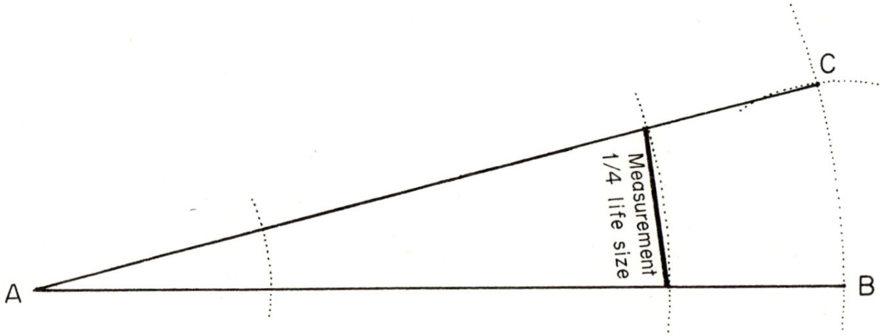

Height of model

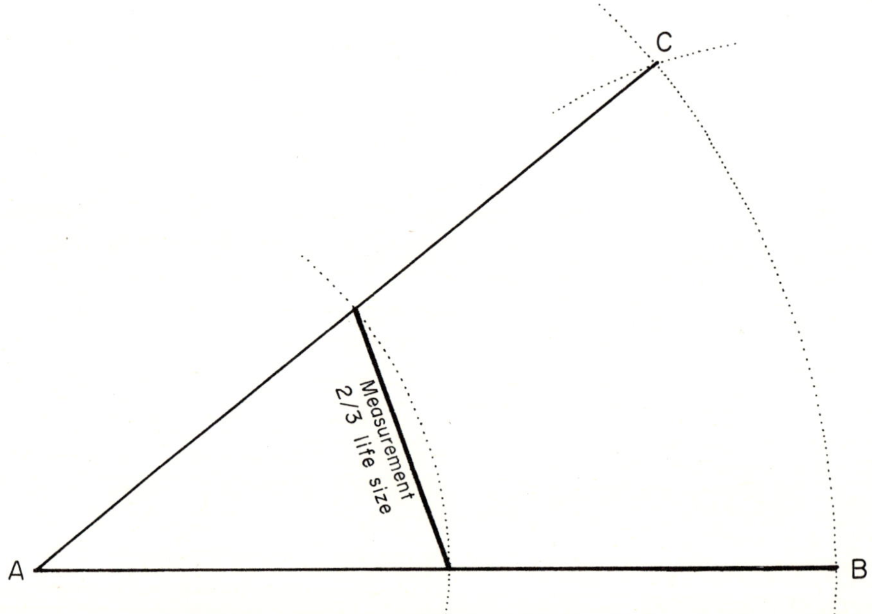

Height of model

Geometric scales used to reduce measurements taken from the model, using calipers. The line *AB* represents the height of the model. *BC* is the proportion of the height to which all future measurements must conform. Connect *AC*. Any measurement taken from the model marked along *AB* and an arc drawn to intersect *AC* will give two points whose measurements will be that required. The three examples are one quarter, a half, and two-thirds life size
See page 111

length of the face also; and so on and so on. Of course these apparent rules can only be offered as guides, and no matter how you draw imaginary grids and construct fantasy scaffolds about the figure, they will not prove to be substitutes for feeling and understanding the visual and physical impact of the unique human being.

Normal humans are endowed with the same physical equipment; each person looks after their sets of parts very well and an accident is by definition something that happens outside the norm. What is breathtaking is that given the uniformity of function and assembly of parts, each assemblage is uniquely different. According to race, global environment, etc., the variety manifest in the human form is almost limitless. The differences one from another are factors that demand study and make the enterprise of figurative sculpture so stimulating. These differences, coupled to their use interpreted by the artists filter, certainly do give an unlimited source of study, which is truly life study.

Anatomy

I was once teaching anatomy and life drawing to a group of diploma students, when the class was visited by one of her Majesty's Inspectors of Art. He demanded to know from one of the students the number of ribs in a rib cage. He was told by the student that as far as she was concerned this was not important information. The visual artist is primarily concerned with the appearance of the torso, and the living model doesn't make it possible to count or comprehend the number of ribs. I think the student was quite right, and the attitude of the Inspector in asking the question indicates the depth of academic mediocrity prevailing at that time. This kind of information is superfluous to an artist's need, and should it be necessary to state the precise number of ribs, there are many reference books that can be referred to for the answer. It is an examinable fact perhaps, but in no way affects the appearance. The HMI was of course indignant, but I could only invite him to view the work being done and the model, and ask him to demonstrate his point as something other than academic.

The point I am drawing to your attention by telling this tale is that the artist needs to know anatomy with quite a different connotation to the knowledge required by medical men. I mentioned in Chapter 1 the work of dissection and anatomical study carried out by such men as da Vinci, Michelangelo, and George Stubbs, but in each case it was to a specific end; mostly to do with an insatiable curiosity. It is unlikely that the figures made after the experience were better than those made before. The artists were men of broader experience after their anatomical studies, but not necessarily better artists. Their example however became an academic discipline, and artists sat in on medical anatomy lectures and on post-mortems, but mostly to little value.

The question that will certainly be in the reader's mind is 'What anatomy do I study then?' So here are some more aids, general in character but useful as points of departure for study.

THE SKELETON

Become as familiar with the appearance of the skeleton as possible. This breaks down into simple forms, the most essential of which is an articulated column of support, the spine. This column is in turn supported above the legs by way of the pelvis, a dish shaped form with bearings at each side to take the leg joints, and a rigid fixing to the spine at the rear. The rib-cage is an admirable description of a flexible basket attached to the upper part of the spine at the back. From the top of the rib-cage a yoke of bones hang which include the arms. The skull surmounts the spine, and is a strong spherical object. Hands and feet are a collection of small bones, constructed in such a way as to give strength and flexibility, like wattle, see diagram on page 124.

The articulation of the skeleton is important of course, so it is essential to appreciate the movement of the spine given by its particular assembly. It can bend forward in a U shape. It can bend sideways to almost a right angle. It cannot normally bend backwards with great freedom without specific exercise. The column has four natural curves, a shape that has evolved to give maximum support and movement. The curves are, in effect, shock absorbers to those items supported along its length. The top curves support the skull and allows it to articulate so that you can nod and shake your head. The next curve holds the rib cage, and the next curve is possibly the main shock absorber. It supports the pelvis and the greater weight. The diagrams on page 118 illustrates the spine in its simplest connotation.

THE PELVIS AND LEGS

The pelvis in its role as articulator is the structure that enables man to stand upright, and its particular form has evolved to this end. It has no movement itself but its rigidity transmits the weight of the torso to the legs and feet, and supports the articulating universal joints of the hips. These joints are particularly deep ball and socket forms designed to withstand forces and shocks of up to two tonnes. The knee and the ankle are subsidiary shock absorbers. The knee is the largest joint in the body, and its job is to provide the best possible support for the weight of the trunk, at the break of the column of the leg. The knee articulates as a simple ball and plate hinge, to alleviate undue tensile stress and increase the mobility of the limb. The ankle is the joint that releases further tensile stress, and by permitting flexing backward and forward contributes to the control, balance and mobility of the figure as a whole. The foot I have described as being like wattle, interwoven small forms. This collection of small bones interlock and arch, whilst at the same time fan out to provide flexible variable support. The big toes bear about a quarter of the load of the body, the heel bears one half the load, the rest being shared by the rest of the toes. By appreciating this principle of load bearing and flexibility, the sculptor can make more sense of the foot as an essential form. The lower leg, below the knee, is made up of two bones that serve to give rotational movement to the leg, in addition to the universal movement afforded by the hip ball and socket joints. These rotating bones form the ankle at the lower ends and are vital to the action and form of the foot.

THE RIB-CAGE AND ARMS

The rib-cage in its skeletal characteristic, is as I have mentioned, like a basket; it carries and protects packages vital to the well being of the body. It is slung in front of the spinal column, attached to it at the back. The shape of this basket accommodates the movement of the shoulders and arms in a compact form. The shoulder girdle is attached to the front of the rib-cage, curves over and around it to the shoulder blades. The front fixing acts like a pivot giving a wide range of swinging movements. The arms fit into a very shallow socket in the shoulder blade, which allows greater mobility than the deep ball and socket bearing of the hips. The swinging, universal turning action of the shoulder and upper arm must be understood and stated clearly to give credence to a figure. The elbow is a more straightforward hinge than the knee; it works like the fingers in giving movement backwards and forwards only. The knee allows some movement from side to side and a degree of rotation. The wrists are complex double hinges, giving upward and downward mobility as well as mobility from side to side. Like the lower leg, the lower arm comprises two bones, that also permit rotational movement whilst retaining great tensile strength. All the hinges of the body have the same kind of vulnerability as door hinges, and can be strained to a point at which they cannot function. This factor too should be borne in mind when modelling these joints especially in extreme action or formalisation.

This brief description of the skeleton and joints, illustrated on page 120, is really all the artist needs to consider in general prin-

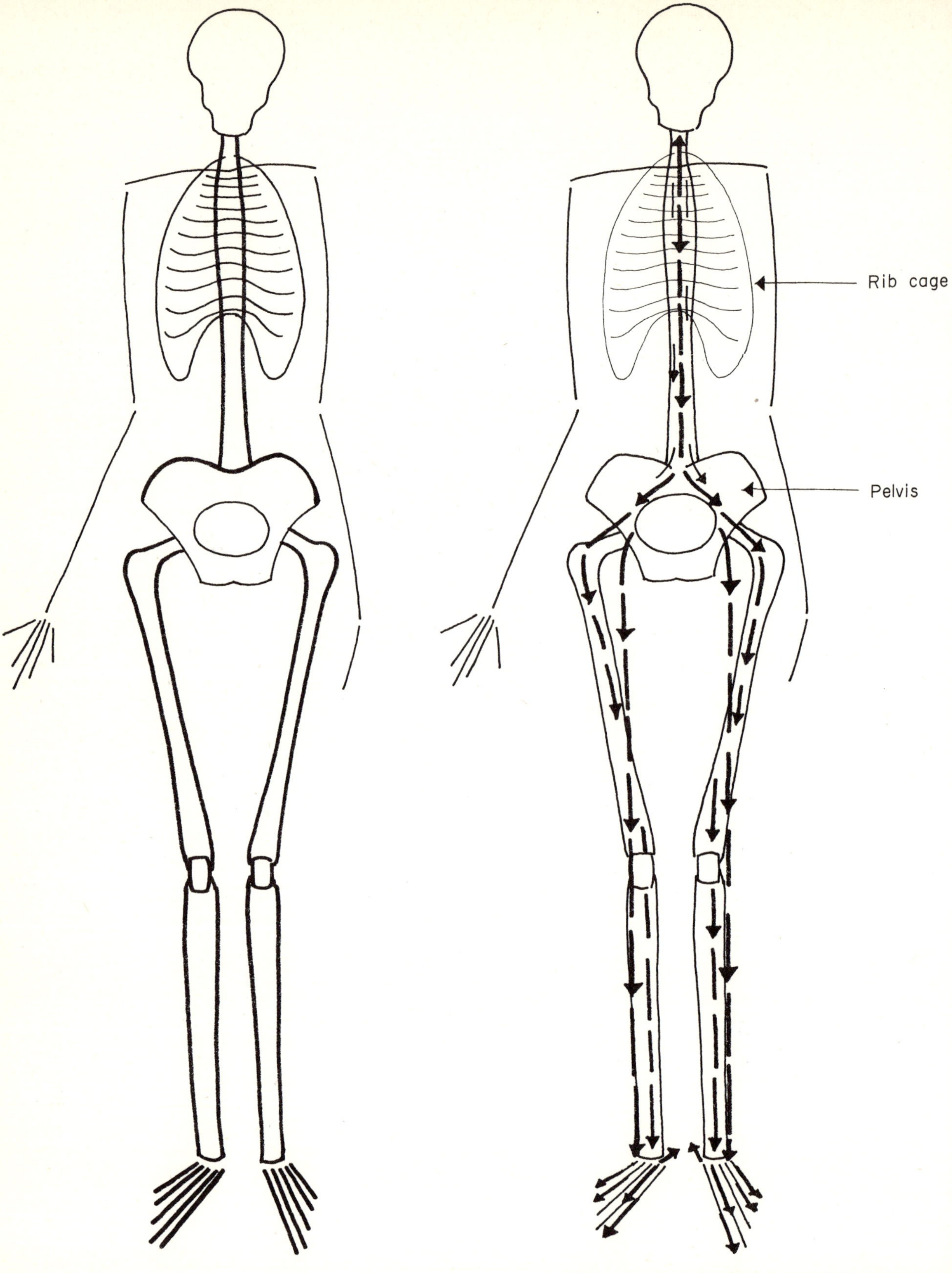

A B

These diagrams describe the simple explanation of the skeleton, useful to remember when constructing a figure, at all stages from the armature onwards. *A* and *C* illustrate the three major columns and their connections. *B* and *D* gives some idea of the directions of support and stress

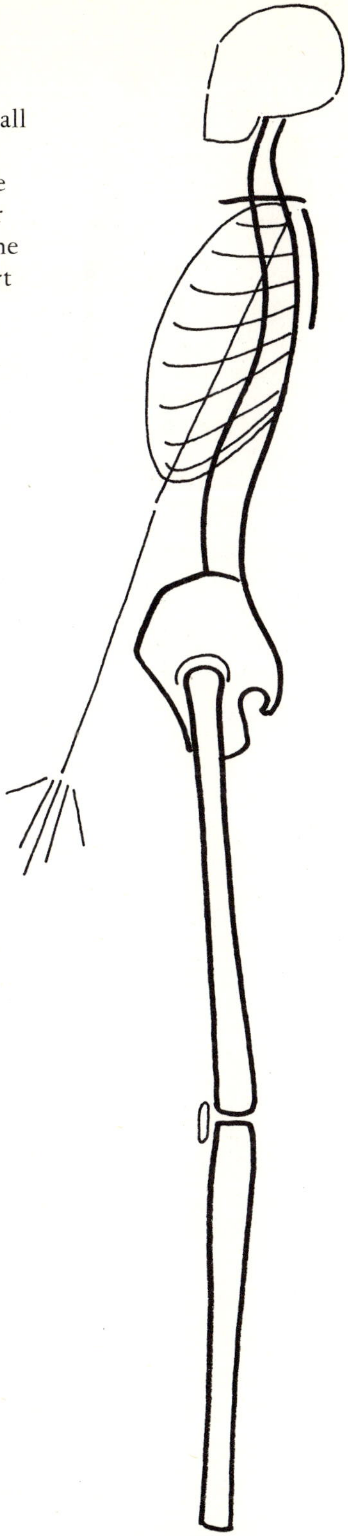

C

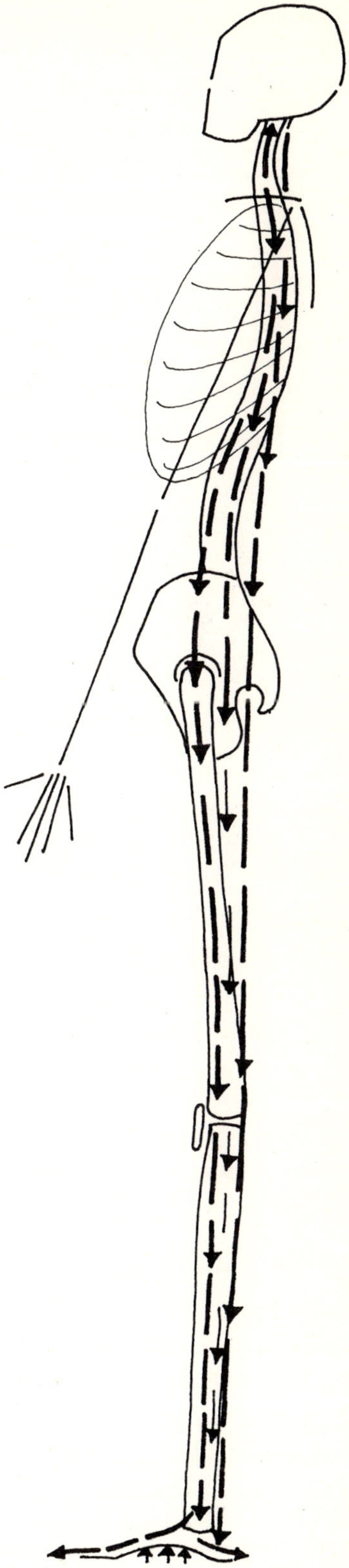

D

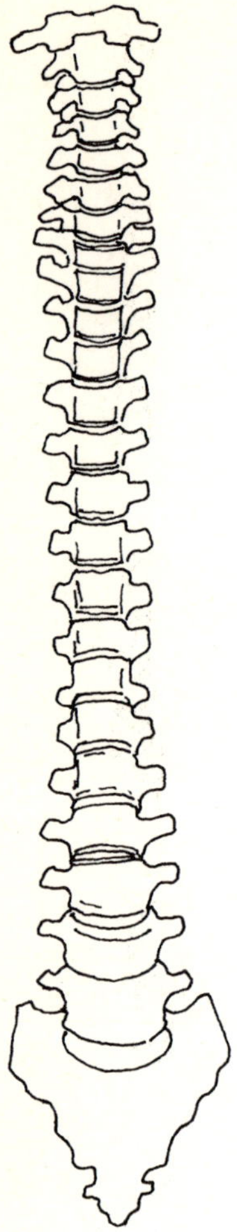

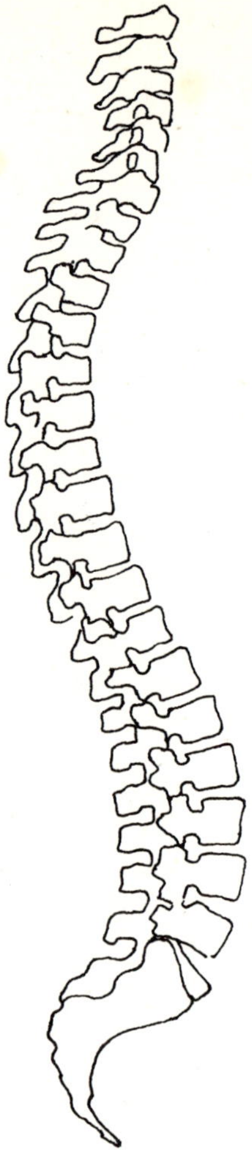

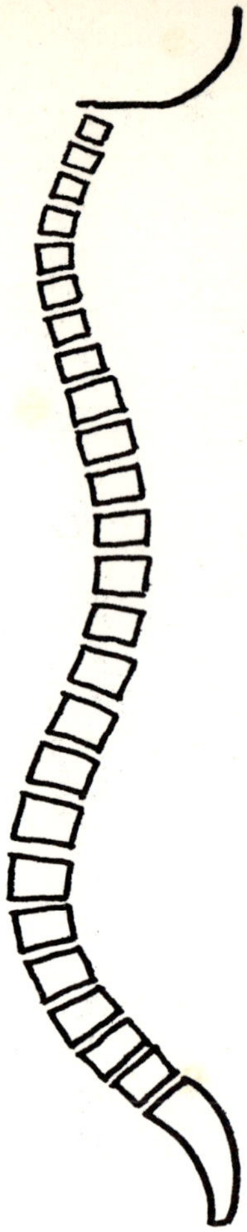

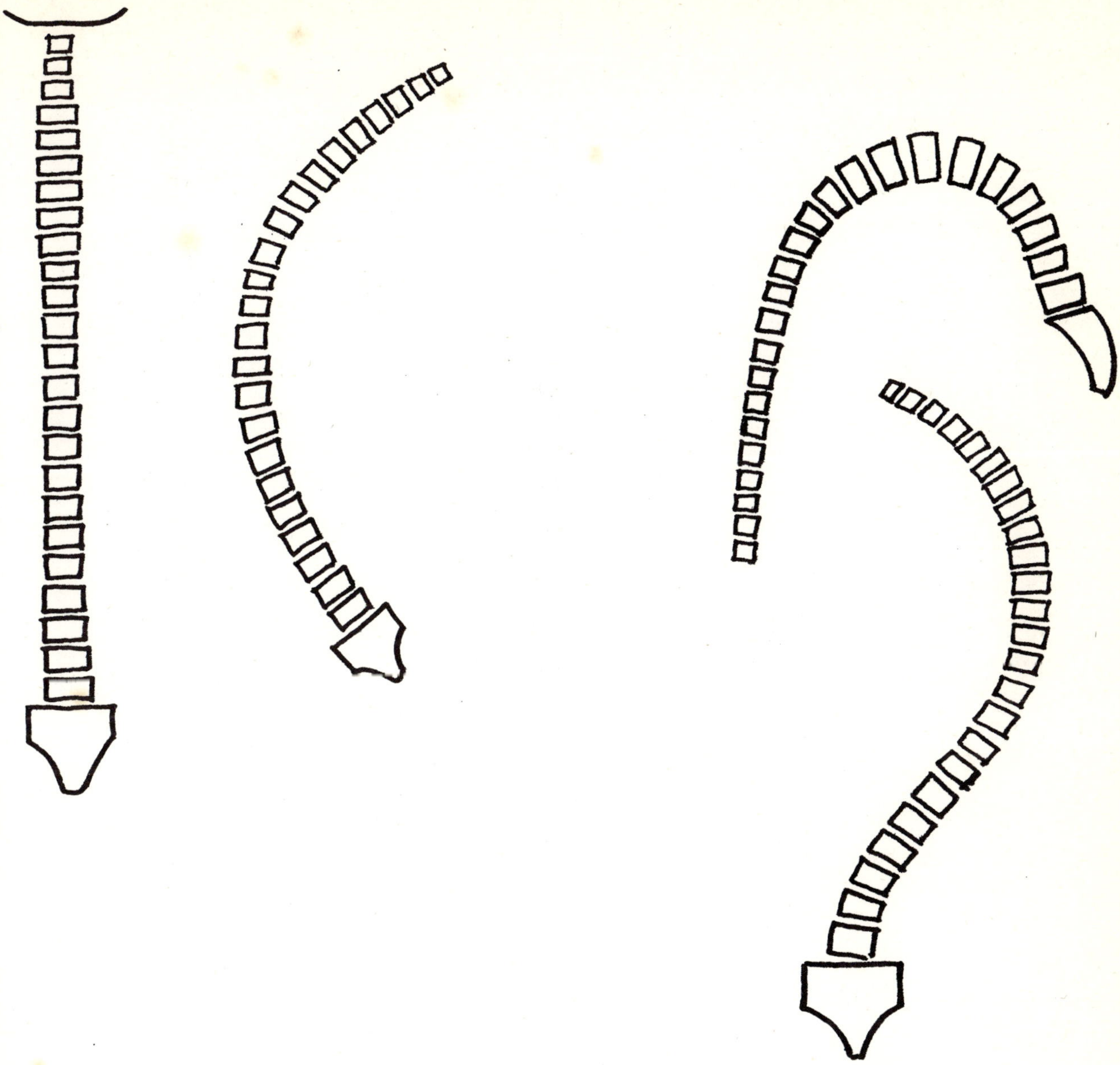

The spine in both simplified form and actual are illustrated here. This column of bones and its flexibility must be understood, as it is the key to balance, poise and convincing study

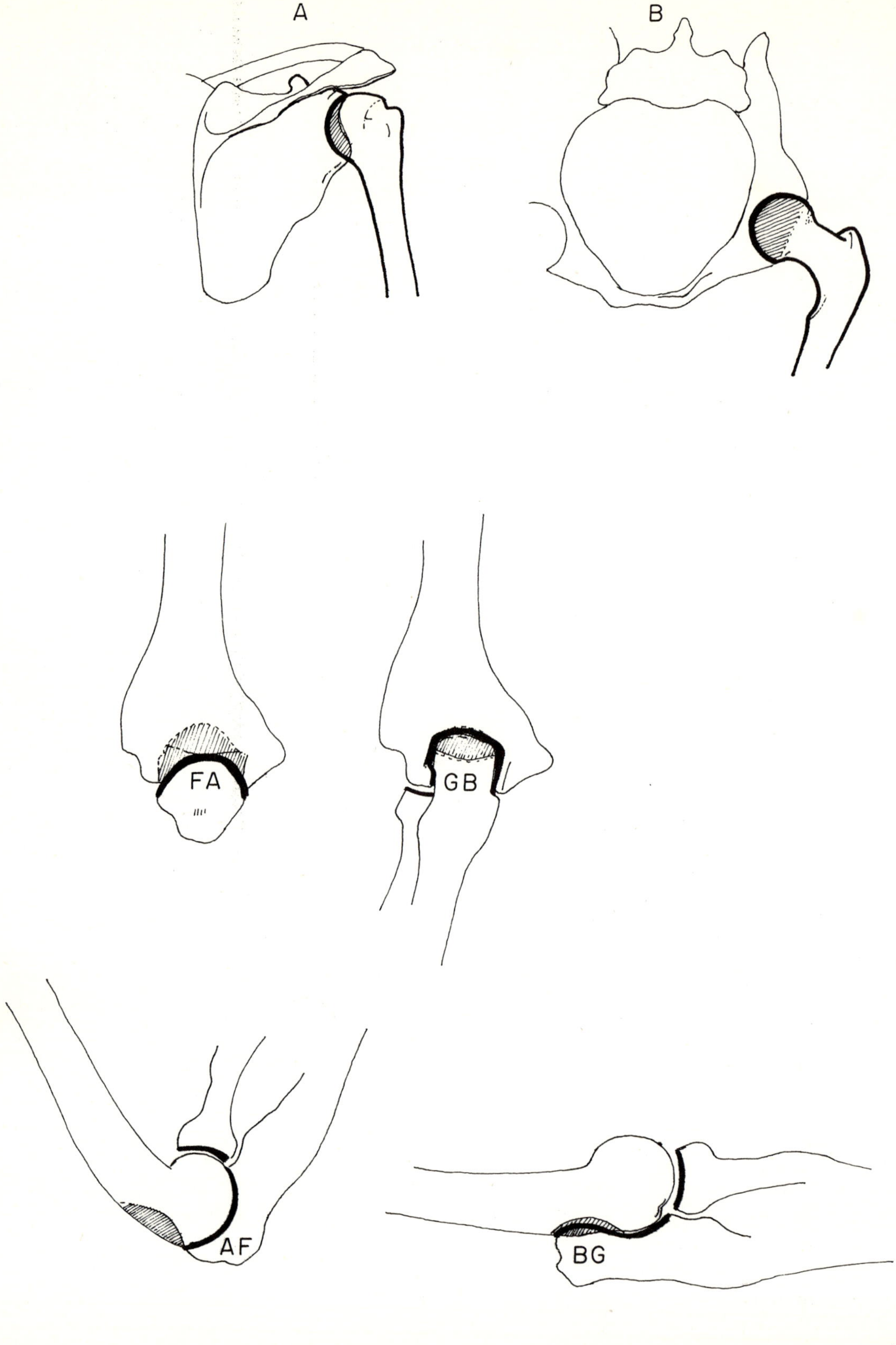
A
B
FA
GB
AF
BG

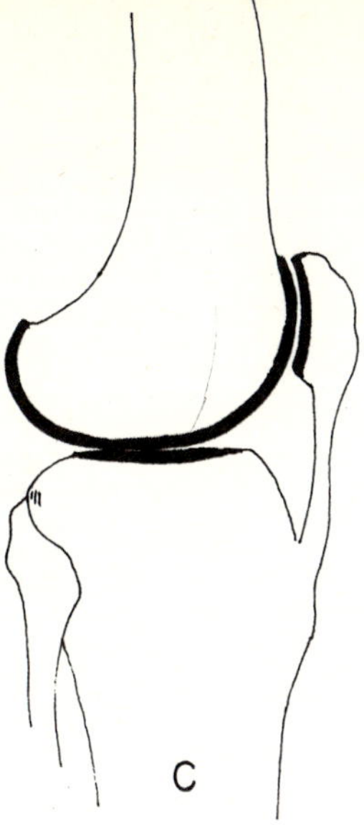

C

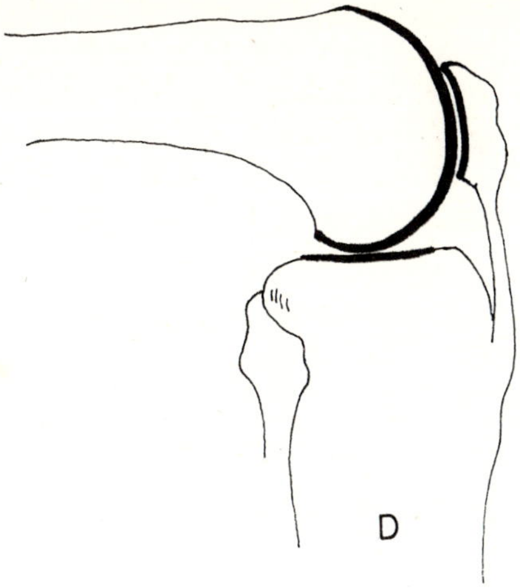

D

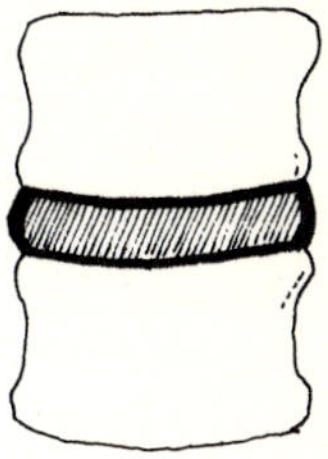

E

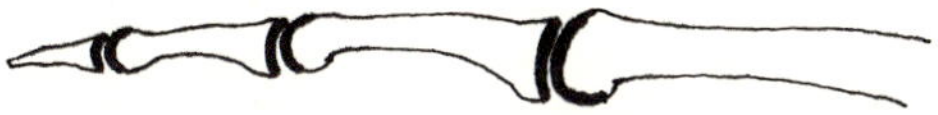

H

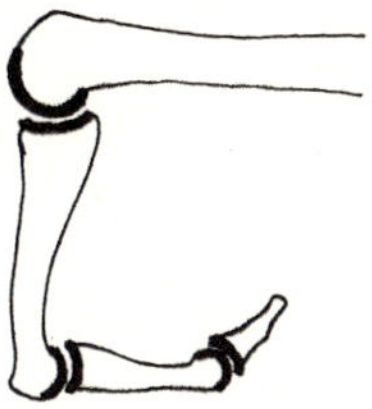

I

Joints simplified. *A* is the shallow ball and socket joint of the shoulder, fitting into the shoulder blade. *B* is the deep ball and socket of the hip joint, deep to be a serviceable load bearing joint. *C* and *D* illustrates the joint of the knee and its articulation. *F* and *G* illustrate the different hinge of the elbow, and its shape in movement. *H* and *I* are the articulations of the fingers which in some respects hinge simply like the knee. *E* shows the cushion between the vertebrae ciple. It provides a set of rules based on fact, that should be visually apparent in figurative sculpture. The degree to which an individual takes anatomical detail is a matter of personal choice; but I add this, I have seen many anatomically correct sculptured figures that amount to nothing, and those that only appear to be correct but are powerful images.

MUSCLES

Musculature is another consideration, and must also be treated with respect, but without awe. There are many fine books on anatomy, and that by Arthur Thomson, *A Handbook of Anatomy for Art Students* is amongst the best. Thomson in 1929 wrote in his preface to the 5 edition, of a first meeting with an artist of repute who said 'the first thing I did after passing my exams was to burn your book'. Thomson wrote that after his initial resentment he too realised that a book is no substitute for demonstration and example, which in turn cannot substitute observation. The visual impact of diverse shapes, the flesh on the skeleton, can only be appreciated by looking at the men, women and children who are our daily companions.

During my National Service I enjoyed the post of physical training instructor. Every two weeks two hundred new men came into the gymnasium for instruction. The picture of two hundred assorted males, exercising and using various apparatus, brought home to me the inadequacy of academic anatomical study for the sculptor. This subject had been an integral part of my art school training for seven years, but the real lesson was there before me in those diverse bodies, each different, each complete, fit and working. The lesson changed and became more interesting with every new intake of men, and the lessons still get more interesting with every new experience.

My experience allows me to pass on the following tips, which I insist are anatomical but not medical. Muscles have the peculiar characteristic of not travelling straight between points. Their job, with the assistance of tendons and ligaments, is to provide the power that combines with and utilises the strength of the skeleton. All factors of course work in unison, in harmony: skeleton, muscles, ligaments, tendons, etc. The muscles are those large observable forms that move, flex and relax as the figure moves. They connect to the skeleton at strategic points, so that a state of equilibrium is maintained as the muscles move. The complex nature of the skeleton, its construction and its function dictate these points and lines of connection. The result is that no muscle describes a straight line, they curve and twist. These curves and turns maybe very slight but are there and should be sought after.

Twisting forms have greater surface tension, as described in chapter 4, and this fact is one reason for the fine spirals that muscles perform. The visual impact of shapes derived from organic forms depends on these curves.

On the figure beginners often miss the curving nature of muscles and although they might realise the correct volume, the effect is wooden and without life. The neck has two large muscles that attach to the front of the rib-cage at the top and gently curves to attach behind the ears. As the neck turns so these muscles move. In female figures and portraits these forms, well modelled, give the air of grace and elegance, typical of extreme femininity. The large muscle in the front of the thigh is similarly characteristic, and the winding curve from inside the knee to the hip, is an important shape. Allusion to strength, power and tension typical of the thigh can be achieved by observing and modelling these muscle forms accurately according to their action. Other obvious muscles that can be studied in this way and are important to the good resolution of figures, are the oblique muscles at the sides of the lower torso. These sets of muscles are typically exploited in Greek Hellenistic male figures. The lateral play of the muscles of the forearm, and those strong shapes below the calf that connect above the heel are features that when modelled well, help towards a convincing figure.

Of course the whole figure has to be studied, and all the visible musculature. The features I have mentioned are given simply as examples easily observed, that indicate the general rule of curving movement.

The rule that every action has an equal and opposite action, is truly observable in the moving figure. Every muscle flexed is counter balanced by a set of relaxed muscles, and their roles change as the movement changes. Therefore a stretched shape, as in the knee of a bent leg, has a relaxed shape, such as that behind the knee and under the thigh of a bent leg. The often mentioned example of muscle binding, an ignorant criticism offered at body builders such as Mr Universe, comes about when one group of muscles develops out of balance with their partners. An example of this in most people is the fingers. Because they are usually clenched, the muscles that clench the fingers are over developed, and are very strong, therefore fingers in repose are usually curved slightly.

The skeleton shown within the outline of the male and female figure. I have indicated by hatching those hard bony anatomical features that can be studied from the skin surface, and provide useful points of reference when making specific study

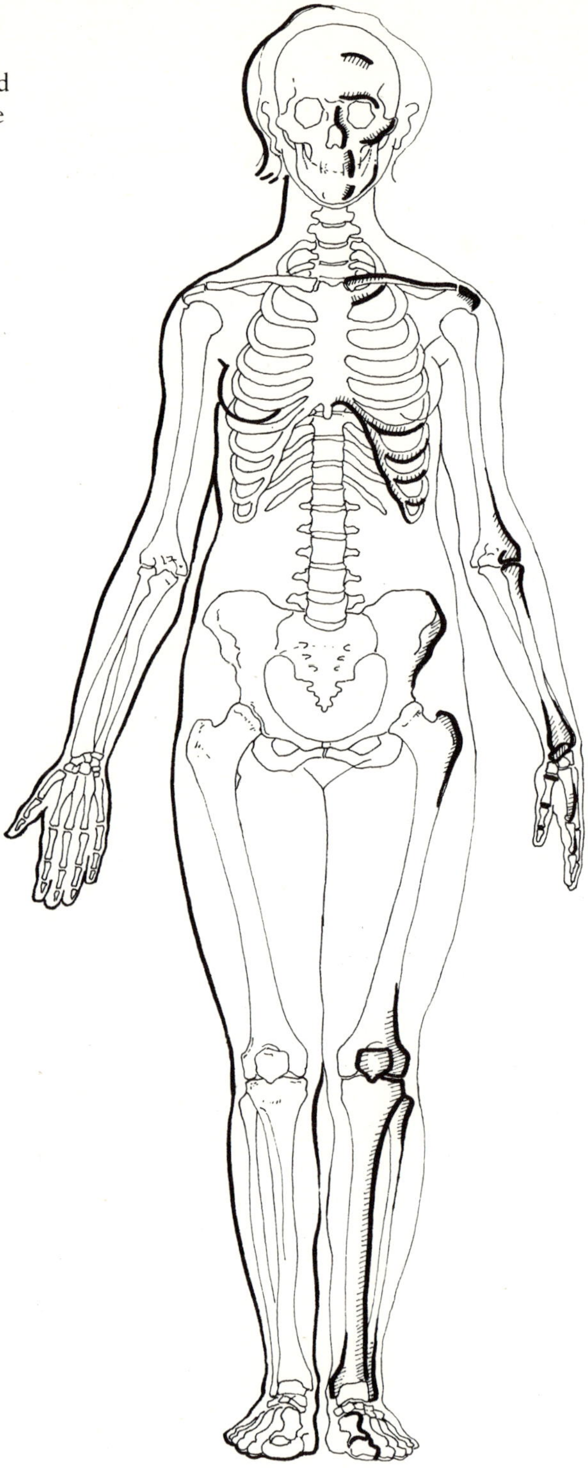

A

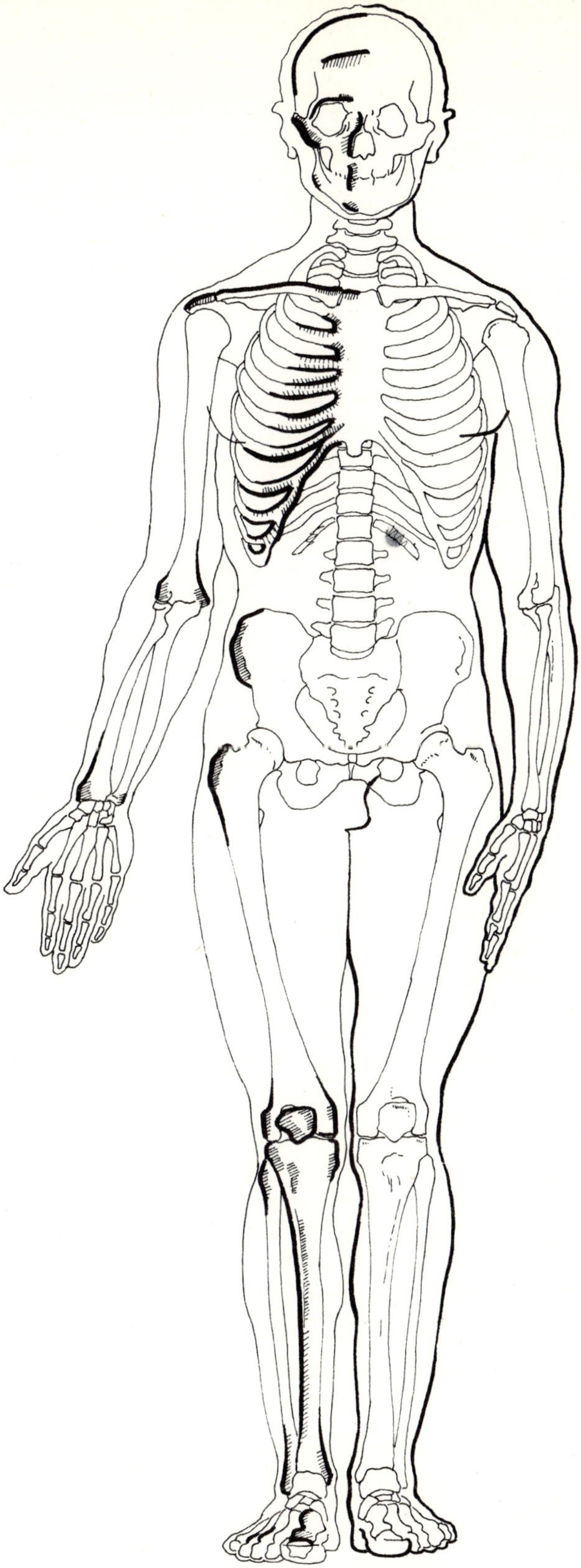

B

ARTICULATION POINTS

At points of articulation, ie elbows, knees, shoulders and armpits, it is necessary to achieve visually the correct sense of strength, and at the same time apply the possibility of movement. The point of connection between the arm and the torso for instance, is often drawn as though one were glued to the other. Too much material is left low down the connecting point. Elbows and knees are often drawn so that they give the sense of immobility, giving the impression that should the figure stand or move an arm the flesh would tear. This is obviously wrong and should be avoided, and can be by careful study. I have already mentioned that the eyes appearing to be attached directly to the bridge of the nose, in poorly drawn portraits, and this is yet another example of poor articulation that should be avoided.

An aid to avoiding visual weakness, is consciously not to put concave shapes opposite one another along a slender form, such as an arm or leg. Concavities are weak shapes anyway, and do not really exist externally in the human form. When they are modelled or drawn opposite one another, the sensation of having been squeezed or pinched is achieved, this is a visual and physical weakness.

MALE AND FEMALE

The basic differences between male and female once pointed out are obvious, but at the risk of being obvious I see the difference as follows: the male form is angular in character and the female is round. Male shoulders are wider than the hips, and in the female the opposite is generally the case. So to model a broad hipped man will probably be wrong, and broad shouldered woman is not really feminine. The muscular detail of the male is clearly defined, and muscular movement easily observed. It is unusual to see muscular detail on a woman, a fatty layer beneath the skin of the female softens detail and smooths out harsh curves. Modelling of the surface can be textured according to these characteristics. It is often better to model male figures with a rough textured surface, than that used for female forms. This is certainly not a rule however and many good sculptures contradict it. The diagram on page 00 illustrates the general classic proportion, seven and a half heads equals the height of the figure.

The breadth of hips of women dictates the shape and flexibility of the arm. Female arms have an exaggerated angle sideways to accommodate the swing of the arm so as not to knock against the hip. This is especially noticeable when a woman carries a weighty object. The male arm doesn't have the same degree of flexibility, the hips being narrower it isn't necessary. The male arm has

These diagrams illustrate the classic proportions for the male and female figure, the height being equal to seven and a half head lengths. The hatched areas indicate the hard skeletal structure detectable from the surface of the flesh.
The contrasting angles of the calf and ankle are also indicated

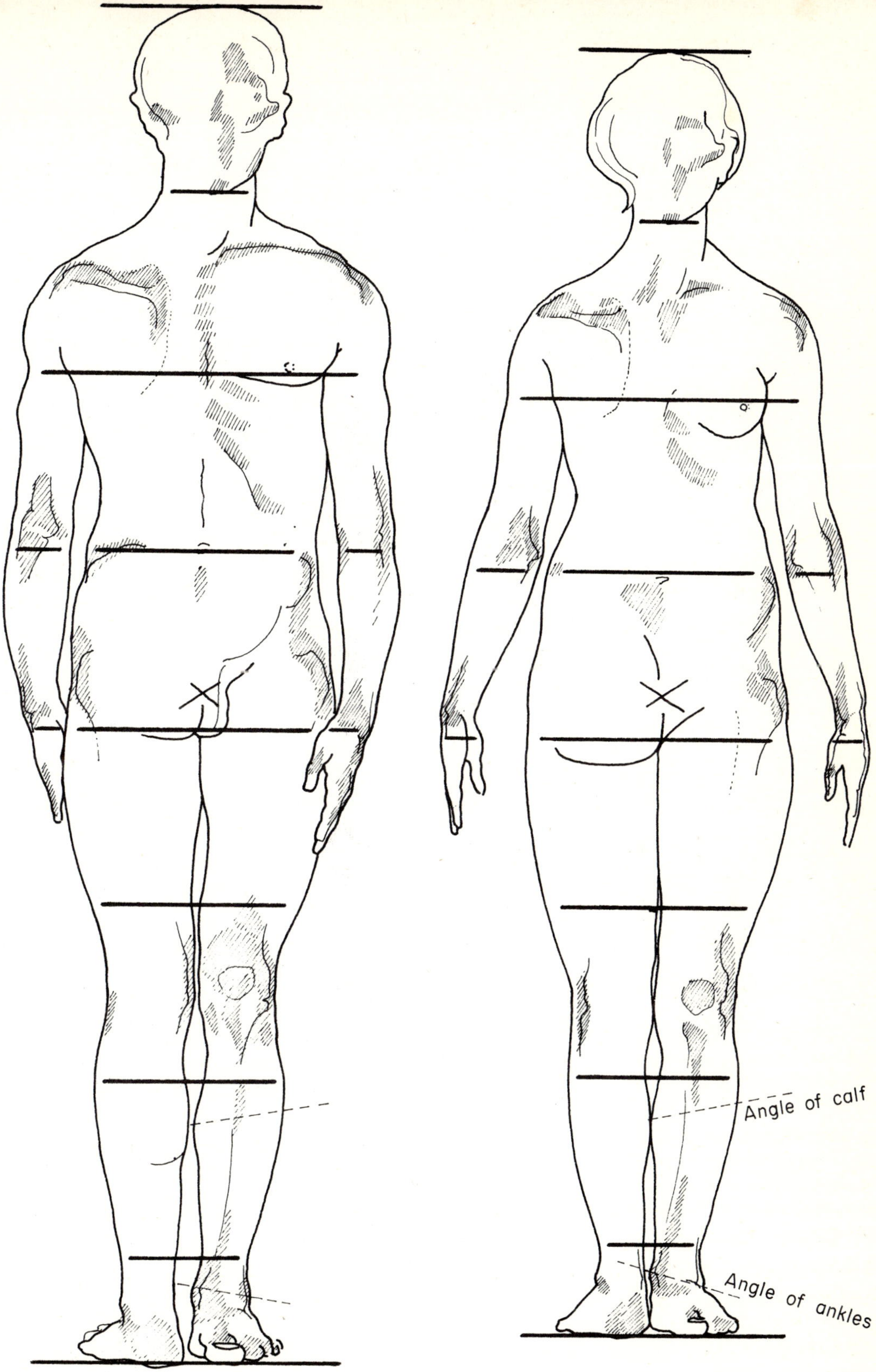
Angle of calf
Angle of ankles

developed a more rugged character too, due possibly to the tasks associated with masculine endeavour, that usually require the lifting of heavy weights. The martial arts all have special exercises for developing the arm, and the arm develops ruggedly accordingly.

THE CURVE OF THE LOWER LEG

Another physical fact that has a kind of jigsaw logic, like the arm and hip, is the fit of curves of the lower leg. A well formed leg, with a full calf has a counter curve just below the knee. This curve accommodates the convex shape of the calf of the opposite leg when walking. It is only when observing a moving figure that this fact becomes obvious. A similar jigsaw fit of curves occurs in the fingers as they move, and an understanding of this dovetailing will help in the modelling of limbs and extremities. Once it is understood and appreciated it will be discernable in many other instances. When limbs are crossed, or cross the torso in comfort, the pattern of convex and concave forms is even more complex and delightful to study. No point at which forms interact should be drawn summarily. I mentioned already that the only true lines occur when forms touch, and these further observations emphasise the importance of closely observing the figure in natural movement

ACCURACY

It is necessary to be accurate when studying a figure, or making a figure that is of a particular type. In other words the shoulders and arms of a trained boxer are extremely different from those of a swimmer. The legs of a racing cyclist develop in quite a different way to those of a dancer. Probably the most evenly balanced figures are those of sprint swimmers, being a sport that demands equal effort of the whole body. A washerwoman's arms are not like the arms of a fashion model; come to think of it fashion models are almost unique physical types. These comments indicate the fallacy of studying just any figure, or the selection of a model because of classical appearance; make particular figures capable of particular actions and work.

Outside the life class away from the life studio is where life begins. This is my message to those sculptors who want to make figurative sculpture that has powerful impact, equivalent to reality, gentle or harsh reality. By this I do not mean narrative. It isn't necessary to have a literal meaning and gesture in the hope that this will make all things right. Outside the studio exists the world into which all artists have to step after work, just like anyone else. It is in this reality that the stuff of fine images resides, and no artist worth his bread ignores it. Therefore the student who seeks reality outside the studio will have more to say than his colleagues who do not. Obvious statements perhaps, but these facts are too often ignored in favour of specialist art magazines and their invidious influence.

Of course every person you meet or see presents a retinal image that your memory stores, so try to train the ability to recall from this computer memory as many images as possible. In addition to this everyday encounter with reality and people, seek out places and facilities that enable you to make particular study. The television for instance presents a veritable barrage of visual information. Sports coverage in particular presents a kind of life class that no art school can copy, except by installing numerous television sets. Wrestling, athletics, swimming, diving, gymnastics, dancing, boxing, ice-skating, ski-ing, football, rugby, tennis and badminton on television provides an incredible amount of information about the figure in action, in a concentrated form unique to the twentieth century artist, who should use it. Wrestling in one programme, usually presents six different physical types, each matched by weight. The constant activity of the camera changing from long focus shots to extreme close up, provides visual changes vital to the correlation of overall statement and detail. The same applies to all film coverage of course, of all subjects, of all sports. The film *68 Olympics* was full of many beautiful images and contained a wide range of physical detail of particular types not possible to study in any other way, and is a fine example of the possible stimuli offered to the sculptor interested in figurative sculpture. To be of use to the artist, he must be able to see the beauty of the film and at the same time take note, for his own use, of the information contained in the imagery. This of course applies to any source of stimulus no matter whether it be film, magazine, other sculpture or reality.

Photography

Whilst on the subject of film and filmed reportage, I must of course refer to still photography. There are some good books devoted to the influence of photography on painters and sculptors, and it is an interesting study. Academic attitudes excluded this influence too, needless to say, and for a very long time, but artists of the calibre of Degas, Rodin, Rosso, Manet, etc, recognised the value of photographic images and used them. The work of Eadweard Muybridge first published in 1888, now known as *The Human Figure in Motion* at first shocked, and then intrigued and delighted artists. For the first time it was possible to study

See end papers

arrested movement, shown in precise sequence, simultaneously photographed from different view points. It was possible to revel in the stimulus of physical peculiarities of actions and gestures. Limbs in movement were seen with new eyes. These photographs in particular opened the eyes of artists to the need for a greater observation of movement. Today the world abounds with photographic stimuli, there to be used, so don't be afraid to make use of an image. Copyright rules can affect the direct reproduction of a photograph, but this anyway will be the same error as making a duplicate instead of an equivalent to reality.

Observation

Swimming pools are a constant source of surprise to the discerning eye. The average municipal pool, on a warm day in particular, houses such an array of diverse physical types, as to provide almost a life-times' stimulus. The same applies, but in less concentration, to running tracks and athletic stadiums during a meeting. Gymnasiums too make it possible to observe fine physiques in action, ranging from the grace of women's gymnastics to the power housing of weightlifting.

Opportunities should be sought to attend these places, and to experience such stimulus. A camera in the hands of an artist will help to recall an image, and by making photographs from which to work, the creative energy so necessary in selection and development of images, can be utilised fully. A photograph helps the memory recall, a fact embodied in every family snapshot album, of which the artist should take advantage. The photograph should not exclude the drawn note, but be used in addition to it. There can be no substitute for the idiosyncratic statements made by hand, that are personal statements. The shortcoming of the photograph can be the lack of the individuals personal imperfections; perfection is often sought after but seldom achieved, thank goodness.

The net result of observation outside the life studio is the factor of surprise. Human beings do make odd shapes as they move. Limbs observed in foreshortening emphasise this, and when used to good effect can add a sparkle to a figure that compels attention from the spectator, and this can only be good. Watch labourers on a building site moving large shovels full of sand, earth or shingle. The shape each individual makes doing similar work is again constantly different. The strain on the arms and back stretch the body into making unique configurations, any group of figures studied in action will provide similar surprises and stimulus.

It will be obvious from the few examples I have given that this subject is endless. By definition Life Study is of unquestionable importance. Man's inventive powers may be greater than any other animal, and makes him dominant on earth, but the degree of invention evident in the various idioms prevalent in the fine arts, is fractional when compared with the examples of diverse form, colour, line, texture, movement and sound that exist in the world about us. Life study therefore offers the most extremely varied stimulus, constantly changing, and is the study of MAN in all his forms, in the reality of his environment. This study plus the artist's unique idiosyncrasies can produce images equivalent to reality by which communication with others can be made. If successful, this activity can be immensely rewarding, frustrating, exciting and constantly surprising. When it has been successful it has produced some of the most beautiful and powerful figurative sculpture yet made.

Index

Suppliers of tools and materials

GREAT BRITAIN

All sculptors' tools and materials
Alec Tiranti Limited
21 Goodge Place, London W1 and
70 High Street, Theale, Berkshire

Clay
Fulham Pottery Limited
210 New Kings Road, London SW6

W Podmore and Sons Limited
Shelton, Stoke-on-Trent,
Staffordshire

Wax
Candle Makers Supplies
4 Beaconsfield Terrace Road
London W14 0PP

Poth-Hille and Co Ltd
37 High Street
Stratford, London E 15

Expanded polystyrene and polyurethane
The Baxenden Chemical Co Limited
Paragon Works, Baxenden,
Accrington, Lancashire

Plaster of paris
British Gypsum Limited
Ferguson House, Marylebone Road
London NW1 5JE

USA

Sculpture Associates
114 East 25th Street, New York,
NY 10010

Sculpture House
38 East 30th Street, New York,
NY 100016

Arthur Brown Inc
2 West 46th Street, New York,
NY 10036

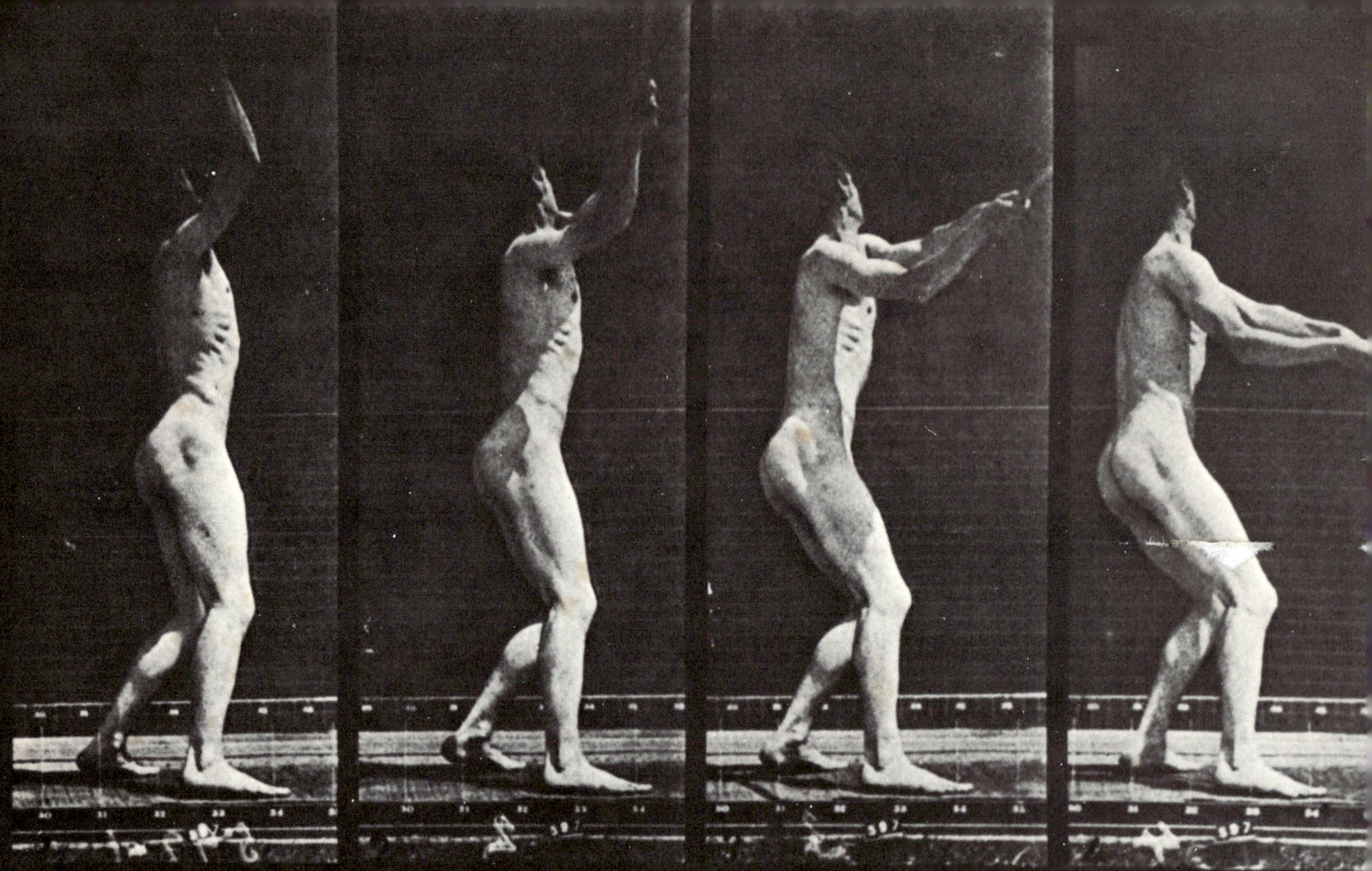

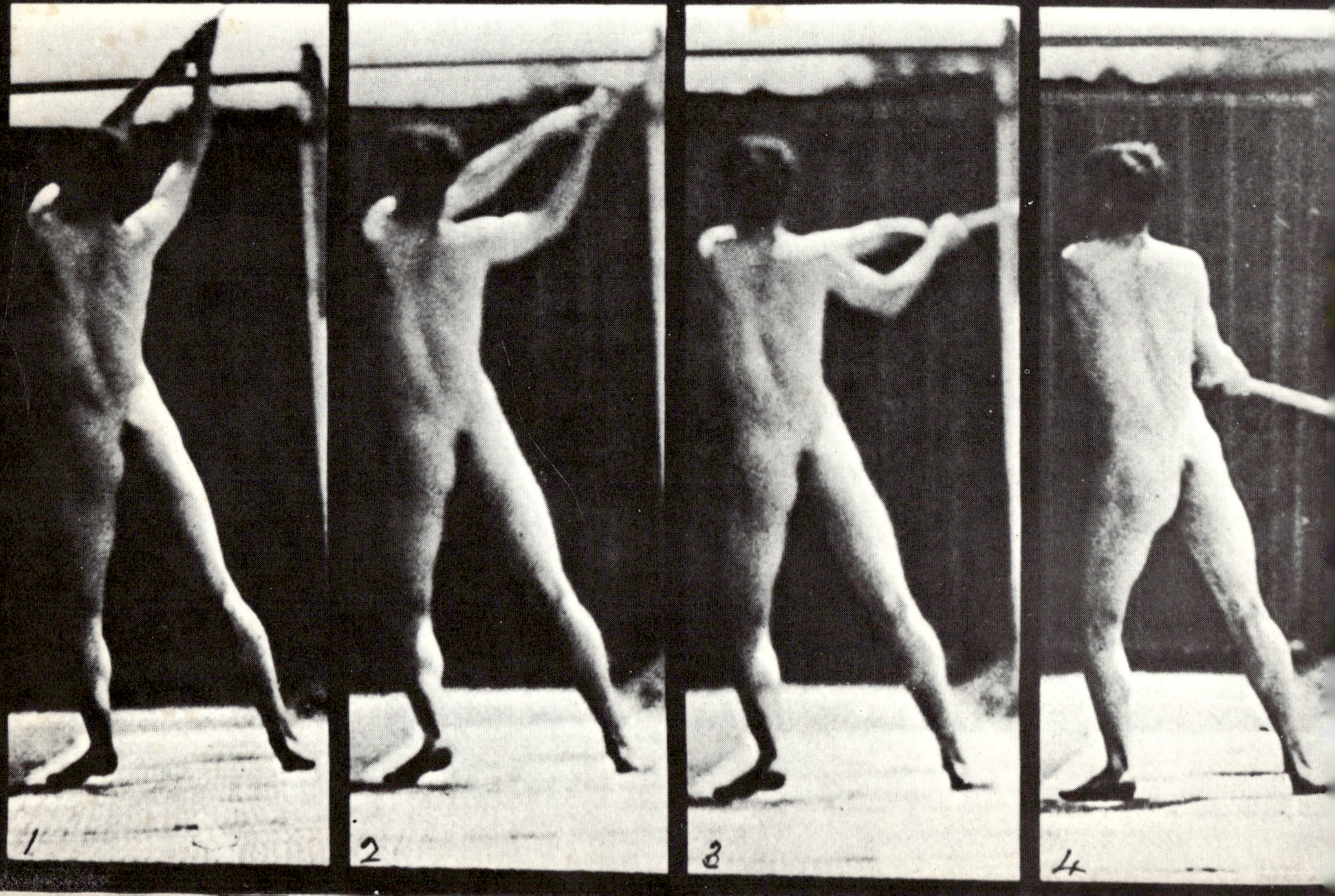
1
2
3
4